A Short Explanation

Of The Epistle

to the

Hebrews

David Dickson

Solid Ground Christian Books
Birmingham, Alabama USA

A

SHORT EXPLANATION

OF

THE EPISTLE OF PAUL

TO THE

HEBREWS.

BY DAVID DICKSON, A.M.

PREACHER OF THE GOSPEL OF JESUS CHRIST,
AND PROFESSOR OF DIVINITY IN THE UNIVERSITY OF GLASGOW.

Reprinted from the Edition of 1649.

LONDON:

THOMAS WARD AND CO.

PATERNOSTER ROW.

Solid Ground Christian Books
2090 Columbiana Rd, Suite 2000
Birmingham AL 35216
(205) 443-0311
sgcb@charter.net
http://solid-ground-books.com

A Short Exposition of the Epistle of Paul to the Hebrews

David Dickson (1583-1662)

Reprinted from the Edition of 1649

First Solid Ground Christian Book edition, September 2005

Cover done by Borgo Design, Tuscaloosa, Alabama
Contact them by e-mail at nelbrown@comcast.net

ISBN: 1-59925-019-5

Table of Contents

TO THE READER.

CHRISTIAN READER,

Before the time that something of mine did pass the press, without my knowledge or allowance, I did not mind to come abroad in this learned age, wherein many more able men than I am do keep silence; my furniture being fitter for my present charge than for more public edification, in my judgment; and my employments so frequent, as my spare time is little, for farther extent of what the Lord hath bestowed upon me. But, since that time, my just fears, from apparent grounds, that numbers of my sermons which were rudely and popularly delivered (as thrice or four times preaching a-week might yield) and taken from my mouth, as it was possible to overtake the current of running speech, the judicious writer making what he had overtaken to cohere the best he could: and copies going from him to many with numbers of faults and mistakings of the transcribers, I being unable to revise, for straitness of time, any thing which was written by them first or last; my just fears, I say, that these should come to thy hands, rude and faulty as they are, made me willing rather, when God should grant me leisure hereafter, to draw up, in short, the points of doctrine delivered by me in these sermons, that thou mightest have a twenty or thirty of them, or more, possible, in the bounds and price of one at large.

With this passage of God's providence another hath concurred, to draw forth this piece unto thy view in the meantime, which is this: when I considered how largely God hath provided helps for understanding of holy Scripture, by large commentaries and sweet sermons, especially from his church in England, whereby increase of knowledge is given to the learned, and such, whose means to buy, and leisure from their calling to read, and victory over their own laziness, for taking pains, doth concur with their capacity for making use of this the Lord's liberality; I have often requested the Father of lights to help such as either could not or would not profit themselves by that which is already granted in his bounty, by some short and plain manner of writing, whereby the weaker judgments might be supported, and all excuse taken away from the witty sluggard, and such whose worldly employments and great affairs have seemed sufficient reasons to excuse their negligence, and [in their estimation] the small and naughty matters of their own salvation, and the kingdom of heaven, and evidences thereof in Scripture.

And to this purpose I have been very instant, with the godly-learned of mine acquaintance, to take this matter in hand, and to divide amongst them the hard parts of Scripture at least, that this work might be done by the hands of many, which could not be done by one. I found their approbation of my desire, and inclinable willingness, to put hand to work also. But some of them, for the weight of their ordinary charge, some of them for age and infirmity of body, some of them for their hands full of the Lord's work in another sort, could not adventure to be straitly engaged in the work. Wherethrough, I was forced either to forsake my desires, which daily were kindled within me more and more, or else come forth with something of this kind, as might be, and seek amongst my readers some to take this matter to heart, and to do therein as the Lord should enable them, by themselves, or by others.

I have made choice of this epistle, which is a piece of hard meat, in the estimation both of the apostle, the writer hereof, (chap. v. and vi.) and of Peter giving his judgment of it, (2 Pet. i. 15, 16,) that if I should attain any part of mine intent, in any measure, in so hard a place, I might encourage others to take in hand a more easy part of Scripture, with more hope of success.

The sum of each chapter, or the contents, do stand instead of analysis, and, in some places, of a paraphrase. The text doth follow, verse by verse. The exposition of the verse serveth for grounds of doctrines, which doctrines, following upon the grounds, are joined, most part, with the note of collection [Then]. Plurality of doctrines from the ground, or from the text where the consequence is easy to be perceived, is distinguished by figures according to their numbers. Terms of art I have eschewed, because I would be plain to all. I have spared all enlargement of the doctrines that I could spare, leaving them, as grains of seed, to get their fruit in thy mind by meditation, which is necessary for such as love to make use of this sort of writing, because I would be short. The special handling of such passages as the apostle citeth out of the Old Testament, I have left to their own proper place. Quotations, for confirmation of my doctrines, drawn from the ground, I have spared also, because I judged if the doctrine was pertinently collected from the ground the text in hand was sufficient confirmation. And if it be not pertinently collected, I am content that thou pass by it, and take only what is pertinent. A quotation could prove the doctrine true, but not prove it pertinent, and so not serve my purpose. Many more, and more pertinent consequences, the learned will find, which I have not observed; but not for the learned, or such as are able and willing to make use of larger writings, do I intend this present.

Therefore, do not look how much thou dost miss, which might have been said, but what, in the first frame of this mould could be done, in such brevity; which mould I trust the learned shall help, if it please the Lord to stir them up to take this matter in hand. I have pressed singly to point out truth without partiality; not wresting the text to reach a blow to any man. And what thou shalt make of this present piece I am not careful, if I can obtain thereby that more able men may be set on work to do what I intend but cannot do.

If the precious jewel of the Scripture may be more esteemed of and made use of, which is more necessary for our souls than the sun in the firmament is for our bodies, and the greatest gift, next after our Lord Jesus' down-sending amongst us, that ever the world saw; if I may by this piece, I say, be an instrument to stir up any to the love of searching the Scriptures, I have not lost my pains, whatsoever shall become of this little book: whereunto I have solicited for no patronage under heaven, but thy Christian good-will to my aim, to have our Lord the more honoured, in the sound knowledge and right use of his Scripture.

I am confident that thou wilt easily judge with me, that the proud and profane despisers of God are worthy to perish amongst his enemies; but consider and judge again, if profane despisers of holy Scripture, who disdain to read, or obey what God commandeth therein, be not to be ranked in the same roll. For God draweth so nigh unto us in his word, speaking unto us as a king unto his subjects, or a master unto his servants, that the obedience or disobedience which we give to his speeches resolveth directly and immediately upon God himself. For what is it else to hear, and believe, and obey God, but to hear, and believe, and obey his speeches? And what is it not to take notice of God, to despise and disobey God, but not to take notice of his speeches, not to read his writings, and not to care for any thing that he commandeth, promiseth, or threateneth? Therefore hath the Lord written the great things of his law unto us, even to be a touchstone not only to try all men's doctrine thereby, but also to try all men's disposition towards himself, and how they stand affected to his honour, whether as foes or as friends. For what readier way is there to get evidence of a man destitute of the knowledge, faith, love, fear, and the rest of the parts of the image of God, than to find him destitute of the knowledge and love of the Scripture? What surer sign of a man who for the present is enemy to God, and to the enlargement of his gracious kingdom, than to find him traducing the perfect law of the Lord, and marring, to his power, the free course of the Scriptures' light, which is the sceptre of Christ's kingdom? Again, what surer sign of a child of promise, begotten of God, than to see him, with David, Psal. cxix., making more of the Scriptures nor [than] of a kingdom, and pouring out all his affections upon it, as the nearest mean whereby God's Spirit may be conveyed into his soul, for perfecting of holiness; and the readiest chariot to carry up his spirit to dwell in God, for perfecting of his happiness.

We shall find also, answerable to God's purpose of trying men by his Scripture, his wisdom giving a due meeting unto men, as they do make use of his Scripture. Do they not read it? or do they read and not consider it? Do they not weigh what is imported by it in sense and meaning? It fareth with them as those to whom Christ said, Matt. xxii. 29, "You err, not knowing the Scriptures, nor the power of God." Do they not love it? Behold their plague, 2 Thess. ii. 10—12, "Because they received not the love of the truth, that they might be saved; for this" very "cause," saith the text, "God shall send them strong delusion, that they should believe a lie, that they might be damned." Do they not steadfastly believe what they learn in Scripture? In God's judgment with the foolish and unstable, they are suffered to wrest the Scriptures to their own destruction, were they never so great wits, 2 Pet. iii. 16. Do they not study to give obedience unto the known truth of it? He dealeth with them as with Israel, Psal. lxxxi. 11, "My people would not hearken unto my voice, and Israel would none of me." (He counteth himself rejected, because his word was rejected.) But what followeth? ver. 12, "So I gave them up unto their own hearts' lust, and they walked in their own counsels." But to such as will be Christ's disciples indeed, students, seeking to grow in knowledge, belief, and obedience of his word, seeking to love him and keep his sayings, he promiseth, John xiv. 26, to send unto them "The Spirit of truth, the Comforter, the Holy Ghost, to teach them all things;" that is, to perfect their knowledge more and more by his Spirit, to fill their hearts with joy and comfort, according to his truth, and to make them holy more and more.

And why are all these styles given? Even to show that such as will have Christ's Spirit to work any of these, must seek him to work all of these jointly, or not to have him for working any of them at all. Neither comfort without truth, nor comfort without holiness. The same is it which Wisdom crieth, Prov. viii. 34—36, "Blessed is the man that heareth me, watching daily at my gates, waiting at the posts of my doors; for whoso findeth me findeth life, and shall obtain favour of the Lord. But he that sinneth against me wrongeth his own soul: all that hate me love death."

Therefore, how thou dost hate death, and love thine own soul; how thou standest affected towards God, and the fellowship of the Comforter, the Holy Spirit, the Spirit of truth, and towards the enlargement of the kingdom of Christ; let thy affection towards the Scriptures, more abundant dwelling in thyself, and for the Scriptures' more free course amongst others, bear witness.

FAREWELL.

EPISTLE OF PAUL

TO

THE HEBREWS.

HEN Peter wrote his second epistle to the scattered Hebrews, there was extant an epistle of Paul, to those same scattered Hebrews also, received in the church, for a part of canonical scripture, and distinguished from Paul's other epistles, 2 Pet. iii. 15, 16. Therefore amongst other reasons, this may be one, to make us think this epistle must be it. For it is without reason to think, that the churches should be negligent in keeping such a jewel, commended unto them by the authority of two chief apostles; or lose Paul's epistle, and keep Peter's; which maketh mention of it.

THE SUM OF THE EPISTLE.

Because the Hebrews were hardly drawn from the observation of Levitical ordinances, unto the simplicity of the Gospel, and in danger of making apostacy from the Christian faith, by persecution, the apostle Paul setteth before their eyes the glory of Jesus Christ, in his person, far above men and angels; by whose ministry the law was given, not only as God, ch. i., but also as man, ch. ii.; and in his office above Moses, ch. iii. Threatening them therefore, if they should misbelieve Christ's doctrine, ch. iii. iv.; and above the Levitical high-priest, ch. v. Threatening them again, if they should make apostacy from him, ch. vi.; yea, above all the glory of the Levitical ordinances; as he in whom all those things had their accomplishment, and period of expiring, ch. vii.—x. Threatening them again, if they should not persevere in the faith of Christ: unto which perseverance, through whatsoever difficulties, he encourageth them, by the example of the faithful before them, ch. x. xi., and by other grounds of Christian comfort, ch. xii. That so in the fruitful obedience of the Gospel, they might follow upon Christ, seeking for that city that is to come, and not for their earthly Jerusalem any more, ch. xiii.

THE SUM OF CHAP. I.

If you shall make comparison, O Hebrews, the ministry of the gospel shall be found more glorious than the ministry of the law: for the manner of God's dispensing his will before Christ came, was by part and part, and subject to his own addition: not after one settled manner, but subject to alteration, and by the ministry of men, the prophets, ver. 1. But now he hath declared his last will gloriously, by his own Son, God and man in one person, ver. 2, 3, who is as far above, not only the prophets, but the angels also, as the native glory of his person and office is above theirs, ver. 4. For he is of the same substance with the Father, ver. 5, and partaker of the same worship with him, ver. 6. The angels but servants to him, ver. 7. He is eternal God, and king over all, ver. 8, and in regard of his manhead and office, filled with the Spirit, ver. 9. Yea, he is Creator, unchangeable and everlasting, ver. 10—12. Joined with the Father, in the government of the world, ver. 13. The angels but servants, both to him, and to his children, ver. 14.

THE DOCTRINE CONTAINED IN CHAP. I.

Ver. 1. God who at sundry times and in divers manners, spake in time past unto the fathers by the prophets.

Albeit the apostle was willing that these Hebrews should understand that this epistle came unto them from him, as appeareth chap. x. 34, yet doth he not prefix his name in the body of it, as in all his other epistles; that by the prudent dealing of these faithful Hebrews, as we may think, others who kept prejudice against his person, might be drawn on, to take notice of his doctrine more impartially, and know his name, after they had tasted of the truth from him, in a fitter time. Whence we learn, 1. That it is lawful for godly men to dispose of the expression of their names in their writings, as they see it expedient. 2. That it is not much to be inquired, who is the writer of any purpose, till we have impartially pondered the matter written. 3. That it is not always necessary, that we should know the name of the writer of every part of scripture; for the authority thereof is not from men, but from God, the inspirer thereof.

1. He saith not simply, The prophet spake,

but God spake to the fathers, by the prophets.—
Then, 1. God was the chief doctor of his own
church, from the beginning. 2. And what the
prophets conveyed from God, to the church, by
Scripture, as it is called here the speaking of
God, so it is to be accounted of still, and not as
a dumb letter.

2. He saith, God spake at sundry times. By
many parts, as the word importeth; now a part
of his will, and then a part farther; at another
time yet a part farther. Then, the Lord was in
the way only, of revealing his whole mind to his
church, before Christ came; letting forth light
by little and little, till the Sun of righteousness,
Jesus Christ, arose, and had not told his whole
will. 2. And for this reason, the Jewish church
was bound to suspend her determination of the
unchangeableness of her Levitical service, till the
lawgiver spake his last word, and uttered his
full mind, in the fulness of time.

3. He saith, before Christ came, God spake in
divers manners.—Not revealing his will after one
manner; but sometimes by *vive* voice, sometimes
by vision, or dream, or inspiration, or Urim and
Thummim, by signs from heaven, by types, and
exercise of shadowing ceremonies. Then, no
reason the Jews should stick so fast to the ordinances of Levi (they being instituted in the
time of the alterable courses of the church's
pedagogy) as not to give way to abolishing of
them by the Messias: which to show, is a part of
the apostle's main scope.

VER. 2. Hath in these last days, spoken unto us
by his Son; whom he hath appointed heir of
all things: by whom also he made the worlds.

1. He saith, God who spake to the fathers,
hath spoken to us. Then, the God, who is author
of the Old Testament, is also author of the doctrine of the New Testament: and the church of
old, and now, is taught of the same God; that the
faith of the elect might depend upon the authority of God only, both then and now; and not
on men.

2. These are called the last days—Then, the
fulness of time is now come: the lawgiver of the
church hath spoken his last will: his mind is
fully revealed; settled course for the faith, and
service of his church, is taken; after which, no
new alteration of his constitutions is to be expected.

3. He saith, God spake to them by the prophets, but hath spoken to us by his Son.—Then,
1. As the Son is above the servants, so is Christ
above the prophets. And no reason, that the
Jews should think so much of Moses, and the
prophets, as for them, to mis-regard Christ's doctrine, and stick to the Levitical service, under
pretence of estimation of the prophets. 2. The
glory of the Gospel is greater than the glory of
the law. 3. The glory of the ministerial calling
of preachers of the gospel, is by so much the
greater, as it hath the Son of God first man in
the roll thereof; as first preacher, and prince of
preachers. 4. Christ's sermons are all of them
directed unto us: and so much more highly
should the doctrine of the Gospel be esteemed of
by us.

4. In describing Christ, he saith, the Son is
heir of all things: that is, he hath received a
domination over all creatures, from the Father;
that as He is Lord over all, so is Christ.—Then,
1. Christ is heir of all things in the church also,
Lord of the Sabbath, and of all the service annexed to it, to whom it is lawful to chop and change
the Levitical ordinances, at his pleasure. 2. And
heir of all the prerogatives and promises, made
to the Jews or others; through whom only, as
the righteous owner of all things, both Jew and
Gentile must seek and keep right to what they
have, or can claim: and therefore it behoved the
Hebrews to enter themselves heirs to their privileges by Christ, or else to be disinherited.

5. He saith, God, by his Son, made the worlds.
—So he calleth the world, for the variety of times,
and ages, and fleeces of the creatures, one succeeding another. Then, 1. Christ is God, Creator of all things. 2. He is a distinct person from
the Father; by whom the Father made all. 3.
That which the Father doth, the Son doth the
same; yet so, as in order of working, the Father
is first, and the Son is next; working with, and
from the Father.

VER. 3. Who being the brightness of his glory,
and the express image of his person, and up-
holding all things by the word of his power,
when he had, by himself, purged our sins, sat
down on the right hand of the majesty on
high.

In describing Christ, he useth borrowed similitudes: for what proper word can be found, to
express so great a mystery? And what can we
conceive of his Godhead, but by resemblance?
Yea, he useth more similitudes than one; for it
is but little we can conceive of him by one: and
what we might misconceive by too hard pressing
of one similitude, by another is corrected; and
so our conception helped.

1. Christ, the Son, is called the brightness of
his Father's glory.—The similitude is borrowed
from the sunbeams. Then, 1. As the Father is
glorious, so is Christ his Son glorious, with the
same glory. Therefore 1 Cor. ii. 8, he is called
the Lord of glory. 2. As the beams of light
have their original from the sun, so hath Christ
his original of the Father, and is unseparable
from him: for as the sun was never without its
light; so neither was the Father ever without
the Son; but coeternally with him. 3. As the
sun is not manifest, but by its own brightness;
so the inaccessible light of the Father's glory is
not revealed to the creature, but by the Son.

2. Christ is called the express image of the
Father's person.—The similitude is borrowed
from a signet's impression, which representeth
all the lineaments of the seal. Then, 1. The
Father is one person, and the Son is one other
person of the Godhead, having his own proper
subsistence distinct from the Father. 2. The
Son resembleth the Father, fully, and perfectly;
so that there is no perfection in the Father, but
the same is substantially in the Son: as the
Father is eternal, omnipotent, omnipresent, infinite in wisdom, goodness, mercy, holiness, and
all other perfections; so is the Son omnipotent,

eternal, and all that the Father is. 3. Whatsoever perfection we can perceive in Christ, shining in his manhead, or word or works; the same we may conclude to be in the Father also; whose resemblance and express image he is. Find we Christ good and merciful, loving and pitiful, meek and lowly; not abhorring the most vile and miserable, whether in soul or body, that cometh unto him for relief; we may be assured, that such a one is the Father; and no otherways minded to such as seek unto him through Christ.

3. Christ upholdeth all things by the word of his power.—Then, 1. The preservation of the creatures, as well as their creation, is from Christ. The Father upholdeth all, so doth the Son. 2. What he doth, he doth as omnipotent God, by his word, without trouble or burthen. As he spake, and all was done; so he but by his word commandeth, and all standeth fast. And this his word is nothing else but his powerful will, ordaining things to be, and continue; and powerfully making them so to be, and continue, so long as he will.

4. Christ by himself purged our sins. To wit, by bearing our sins upon his body on the tree, 1 Pet. ii. 24.—Then, 1. Our sins are a filthiness that must be purged. 2. The satisfactory cleansing of our sins, is not a thing to be done by men's meritorious doings or sufferings; but already done and ended by Christ, before he ascended; and that by himself alone, all creatures being secluded. 3. He that upholdeth all things by the word of his own power, and he that purged our sins by his own blood, is but one selfsame person; God and man is he in one person.

5. Christ sat down on the right hand of the Majesty on high.—That is, when Christ had cleansed our sins by his death, he ascended to heaven, and possessed himself as man, in the fellowship of the same glory, which as God he had before the world was, John xvii. 4, 5.

Then, 1. The Son is joined in the fellowship of the same glory with the Father, as well in his manhead after his resurrection, as in his Godhead before his incarnation. For, though the glory of Christ's Godhead was hid for a while, by the sufferings of his manhead, yet was it not abolished, nor in itself abated thereby: but the manhead first assumed unto the unity of person with the Godhead, that our ransom might be rich; and then, to the union of the same glory, that the Redeemer, after the ransom's paying, might be altogether glorious.

2. Seeing he that hath cleansed our sins is so glorious a person, all the means of his cleansing us, how base soever, such as were his hunger and thirst, his poverty and weakness, his shameful and painful death, should be glorious in our eyes also.

3. Majesty, and magnificence, and grandeur, properly so called, is the Lord's. The highest excellences of the creature, are but sparks of his majesty, and weak resemblances only, albeit their earthly glory often holds men's eyes so, as they forget the Lord's greatness.

Ver. 4. Being made so much better than the angels, as he hath by inheritance obtained a more excellent name than they.

1. He proveth Christ to be greater than the angels, because his name is more excellent than theirs.—For they are called angels, and he God's Son: which he is said to have by inheritance as due to him; both as God by eternal generation, and as man by assumption of our nature in unity of one person; according to which he is not the adopted, but natural Son of God: *filius natus, non filius factus.* Then God giveth not idle titles; as God calleth things, so they are, or are made to be. Christ, as God, is called God's Son, because by eternal generation he is so: as man he is called God's Son, because by assumption of the human nature unto the personal union of his Godhead, he is made so to be.

2. As far as Sonship is above servile employment, as far is Christ more excellent than the angels.

Ver. 5. For unto which of the angels said he at any time, Thou art my Son, this day have I begotten thee? And again, I will be him a Father, and he shall be to me a Son?

1. He proveth this point by Scripture, Psal. ii. 7; 2 Sam. vii. 14, and putteth them to improbation of his doctrine by Scripture, if they could.

Then, 1. In the primitive church, in matters of religion, all authority was silent, and Divine Scripture spake, and determined questioned points of truth. 2. The apostle counted it sufficient to bring Scripture for his doctrine; and permitteth no impugning of it, but by Scripture.

2. Only of Christ, saith God, I have begotten thee.

Then, 1. Howsoever God hath many sons by creation, by office, by grace, and adoption; yet a Son by generation, a native son, hath none but Christ. 2. Christ is of the same nature and essence with the Father, consubstantial with him; because begotten of him in himself, without beginning; the Son being eternally in the Father, and the Father eternally in the Son, of the selfsame nature and Godhead.

3. This day have I begotten thee.—Being understood of Christ, according to his Godhead, signifieth the Father's timeless, eternal, perpetually constant, and present generation of his Son, in himself; being understood according to his state, in his manhead, it signifieth the Father's bringing forth of the Son, to the knowledge of the world, and declaring him to be Son of God, with power, by his resurrection from the dead, Rom. i. 4. These places, it is true, were spoken of David and Solomon, as types of Christ, typically in a slender resemblance, Psal. ii. 7; 2 Sam. vii. 19. But the body of the truth aimed at and signified, was Christ resembled by them, as here we see. Whence we learn, that typical speeches in Scripture have not their perfect meaning, neither can be fully expounded nor truly understood, till they be drawn to Christ, in whom they have their accomplishment, and of whom they mean to speak, under the name of the types. And therefore neither could the old church of the Jews, nor can we get comfort in any of them, till Christ, in whom all the promises are yea and amen, be found included in them.

Ver. 6. And again, when he bringeth in the

first-begotten into the world, he saith, And let all the angels of God worship him.

1. He saith, that is, the Father saith, Psal. xcvii. 7. Then the Scripture which elsewhere is called the speech of the Holy Ghost, is also the speech of the Father.

2. He bringeth in his first-begotten into the world.—Then,

1. The Father is the Author of Christ's incarnation, and of his kingdom amongst men, and of divine glory given to him in his kingdom. 2. Christ is the Father's first-begotten, both for the eternity of his person, begotten without beginning, before the world was; and for the excellency of his person, being more glorious than all angels, or men, which get the name of children, either by creation or adoption. 3. The Father commandeth; let all the angels of God adore him. Then, 1. The Father communicateth to Christ, as his own nature and Godhead, by generation; so also his own glory, by commanding the creatures to adore him. 2. What the creatures adore, they acknowledge by adoration, to be God; so God esteemeth. 3. And Christ is the angels' God, because they must adore him.

Ver. 7. And of the angels he saith, Who maketh his angels spirits, and his ministers a flame of fire.

He maketh his angels spirits, &c., Psal. civ. 5. Then 1. God made not the angels, to get any part of Christ's room in the church's worship; but to serve Christ, as lowly as any of the meanest creatures. 2. And the angels, indeed, are as ready to do so, and as swift and active in their service, as the winds, and fire-slaughts.

Ver. 8. But unto the Son he saith, Thy throne, O God, is for ever and ever : a sceptre of righteousness is the sceptre of thy kingdom.

Ver. 9. Thou hast loved righteousness and hated iniquity : therefore God, even thy God, hath anointed thee with the oil of gladness above thy fellows.

1. By this place, cited out of Psal. xlv. 7, it is evident that Psal. xlv. is a song of the mystical marriage of Christ and his church; and in this passage a number of notable doctrines concerning Christ are pointed at. 1. He is called God; and so is fit to reconcile us to God; able and all sufficient to accomplish our salvation : a rock to lean unto. 2. A king enthroned, not only over the world, but in a gracious manner, over the church, which he marrieth to himself in this Psalm : and therefore shall his church have laws, and direction, and protection from him. 3. He hath a throne for ever and ever; and therefore shall his church, which is his kingdom, endure for ever and ever. 4. He hath a sceptre to rule with, and therefore power and authority, to take order with his subjects, and with his enemies also. 5. His sceptre is a sceptre of righteousness, because he cannot abuse his power, to do wrong to any, but will do right to all; yea, and lead on his subjects to

righteousness of faith, to justify them before God; and righteousness of conversation, to adorn them before men.

2. He loveth righteousness and hateth iniquity. —And therefore, 1. His sceptre cannot be swayed but righteously. 2. And so must his subjects set themselves to do, if they will please him. 3. Therefore, Christ's God hath anointed him with the oil of gladness above his fellows. Then, 1. As Christ is God himself, so also is he man under God, in regard of his manhead, and office therein. 2. And God is his God by covenant : Christ as man is confederate with God. 3. And he hath fellows in the covenant : that is, others of mankind, with whom he is partaker of flesh and blood, fellow brethren, and co-heirs, sharesmen in all the Father's goods with him. 4. He is anointed with the oil of gladness; furnished with the Spirit that bringeth joy unto him, and all his subjects, who get conveyed unto them by Christ, righteousness and peace, and joy in the Holy Ghost. 5. He is anointed above his fellows. The rest of the confederate saints are anointed also; yet by measure receive they the Spirit. But Christ is anointed above them : the Spirit is not given to him by measure; but to dwell bodily or substantially, that we of his fulness may all receive grace for grace.

4. Because he loveth righteousness, &c. Therefore he is anointed. Then, the righteousness of Christ is the procuring and meritorious cause of this joy to him and his subjects, fellows in the covenant.

Ver. 10. And thou, Lord, in the beginning hast laid the foundation of the earth; and the heavens are the works of thine hands.

Ver. 11. They shall perish, but thou remainest; and they all shall wax old as doth a garment ;

Ver. 12. And as a vesture shalt thou fold them up, and they shall be changed : but thou art the same, and thy years shall not fail.

1. Another testimony of Christ, from Psal. cii. 25, 26, wherein he is expressly called, 1. Jehovah, God in essence, the same God with the Father, and the Holy Ghost; who giveth being to the creatures, and performance to the promises. 2. Who laid the foundation of the earth, &c. and so Creator of heaven and earth. 3. And by consequence, who can create in us a right spirit, and make us, of naughty sinners, sons.

2. They shall perish, wax old, and be changed. Then the heavens and the earth, now subject to corruption, shall both not continue; and yet they shall not utterly be abolished, but changed into an incorruptible estate, for man's cause, Rom. viii. 21.

3. Christ remaineth, and is the same; and his years fail not. Then, 1. Christ is eternal : and our Mediator cannot be missing, cannot die. 2. Constant and immutable; and cannot change his purpose of love, to his called ones, whatsoever changes befal them. And this is the rock of the church's comfort, when she looketh to her own frailty and changeableness.

VER. 13. But to which of the angels said he at any time, Sit on my right hand, until I make thine enemies thy footstool? Psal. cx.

1. To which of the angels said he?—He asketh for Scripture, to show what is due to angels. Then, 1. The Scripture must determine what is due to angels, and other creatures; what is to be thought of them, and done to them also. 2. And no word in Scripture doth countenance the giving the glory of the Mediator to any angel.

2. The Father hath said to Christ, Sit thou on my right hand, until I make thine enemies thy footstool.—Then, 1. Christ's kingdom will not want enemies. 2. Yea, his enemies shall be such, as there shall be need of divine wisdom and power to overcome them. 3. God professeth himself party against all the enemies of Christ's church and kingdom. 4. God will put them under, piece and piece; and altogether at length. 5. Their opposition and overthrow shall serve to glorify Christ's kingdom and government: they shall be his footstool. 6. In the mean time of this battle, Christ in his own person shall continue equal with glory and majesty with the Father; beholding the victory brought about; and bringing it about, with the Father, unto the soldiers' comfort.

VER. 14. Are they not all ministering spirits, sent forth to minister for them who shall be heirs of salvation?

The angels are all ministering spirits. Then, 1. Angels are not bodies, but their substance is invisible. 2. They are all of them, even these that are called archangels, the greatest of them, but servants to Christ; and none of them must have their master's honour: that is, any religious worship of prayer or invocation made to them.

2. They are sent forth for service or ministering.—Then, their employment is about God's children, to attend us, and serve us, at Christ's direction; not to be served by us, by any devotion.

3. Christ's subjects are called heirs of salvation.—Then, 1. They are sons. 2. And what they get is by heirship, by virtue of their adoption and sonship; not by merit of their works. 3. And they shall surely get salvation, as an heritage never to be taken from them.

THE SUM OF CHAP. II.

From the former doctrine he inferreth, seeing Christ is so glorious, let his gospel be stedfastly believed, ver. 1; for if the disobedience of the law given by the ministry of angels, was punished, ver. 2, far more the disobedience of the gospel, so gloriously confirmed, ver. 3, 4. For Christ is greater than the angels, even as man, and hath all things in subjection to him, ver. 5. As David witnesseth, speaking of elected men, with their head, the man Christ, ver. 6—8. And albeit we see not that subjection yet fully accomplished, ver. 8, yet it is begun in Christ's personal exaltation. And for his short humiliation, under the estate of angels, by suffering, we must not stumble; for it is both glorious to himself and pro-

fitable for us, ver. 9. For God's glory required that our salvation should be wrought by sufferings of the Mediator, ver. 10. And to this end he behoved to be partaker of our nature, as was foretold, ver. 11—13. That he might take on our due punishment, that is, death, ver. 14. And deliver his own from the fear thereof, ver. 15. And herein we have a privilege above the angels, in that he took on our nature and not theirs, ver. 16. And by his sufferings, a ground of so much greater comfort in him, ver. 17, 18.

THE DOCTRINE OF CHAP. II.

VER. 1. Therefore we ought to give the more earnest heed to the things which we have heard, lest at any time we should let them slip.

1. Therefore we ought to give heed, &c.—From the excellency of Christ's person, he urgeth the belief of his doctrine. Then, 1. Christ must be esteemed of, as becometh the excellency of his person. 2. The way how Christ will be respected of us, is by respecting his doctrine. And the excellency of his person should procure our reverend receiving of his word, and stedfast holding of it.

2. He will have us to take heed, lest we let it slip. The word is borrowed from rent and leaking vessels, or sandy ground. Then, 1. The gospel is a precious liquor, worthy to be well kept; and we, of ourselves, are as rent vessels, ready to let it slip when we have heard it; or like sandy ground, which keepeth not the rain.

3. For this we ought to give the more earnest heed.—Then the conscience of the worth of Christ, and his gospel, and of our own unfitness to retain it, should sharpen our vigilance and attendance to keep it; else we will doubtless let it slip.

4. He saith not, lest shortly, but lest at *any* time.—Then, it is not sufficient to believe the word for a while, and for a while to remember it; but we must gripe it so as never to quit it by misregard or misbelief. For faith, and love of the truth, is the good memory that specially he requireth here.

VER. 2. For if the word spoken by angels was stedfast, and every transgression and disobedience received a just recompense of reward;

1. He reasoneth from the law spoken by angels.—Then, the angels were employed in giving of the law; they did blow the trumpet; they, from God, uttered the word to Moses.

2. The word spoken by them was stedfast.—Then, what God delivereth by the ministry of messengers, is authorised and ratified by God.

3. Every transgression was punished.—Then, the punishment of transgressors of his law is a proof of God's authorising the doctrine.

4. He calleth the punishment a just recompense.—Then, there is no evil befalleth sinners more than they do deserve. None hath cause to complain of injustice.

VER. 3. How shall we escape, if we neglect so great salvation, which, at the first, began to be spoken by the Lord, and was confirmed unto us by them that heard him ;

1. How shall we escape?—The apostle joineth with them in the threatening. Then, so should preachers threaten their people, as willing to undergo the same punishment, except they flee the sin for which they threaten others.

2. He reasoneth for the punishment of the law breaking, to prove the punishment of misbelieving the gospel.—Then, 1. The not embracing of the gospel is a greater sin than the breach of the law. The despising of forgiveness is much worse nor the making of the fault. 2. Examples of judgment upon transgressors of the law are evidences of greater judgments to come on the misregarders of the gospel.

3. He calleth the gospel so great a salvation, because of the free offer of remission of sins, and eternal life, in it.—Then the greatness of the benefit to be gotten by the gospel, aggravateth the sin of the misregarders of it.

4. He saith not, if we reject, deny, or persecute the gospel; but if we neglect.—Then, the neglect of the doctrine of the gospel, the careless receiving of it, the not studying to know it, is sufficient to draw down heavier judgments than ever fell on the breakers of the law ; albeit a man be not an underminer or open enemy to the gospel.

5. He describeth the gospel to be that doctrine which Christ himself preached, and his apostles from him. Then, we are not bound to believe any more for gospel than that which is made clear unto us by his apostles' word. And the misregarding of other doctrine, which is not conveyed so from him, falleth under the threatening.

6. He marketh the apostles' certainty of what they have delivered unto us, in that they were ear-witnesses of his doctrine. Then, the more certainty the apostles had from Christ of their doctrine, the surer is the groundwork of our belief, and the greater is the contempt done to Christ, in their message, by unbelief.

Ver. 4. God also bearing them witness, both with signs and wonders, and with divers miracles, and gifts of the Holy Ghost, according to his own will?

1. He saith, God bare witness to the apostles' doctrine, by signs and wonders.

Then, 1, What the apostles have spoken from Christ, they spake not alone, but God with them, witnessed with them. 2. The proper use of miracles and extraordinary gifts poured out in the apostolic times was to testify that the apostles' doctrine was divine truth. Those then, must be lying wonders which are alleged for confirming any doctrine beside theirs.

2. The distribution of the gifts of the Holy Ghost, was according to his own will; not as possibly the apostles would have carved, either to themselves, or others, in the nature of the gift, or measure of it. Then, the apostles were so employed in the working of miracles, as it was evident, even then, that not they, but God was the worker of them, while he was seen to follow his own will therein, and not man's carving, in distributing his gifts. And the more God's overruling will was seen in the miracles then, the more confirmation have we of that doctrine now.

Ver. 5. For unto the angels hath he not put in subjection the world to come, whereof we speak.

He calleth the world under the kingdom of the Messias, "the world to come :" first to put a difference betwixt the estate of the world considered as under sin, and under the Messias. For as it is under sin it is said of it, old things are past away, 2 Cor. v. 17 ; Isa. xliii. 19. The creature is waxing old and running to ruin. But under the Messias it is said of it, "behold I make all things new," 2 Cor. v. 17. The creature is lifting up its head, and waiting for the day of liberation from vanity, and the manifestation of the sons of God, Rom. viii. 19. Then the kingdom of the Messias maketh another world, in effect, of that which was of old ; changing the holding and nature and use of all things to his subjects. For a man, ere he come into Christ, is God's enemy ; and to him all things in the world are enemies, the host and soldiers of his dreadful judge. But after a man is made Christ's subject, they turn all to be his friends, and his Father's servants, working altogether for his good. That is another and a new world indeed.

2. It is called the world to come ; because albeit this change began with the work of grace, before Christ came, yet it was nothing in comparison of the world to come under the Messias. And that which is now under the gospel, is little or nothing, in comparison of that glorious change of the nature and use of all things, unto Christ's subjects, which is to be revealed at his last coming. Then whatsoever thing we have hitherto found to our good, since we knew Christ, it is but little to what shall be. Our world is but to come, 1 Cor. xv. 9.

3. The world is put in subjection to Christ, that he may dispose of it at his pleasure. Then Christ is twice sovereign Lord of the world: once as Creator, again as Mediator, in his manhead, to make all the creatures in heaven and earth serve, nill they, will they, to further the work of full redemption which he hath undertaken.

4. He excludeth the angels from this honour. Then, in Christ's kingdom the angels are in subjection to Christ, for the good of his subjects, no less nor sheep and oxen, as the psalm saith, and not to be adored with him, as sovereigns over us.

Ver. 6. But one in a certain place testified, saying, What is man, that thou art mindful of him? or the son of man, that thou visitest him?

Ver. 7. Thou madest him a little lower than the angels ; thou crownedst him with glory and honour, and didst set him over the works of thine hands;

1. Being to prove, by Scripture, his purpose, he citeth neither book, nor chapter, but the words

which are of the eighth psalm, and fourth verse. Then, the apostle will have the church so well acquainted with text of scripture, that at the hearing of the words, they might know where it is written, though neither book nor verse were cited.

2. The prophet looking on man, even on Christ's manhead, wherein he was humbled, he wondereth to see man's nature so highly dignified above all creatures. Then, 1. The baseness of man's natural being, compared with other more glorious creatures, maketh God's love to us above all other creatures, so much the more wonderful. 2. Christ's humiliation and exaltation were both foreseen, and revealed, by the prophets.

VER. 8. Thou hast put all things in subjection under his feet. For, in that he put all in subjection under him, he left nothing that is not put under him. But now we see not yet all things put under him.

1. He proveth that angels are in subjection to Christ, because the text of the psalm saith, all is put in subjection; and so neither angels nor other creatures are excepted. Then, 1. For understanding of the meaning of scripture, it is necessary to consider, not only what it saith expressly, but also what it saith by consequence of sound reason. 2. And whatsoever is rightly deduced by evidence of sound reason of the words of scripture, is the meaning of the scripture, as if it were spoken expressly.

2. He saith, There is nothing left that is not put under Christ. Then, not good angels only, but all spirits, and all that they can do also, are subject to Christ; and he can make them, nill they, will they, contribute to the furtherance of his own purpose, for the good of his subjects, and hurt of his foes.

3. Because Christ's enemies are still troubling his kingdom, he moveth a doubt, saying, we see not yet all things put under him. Then, 1. The troubles of Christ's subjects hinder the natural mind to perceive the glory of Christ's advancement. 2. Carnal reason, the proctor of misbelief, will admit no more of divine truth, nor it is capable of, by sense.

VER. 9. But we see Jesus, who was made a little lower than the angels, for the suffering of death, crowned with glory and honour, that he, by the grace of God, should taste death for every man.

1. He answereth the doubt, saying, we see Jesus crowned with glory and honour, and so a course taken for putting all that oppose him farther and farther under him. Then, 1. The subjection of all things to Christ's throne cannot be seen, but in the exaltation of his person. 2. When we see his person exalted to such high dignity in heaven, it is easy to see him put all under that riseth up against him. 3. That which may be taken up of Christ, partly by his word and doctrine, partly by his miraculous works and extraordinary gifts of the spirit, poured out upon the primitive church, partly by his ordinary and powerful working upon the souls of his own, since

that time, unto this day, humbling and comforting, changing and reforming men's hearts and lives: I say these evidences of his power do make a spiritual eye, in a manner, to see Jesus, the worker of these works, crowned with glory and honour.

2. He meeteth another doubt, arising from the abasement of Christ, in his sufferings and death, to which he answereth, in the words of the psalm: first, that it was foretold in that same psalm, that he was to be made, for a little, lower than the angels; to wit, by suffering of death. Then, 1. The cross of Christ is a ready stumbling block for a carnal mind; else, what needed the removal of the scandal? 2. It is true, indeed, Christ, in his humiliation, was abased under the angels, and emptied. 3. This abasement was but a little and for a short time. 4. It was foretold in the psalm that speaketh of his exaltation. 5. If we look to the scripture foretelling, we shall not stumble at Christ's humiliation.

3. He giveth a further answer, by showing the end of Christ's sufferings, to be for our cause, in the favour of God to us, that he should, by the grace of God, taste death for every one of us.

Then, 1. Christ's suffering was not for his own deserving, but for ours; and therefore should be glorious in our eyes. 2. Every believer and elect soul hath interest in that death of his; and so every man bound to love him and magnify him for it, and to apply the fruit of it to himself. 3. This death was but a tasting of death, because he continued but a short time under it; for his short suffering was so precious that he could not be holden by the sorrows of death; but death for a little was sufficient; and therefore should diminish no man's estimation of him. 4. It was by the grace of God that his death, for a short, should stand for our eternal; and therefore, gracious and glorious should these sufferings be esteemed by us.

VER. 10. For it became him, for whom are all things, and by whom are all things, in bringing many sons unto glory, to make the captain of their salvation perfect through sufferings.

1. Another reason of Christ's sufferings. This way of our saving by Christ's sufferings, made for the glory of God, and our good.

Then, when the reasons of Christ's death are seen, the scandal of his cross ceaseth.

2. There is a work to do here; a great many of sons to be brought to glory.

Then, 1. All the elect, and saved souls, are in the rank of children. 2. Albeit, they be few in comparison of the world, yet are they, many of them, all together. 3. There is not one of them all who can go to heaven or salvation, but by Christ's leading and conduct.

3. The captain of their salvation must be made perfect, through suffering. Then, 1. How perfect soever Christ be in himself, yet before his suffering he lacked one thing which his office towards us required; to wit, experimental suffering of such sorrows as his soldiers and followers are subject unto. 2. When his sufferings were ended he was perfectly fitted to comfort us, seeing he found our sorrows in himself sometime.

4. He saith, it became God, for whom and by

whom are all things, that the matter should be so brought about. Then, 1. All things are for God's glory at the end; and so should the manner of our salvation be also. 2. All things are by God's hand and power brought about; and reason too, that he dispose of the means of our salvation as he pleaseth. This way became God most of any; it brought him greatest glory, by the shame, sorrow, and death of one, to bring glory, and joy, and life to many.

Ver. 11. For both he that sanctifieth, and they who are sanctified, are all of one; for which cause he is not ashamed to call them brethren.

1. If any should further ask how could he die? or how could justice accept him in our stead? he answereth, because he is one of our kind and nature. Then, 1. There is a natural band betwixt Christ and his followers; they are of the same stock, the same natural substance. 2. Christ's natural band with us maketh him a direct entress [suitable person] to redeem us.

2. He calleth Christ him that sanctifieth; and the believers they who are sanctified. Then, 1. The band of nature betwixt Christ and men is reckoned unto those only who are sanctified; with none other will Christ reckon kindred. Therefore they must study to holiness that would claim kindred to Christ. 3. The sanctification which it behoveth us to have must proceed from Christ; no holiness until a man be in him.

3. He saith Christ is not ashamed to call the sanctified, brethren.—Then, 1. As Christ hath dimitted [condescended] himself to our nature, so also to the styles of consanguinity with us. 2. Christ is as kindly affectioned to his followers as ever brother was to another; he will not misken [neglect] his own, albeit unworthy. That which may serve to our glory and comfort, Christ will think it no disgrace to himself.

Ver. 12. Saying, I will declare thy name unto my brethren; in the midst of the church will I sing praise unto thee.

He proveth that he calleth us brethren from Psal. xx. ver. 22. The Messias there taketh upon him to preach to men, and to praise the Father, Then, 1. With our nature Christ took on also the yoke of the exercises of religion. 2. He joineth with us in the discharge of them. 3. He is first in the exercise; not only because he discharged them in his own proper person; but also because still by his Spirit, where two or three are gathered together in his name, he is in the midst of them; moving and moderating the spirits of his own delectable organs.

Ver. 13. And again, I will put my trust in him. And again, Behold, I and the children which God hath given me.

1. The next proof is from Psal. xviii. ver. 2, where Christ, under the type of David, promiseth to believe in the Father. Then, 1. Christ is one of the number of believers, one of the Covenant of Grace, confederate by faith; and therefore he behoved to be a

man to this end. 2. Then have we in the sense of our unbelief the comfort of the soundness and strength of Christ's believing, as well as of his other perfections.

2. The third proof is from Isa. viii. 18, wherein Christ, under the type of the prophet Isaiah, presenteth himself with his chosen children before the Father. Then, 1. Christ is our father also. and we his children. 2. We are given to him of the Father. 3. We are not presented before the Father without our Mediator Christ. 4. Christ, and we his little ones, joined together and separated from the world, are a pleasant sight for the Father to behold.

Ver. 14. Forasmuch then as the children are partakers of flesh and blood, he also himself likewise took part of the same; that through death he might destroy him that had the power of death, that is, the devil.

1. He giveth farther reasons of his incarnation. And first, he behoved by death to destroy the devil, that had the power of death; and so behoved to be a man, that he might die. Then, 1. Sinners without Christ are under the sentence of death, temporal and eternal. 2. Satan hath power of death, as the burly [court officer] hath power over the pit and gallows, at death, to take them away to torment who are not delivered from his power. 3. Christ hath destroyed Satan's power and tyranny in this point, in behalf of all his elect and true believers. 4. The way how Christ hath overcome Satan, is by his own death, ransoming his own. 5. Fray [a combat with] death behoved to be the way, it behoved also Christ to be a mortal man, as well as God, that he might die.

2. Again he saith, Christ took part of flesh and blood with the children, that is, with the elect given to him.—Then, 1. Love to the elect made the Son of God come down, and make himself a man also. 2. Christ, in his human nature, is as kindly a man as any of the elect; having flesh and blood and bones, as well as we. His flesh and blood is not only like ours, but is a part of our substance; who is come of the same stock of Adam and Eve, as surely as ours; and not made either by creation of nothing, or by transubstantiation of some other thing than our substance.

Ver. 15. And deliver them, who through fear of death, were all their life-time subject to bondage.

Another fruit of Christ's death is the delivery of believers from the bondage of the fear of death, wherein they do lie before belief. Then, 1. There is a natural fear of death, and the devil, and hell rooted in all men always; albeit not aye [always] felt, yet easily wakened. 2. This fear putteth men in bondage, that they dare not meditate on death, or God's judgment, or hell, as deserved by themselves. 3. Christ's death delivereth his subjects from the danger of this evil, and from the bondage of this fear also. 4. None but a child of Christ's can have solid and true courage against death; neither is there a free man in the world, except true Christians.

Ver. 16. For verily, he took not on him the nature of angels; but he took on him the seed of Abraham.

He insisteth in the doctrine of Christ's incarnation, because it is the ground of all our comfort, and secludeth the angels from such an honour as we have thereby. The Son of God took on him the seed of Abraham, and not the nature of angels, saith the apostle. Then, 1. Christ hath his proper subsistence, and being in himself, before the incarnation, even his own Divine nature, with personal properties existing; for he is the Son of God, the second person of the Godhead, before he took on our nature. 2. He chose to assume our nature for our delivery, and not the angels' nature, for delivery of such as were fallen of their kind. 3. The nature that he taketh on is man's very nature, the seed of Abraham. 4. He preventeth the personal subsistence of our nature, he assumeth the seed of Abraham. 5. He maketh an union of our nature with his Divine nature. 6. The way of making the union is assumption, or taking of our nature unto his own, whereby remaining the same which he was before; to wit, the Son of God, he joineth our nature to himself, and becometh what he was not before, to wit, the Son of man. 7. He assumeth the seed of Abraham, that he may be known to be no other but the same Messias which was promised by the prophets to the fathers. 8. When he hath assumed man's nature to his own Divine nature, he remaineth the same He that he was before, still one person. So Christ Jesus is the promised Messias, the second person of the Godhead; very God from everlasting, and very man since the conception of the Virgin Mary; before his incarnation having only his own Divine nature in his person, but now since that time having our nature also personally united with his Divine nature, so to remain, both God and man in one person for our good for ever.

Ver. 17. Wherefore in all things it behoved him to be made like unto his brethren, that he might be a merciful and faithful high priest in things pertaining to God, to make reconciliation for the sins of the people.

He concludeth that Christ behoved to partake both of our nature and punishment or misery, that we might receive the more good of him. 1. First, he saith, he behoved to be like his brethren in all things; that is, for substance of nature, for natural properties, for sinless infirmities, for fellowship in temptations and miseries, and in all things whatsoever our good did require his making like unto us. Then, 1. They who imagine and worship a Christ not like to us in all these things, wherein the Scripture pronounceth him like unto us, do mistake the true Christ and worship a false. 2. It is very necessary that we conceive rightly of Christ's person, seeing the Scripture doth press the knowledge thereof upon us so particularly. 2. He showeth the end of his conforming himself unto us to be that he might be a faithful and merciful high-priest. Then, 1. As Christ took on our nature, so in our nature, he took on a special office of priesthood to do us good. 2. In this his office, he is faithful, and will neglect nothing night nor day that may help us. 3. In our slips and oversights he will be merciful unto us. 4. Seeing he hath conformed himself to us for this end, we may take his communion of nature and miseries with us for a pawn and pledge to assure us that he will both pity and help us.

3. The extent of his priesthood he maketh in general to be in all things pertaining to God; and in special to make reconciliation for the sins of the people. Then, 1. If God have any thing to do with us, any direction, or comfort, or blessing to bestow upon us, it must come by our High-priest, Jesus, unto us. 2. If he command us in any thing, or be to make covenant with us, or have controversy to debate with us, our High-priest will answer for us. 3. If we have any thing to do with God, to seek any good thing of him, or deprecate any evil, or to offer any offering of praise or service, Christ's office stretcheth itself to all this to do for us. 4. In special, as our sins daily deserve and provoke God's anger, so doth Christ's priesthood pacify God's wrath, and work reconciliation to us.

Ver. 18. For in that he himself hath suffered, being tempted, he is able to succour them that are tempted.

1. He showeth Christ's experience to be both of sufferings and temptations; that whether of the two annoy us, we may get comfort for either or both from him.

Then, 1. There are two evils which attend the children of God, to annoy them; to wit, troubles and sin, or sin and misery. 2. Christ hath experience albeit not of sin, in his own person; yet of temptation to sin, and of suffering of trouble.

2. He applieth the comfort expressly to the tempted. Then, 1. Men in trouble have need of comfort and relief; but men under temptation to sin, much more. 2. Yea, sin, and temptation to sin, is more grievous to a true child of God, when he seeth matters rightly, than any trouble. 3. No bearing out under trials, or standing in temptations, but by succour and help from Christ. 4. Christ's experience of temptation may assure us both of his ability and willingness to succour such as seek relief from him in this case.

THE SUM OF CHAP. III.

Therefore weigh well what a one Christ is, and prefer none before him, ver. 1; for he is as faithful in his message for changing the typical priesthood, as Moses was in his message when he delivered it, ver. 2, and so much more honourable than Moses, as the builder is over the stones builded, ver. 3, 4. And Moses was faithful as a servant in the church, ver. 5; but Christ, as Son and Lord over the church, to dispose of the service thereof at his pleasure, ver. 6. Therefore beware of old Israel's hard heart, lest you be debarred of God's rest, ver. 7—11. Beware of like unbelief, for it is the ground of apostasy, ver. 12, and do your best to preserve others from it also, ver. 13; for perseverance in faith is necessary to salvation, ver. 14. For David's words do prove that there were some, albeit not all hearers of God's word of old, that did provoke him, ver. 15, 16; and who were these, but such as he punished? ver. 17. And whom punished he but unbelievers? ver. 18. So misbelief debarred them out of God's rest of old, and will also do the like yet, if men continue in it, ver. 19.

THE DOCTRINE OF CHAP. III.

VER. 1. Wherefore, holy brethren, partakers of the heavenly calling, consider the Apostle and High-priest of our profession, Christ Jesus.

1. After he had taught them somewhat more of Christ, he exhorteth them of new to consider of him.—Then, 1. As we get farther light of Christ, we are bound to farther use making of our light. 2. As farther is revealed unto us of Christ, so must we set our minds on work to ponder and weigh what is revealed, that the matter may sink deeper in our mind and in our heart. 3. Except we shall consider seriously what is spoken of Christ, we can make no profitable use of the doctrine; for such high mysteries are not soon taken up, and the heart is not soon wrought upon, so as to receive impression of his excellency, except after due consideration.

2. He calleth Christ Jesus the High-priest and the Apostle of our profession.—The high-priesthood was the highest calling in the Jewish church; the apostleship the highest calling in the Christian church. Christ is here styled by both. Then Christ hath inclosed in his office the perfection and dignities of the highest callings both in the Jewish and Christian church,—those dignities which were divided in men, or conjoined in him; in men, by way of ministerial employment under him; in Christ, by original authority above all.

3. He calleth the Christian religion, our profession, or confession. Then it is the nature of the Christian religion not to be smothered, but to be openly brought forth, confessed, and avowed, in word and deed, to the glory of Christ, who is the author thereof.

4. He styleth these Hebrews to whom he writeth, holy brethren, partakers of the heavenly calling. Then, 1. Christians do not possess their prerogatives without a warrantable title: they have a calling thereto. 2. The calling is heavenly, because God, by his word and Spirit, calleth men to the communion of his grace and glory, by forsaking of themselves and things earthly, and following Christ in an holy conversation: all is heavenly here. 3. Christians are partakers alike of this vocation: that is, have a like warrant and obligation to follow him that calleth them, albeit all do not alike follow the calling. 4. They are brethren amongst themselves, for their adoption, albeit some weaker, some stronger. 5. And holy is this brotherhood, that is, spiritual; and so superior to civil or natural or earthly bands whatsoever.

VER. 2. Who was faithful to him that appointed him, as also Moses was faithful in all his house.

1. Because the Jews did too highly esteem of Moses, in appointing of the legal service, and not so highly of Christ, as became in abrogating thereof, the apostle compareth Moses and Christ, giving to Moses his due place of a servant, and to Christ the place due to the master.

Then, it is no new thing that people incline so to esteem of good men's authority, as to forget to give Christ his own room. 2. The way to help this is, so to esteem of God's servants, fathers, or councils, more or fewer, as the estimation that men have of them, derogate nothing from the estimation due to Christ.

2. In special he maketh all the points of Moses's commendations duly deserved points of Christ's commendation. 1. Did Moses's office reach itself to all the house of God under the law, and all the service of it? so did Christ's office reach to all the church of God, and all the service of it, under the gospel. 2. Was Moses appointed to give out what he delivered? so was Christ appointed to institute what he did institute, and abrogate what he did abrogate. 3. Was Moses faithful to him who appointed him, in all the matters of God's house, keeping back nothing that he was directed to reveal? so is Christ faithful to the Father, who did appoint him in like manner.

Then, like as if any man should have added or pared, chopped or changed the ordinances of God's house under the law, it had been an imputation, either unto God, of not sufficient directing his church, or unto Moses and the prophets, of unfaithful discharge of their duty in the church of the Old Testament. So is it a like imputation to God and Christ, if any shall add or diminish, chop or change the ordinance of God's church under the New Testament.

VER. 3. For this man was counted worthy of more glory than Moses, inasmuch as he who hath builded the house hath more honour than the house.

1. Having equalled Christ unto Moses, he now preferreth Christ to Moses.

Then Christ is not rightly esteemed of, except he be preferred as far above all his servants, as the Father hath counted him worthy of more glory than his servants.

2. He preferreth Christ above Moses, as the builder is above the house. Then, as no stone in the house, nor all the house together, is comparable in honour with the builder of the house; so the honour and authority of no particular member of the church, nor of the whole catholic church together, is comparable to the honour and authority of Christ. Yea, as far as the builder is above the house in honour, as far is Christ's authority above the church's authority, which is his house.

VER. 4. For every house is builded by some man, but he that built all things is God.

He proveth Christ to be the builder of the church, because some builder it must have, as every house hath. But only God that buildeth all things is able for this work : therefore Christ, who builded all things, is the builder of it.

Then, 1. Whatsoever employment a man get of God, in edifying of the church, yet, in proper speech, he is a part of the building builded by another. 2. The honour of building the church belongeth to God alone properly. 3. The building of the church is a work requiring omnipotency in the builder ; for to make a saint of a sinner, is as hard as to make a man of the dust of the earth, or of nothing.

Ver. 5. And Moses, verily, was faithful in all his house, as a servant, for a testimony of those things which were to be spoken after.

Moses was faithful as a servant.—Now a servant's part is to do and say by direction, and not of his own authority. Then, he is the faithfulest servant that doth least in his own authority, and most attendeth unto the direction of God, beareth testimony to what God hath commanded, and teacheth not for doctrine the precepts of men.

Ver. 6. But Christ, as a Son over his own house, whose house are we, if we hold fast the confidence and the rejoicing of the hope firm unto the end.

Moses was faithful as a servant, but Christ as a son, over his own house.—Then, as much difference betwixt Christ's authority in the church, and men's, how excellent soever, as betwixt the authority of the master and the servants. 2. Christ's authority is native over his church, by virtue of his Sonship : by his eternal generation of the Father, he hath this prerogative. 3. The church is Christ's own house, and he may dispose of it, and of the service thereof, as pleaseth him. Men who are but servants, must change none of the ordinances of God's worship in it : but Christ may change the ordinances of his own worship, and therefore alter the ordinances of Levi, and appoint a more simple form of external worship in place thereof. 2. He expoundeth this house to be the company of true believers. Then, 1. The church of God under the law, and under the gospel, are one church, one house of God in substance, and all the faithful, then and now, lively stones of this house. 2. The church have God dwelling, and conversing, and familiarly manifesting himself amongst them. 3. He addeth a condition, If we hold fast the confidence, and the rejoicing of the hope, firm unto the end. That is, if we continue stedfast in the faith, inwardly griping the promised glory by hope, and outwardly avowing by confession Christ's truth ; whereby he neither importeth the possibility of final apostasy of the saints, nor yet mindeth he to weaken the confidence of believers, more than he doubteth of his own perseverance, or mindeth to weaken his own faith ; for he joineth himself with them, saying, " If we hold fast." But writing to the number of the visible church, of whom some, not being sound, might fall away, and by their example

make some weak ones, though sound, stumble for a time, to the dishonour of the gospel ; he putteth a difference betwixt true believers, who do indeed persevere, and time-servers, who do not persevere, to whom he doth not grant, for the present, the privilege of being God's house.

This conditional speech then importeth, 1. That some professors in the visible church may make defection, and not persevere to the end. 2. That such as shall make final defection hereafter are not a part of God's house for the present, howsoever they be esteemed. 3. That true believers must take warning, from the possibility of some professors' apostasy, to look the better to themselves, and to take a better gripe of Christ, who is able to keep them. 4. That true believers both may and should hold fast their confidence unto the end ; yea, and must aim to do so, if they would persevere. 5. That true believers have ground and warrant, in the promises of the gospel, both to hope for salvation, and to rejoice and glory in that hope, as if it were present possession. 6. That the more a man aimeth at this solid confidence and gloriation of hope, the more evidence he giveth that he is of the true house of God.

Ver. 7. Wherefore as the Holy Ghost saith, To-day, if ye will hear my voice.

1. In the words of the Psal. xcv. 9, he exhorteth them to beware of hardening their heart in unbelief. The words of the psalm are called here, The saying of the Holy Ghost, and of the God of Israel, 2 Sam. xxiii. 2, 3.

Then, 1. The authority of the Scripture is not of man, but of the Holy Ghost. 2. The Scriptures are no dumb letter, but the voice of the Holy Ghost, who by them speaketh. 3. The Holy Ghost is God, the inspirer of the prophets that wrote the Scripture. 4. The Holy Ghost is a distinct person of the Godhead, from the Father and the Son, exercising the proper actions of a person, inspiring the prophets, inditing the Scriptures, and speaking to the church.

2. In the words of the exhortation, To-day, if ye will hear his voice, harden not your hearts ; Observe, 1. That while men have the offer of salvation, and the word preached unto them, it is their day. 2. That by the outward hearing, God requireth the heart to be brought down and mollified. 3. That he requireth present yielding, to-day, while he calleth, without delay, because we cannot be sure how long God will spare or continue his offer, beyond this present. 4. He that studieth not to yield his heart to believe, and obey God's word, sounding in his ears, hardeneth his heart. For what is it else, not to harden their heart, but heartily to believe, and give obedience ?

Ver. 8. Harden not your hearts, as in the provocation, in the day of temptation in the wilderness.

Ver. 9. When your fathers tempted me, proved me, and saw my works, forty years.

He proveth the danger of this sin, in the example of their fathers : as in the day of provocation, when your fathers tempted me, Exod. xvii. 7 ; whence we learn,

1. That the evil of sin is not seen, till the consequences thereof be seen, what provocation it giveth to God, and what wrath it draweth down on the sinner. 2. It is safest, to take a view of our danger by any sin, in the person of others, who have fallen in the like, and have been punished. 3. The sins that our predecessors have been given unto, we should most carefully watch against. 4. That God's bounty, patience, and means of grace, the longer they be abused, aggravateth sin the more.

VER. 10. Wherefore I was grieved with that generation and said, They do alway err in their hearts ; and they have not known my ways.

God pronounceth the offenders guilty, and then giveth sentence of doom upon them, for their guiltiness : they err in heart, saith the Lord. Then, 1. Misbelieving and disobeying of the word preached, is not reckoned with God, for simple ignorance of the mind, but for a wilful ignorance, and erring of the heart, which is worse. For the ignorance of the mind simply is, I know not, but the error of the heart is, I will not know, I care not, I desire not, I love not to know, nor obey. And such is the ignorance of those who have the means of knowledge, and reformation, and yet remain in their sins. 2. Such obstinate ignorance and wilful disobedience, provoketh God to cast away the sinner, and not to deal any more with him.

VER. 11. So I sware in my wrath, they shall not enter into my rest.

For their doom God debarreth them from his rest, that is, from all the comforts of his fellowship, and giveth them torment, instead of rest. Then, 1. Obstinate disobedients of the voice of the gospel, lie near hand final off-cutting. 2. If God give over a man to such hardness of heart, as still to work contrary to the light of God's word, he hath apparently denounced and sworn to condemn and seclude from heaven, such a soul. 3. It is only such obstinate ones, as go on hardening their heart against admonitions of the word, that God hath sworn to debar. If a man be found mourning for his former obstinacy, the decree is not gone forth against him.

VER. 12. Take heed, brethren, lest there be in any of you an evil heart of unbelief, in departing from the living God.

1. From the former example, he warneth them to beware of an evil heart of unbelief, and so to eschew apostasy.
Then, 1. Misbelief is the main root of apostasy. As belief draweth us to an union with God ; so misbelief maketh a separation. 2. Misbelief is a special part of the heart's wickedness, bewraying the enmity which naturally we have against God, as much as any ill : for misbelief denieth to God the honour of truth, mercy, and goodness ; and importeth blasphemies in the contrary. 3. Misbelief is an ill in the heart, making the heart yet worse and worse where it is, and barring forth all the remedies which might come by faith to cure the heart.

2. He warneth to take heed, lest there be such a heart in any of them at any time.
Then, 1. Misbelief is a subtle and deceitful sin, having colours and pretences a number to hide it ; and must be watched over, lest it deceive, and getting strength overcome. 2. The watch must be constant at all occasions, lest this ill get advantage, when we are careless and inattentive at any time. 3. Watch must be kept as over ourselves, so also over others : lest any others' misbelief not being marked, draw us in the same snare with them.

3. He describeth apostasy by misbelief, and departing from the living God.
Then, 1. Believing is a drawing near to the living God, and staying with him. 2. The loss that misbelief bringeth, should scare us from so fearful a sin. 3. Departing from the true Christian religion, is a departing from the living God, whatsoever the apostate or his followers do conceive : for God is not, where truth is not.

VER. 13. But exhort one another daily, while it is called to-day ; lest any of you be hardened, through the deceitfulness of sin.

1. He prescribeth a remedy to prevent this ill : to wit, that they exhort one another daily, while it is called to day, that is, beside the public exhortation from the preachers, that every one of them mutually confer and stir up one another by speeches that make for decyphering the deceitfulness of sin, or preventing hardness of heart, or confirming one another in the truth of religion and constant profession thereof.
Then, 1. Private Christians not only may, but should, keep Christian communion amongst themselves, and mutually exhort and stir up one another. 2. This is a necessary mean of preserving people from defection. 3. And a duty daily to be discharged, while it is to-day ; that is, as oft, and as long, as God giveth present occasion and opportunity for it ; lest a scattering come.

2. The inconvenience that may follow, if this be neglected, is, lest any of you be hardened through the deceitfulness of sin.
Then, 1. There is none, even the strongest of the flock, but they have need of this mutual help of other private Christians. 2. Neither is there any so base, or contemptible, but the care of their standing in the faith, and of their safety, belongeth to all. 3. Sin hath many ways and colours, whereby it may beguile a man : and therefore we have need of more eyes than our own, and more observers. 4. If it be not timeously discovered, it will draw on hardness of heart, so as a man will grow senseless of it, confirmed in the habit of it, and loath to quit it.

3. In the former verse he warneth them to beware of apostasy in religion ; and in this verse, that they take course, that they be not hardened in any sin in their conversation.
Then, The ready way to draw on defection in religion, is defection from a godly conversation. And the way to prevent defection in religion, is to study to holiness of conversation.

VER. 14. For we are made partakers of Christ, if we hold the beginning of our confidence stedfast unto the end.

To stir them up to perseverance, he layeth a necessity of holding fast gripe of the principles of Christian religion, whereby they were persuaded to become Christians : because only so, fellowship with Christ is gotten. The truth whereby they were begotten to Christian religion he calleth, The beginning of our confidence : yea, and of our spiritual subsistence ; as the word in the original importeth.

Then, 1. The gospel is the beginning of our confidence ; yea, and of our spiritual subsistence ; of our new being that we have, as spiritual men, in the state of grace. 2. The man that renounceth the grounds of the gospel, and persevereth not, was never partaker of Christ. 3. Christian religion is not a thing that a man may say, and unsay : keep or quit, as prosperity or adversity, threatenings or allurements, do offer ; but such as must in all estates, upon all hazard be avowed.

VER. 15. Whilst it is said, To-day if ye will hear his voice, harden not your hearts, as in the provocation.

VER. 16. For some when they had heard, did provoke ; howbeit not all that came out of Egypt by Moses.

Now, the apostle draweth collections from the words of the prophet in the psalm repeating the words of the text, which speak of the provocation of the fathers, ver. 25. Whereupon he inferreth that there were some, at least, hearers of the word, which provoked God ; albeit not all. For whose cause, David had reason to give advertisement to their posterity, to beware of the like ; and the writer of the epistle, reason to apply the same unto them, ver. 16.

Then, 1. From the apostle's handling of the text which he hath in hand, all must learn, not lightly to pass Scripture, but to consider both what is said expressly in it, and what is imported by consequence. 2. Preachers' practice is justified when they consider the circumstances of a text, and do urge duties upon their people, or teach them doctrine from the text.

VER. 17. But with whom was he grieved forty years ? Was it not with them that had sinned, whose carcasses fell in the wilderness ?

He observeth another thing in his text, upon the persons with whom God was grieved : that first, they are marked to have sinned, and afterwards punished, leaving to them to gather,

That where sin went before, the anger of God would follow upon the sin : and, after the grieving of God, judgment light upon the sinner.

VER. 18. And to whom sware he, that they should not enter into his rest, but to them that believed not ?

VER. 19. So we see, that they could not enter in because of unbelief.

He hath yet another observation, upon the nature of the sin, whereby God was provoked to swear their damnation that sinned, that it was unbelief, ver. 18. And formally deduceth his doctrine by consequence ; that misbelief did stop the sinner's entry into the rest, and made the sinner to lie under an impossibility of entering, ver. 19. The use of which doctrine he presseth in the next chapter.

Then, 1. The apostle leaveth us to gather. That above all other sins, misbelief provoketh God to indignation most. 2. That as long as this sin lieth on, and getteth way, it is impossible for a man to enter into God's rest. This sin alone is able to seclude him.

THE SUM OF CHAP. IV.

He presseth the use of the former doctrine, saying in substance, Therefore, be afraid, to be debarred from God's rest, ver. 1. For we have the offer of it, as well as they ; only here are the odds, they believed not, ver. 2. But we who do believe enter into a rest, as David's words import. For there are three rests in the Scripture, which may be called God's rest : 1. God's rest upon the first Sabbath : 2. The rest of Canaan, typical. 3. The spiritual and true rest of God's people, in Christ's kingdom, which is a deliverance, and ceasing from sin and misery. David doth not mean of the rest of the Sabbath, in his threatening ; because albeit the work of creation was finished in the beginning of the world, and that rest come and gone ; yet David speaketh of another rest after that, in the word threatening, ver. 3. That God's rest was past at the founding of the world, is plain from Moses's words, ver. 4. After which rest, David speaketh here of another rest, ver. 5. Wherein, seeing unbelievers entered not, believers must enter, ver. 6. Again, David meaneth not of the rest of Canaan ; for after they had, a long time, dwelt in Canaan, David yet setteth them a day, during which they might enter into God's rest, ver. 7. For if the rest of Canaan, which Jesus or Joshua gave unto them, had been this true rest, then David would not have spoken of another rest after that, ver. 8. But speak he doth. Therefore there is a rest beside these, even that spiritual rest, proper to God's people, ver. 9. I call this a rest, because when God's people cease to do their own works, and will, it is like God's rest, ver. 10. Therefore, let us beware to be debarred from this rest by unbelief as they were, ver. 11. For God's word is as effectual now, as ever it was, to discover the lurking sins of the heart, howsoever men would cloak them, ver. 12. And God, with whom we have to do, seeth us thoroughly, ver. 33. But rather seeing we have so great encouragement, to get entry through Jesus Christ, so merciful and pitiful a high priest, ver. 14, 15, let us be stedfast in our faith, and come, confidently, to get God's grace, to help us through all difficulties in the way to that full rest, ver. 16.

THE DOCTRINE OF CHAP. IV.

VER. 1. Let us therefore fear, lest a promise being left us of entering into his rest, any of you should seem to come short of it.

1. In the exhortation he layeth down this

ground, that there is a promise of entry to this rest left unto us.

Then, 1. The entry into God's rest is cast open to the Christian church, and encouragement given by offer and promise of entry. 2. While it is to-day this promise and invitation to it is left unto us, notwithstanding that many bye-gone occasions of getting good and doing good be spent and away. 3. As long as this merciful offer and promise is kept to the fore unto [remains before] us, we should stir up ourselves to lay hold on it in time.

2. Therefore let us fear lest any of you seem to come short of it. The similitude is borrowed from the price of a race. Then, 1. A race must be run ere we come to our full rest. 2. The constant runner to the end getteth rest from sin and misery, and a quiet possession of happiness at the race's end. 3. The apostate, and he who by misbelief breaketh off his course, and runneth not on, as may be, cometh short, and attaineth not unto it. 4. The apostasy of some, and possibility of apostasy of mere professors, should not weaken any man's faith; but rather terrify him from misbelief. There is a right kind of fear of perishing; to wit, such as hindereth not assurance of faith; but rather serveth to guard it, and spurreth on a man to perseverance. 6. We must not only fear, by misbelieving to come short; but to seem or give any appearance of coming short.

VER. 2. For unto us was the gospel preached, as well as unto them; but the word preached did not profit them, not being mixed with faith in them that heard it.

1. To make the example the more to urge them, he saith, the gospel was preached to them whom God debarred, for misbelief, from his rest. Then, 1. The gospel was preached in the wilderness for substance of truth, albeit not in such fulness of doctrine and clearness of truth as now. The preaching of it in clearness now must make the misbelievers of it in no less danger of being debarred from that rest than the old Israelites, yea, rather in more.

2. The cause of their debarring, is: The word was not mixed with faith in them, and so profited them not. Then, 1. As a medicinal drink must have the true ingredients mixed with it, so must the word have faith mixed with it, joining itself with all the parts of truth closely. 2. Faith can wall [stand] with nothing, nor be mixed with truth but the word; and the word will not join, nor wall, nor mix with conceits, opinions, presumptions, but with faith; that is, it will be received, not as a conjecture, or possible truth, but for divine and infallible truth; else it profiteth not. 3. Hearers of the word may blame their misbelief, if they get not profit. 4. Albeit a man get light by the word, and some tasting of temporary joy, and honour, and riches also, by professing or preaching of it, yet he receiveth not profit, except he get entry into God's rest thereby; for all these turn to conviction.

VER. 3. For, we which have believed, do enter into rest, as he said, As I have sworn in my wrath, if they shall enter into my rest, although the works were finished from the foundation of the world.

Read the sum of this chapter, verses 2, 3, 5, for clearing of his reasoning.

He proveth that believers enter into God's rest, because God excludeth, by his threatening, misbelievers only. Then, 1. Fearful threatenings of the wicked, carry in their bosom sweetest promises to the godly and the faithful.

2. Believers get a beginning of this rest in this world, and a possession of it, in some degree, by faith. Their delivery from sin and misery is begun. Their life and peace and joy is begun.

VER. 4. For he spake in a certain place of the seventh day, on this wise; And God did rest the seventh day from all his works.

VER. 5. And in this place again: If they shall enter into my rest.

He compareth places of Scripture, and showeth the significations of rest.

Then, 1 Words in Scripture are taken in sundry places, in sundry significations. 2. Comparison of places will both show the divers acceptations of any word, and the proper meaning of it in every place.

VER. 6. Seeing therefore it remaineth, that some must enter therein; and they to whom it was first preached entered not in, because of unbelief

The full sentence of the first verse is this: Seeing therefore it remaineth that some must enter in; and they to whom it was first preached, entered not in because of unbelief; it will follow by consequence that believers do enter in. This latter part is not expressed in the text, but left unto us, to gather by consequence. Whence we learn: 1. That God alloweth us to draw consequences from his Scripture. 2. Yea, traineth us on by his own example, to draw them forth by reason. 3. Yea, he will, of necessity, force us to draw consequences from his words; or else, not let us understand his meaning, by leaving something not expressed to be collected by us.

VER. 7. Again, he limiteth a certain day, saying in David, To-day; after so long a time, as it is said, To-day, if ye will hear his voice, harden not your hearts.

In that he reasoneth from the circumstance of time when David uttered these words, he teacheth us, that oftentimes there is matter of great moment imported in the least circumstances of the Scripture's writing; and therefore, that the circumstances of time, place, and person, who speaketh, and to whom, and at what time, &c. should not be passed over in our consideration of a text, but diligently be marked.

VER. 8. For if Jesus had given them rest, then would he not afterwards have spoken of another day.

VER. 9. There remaineth therefore a rest to the people of God.

VER. 10. For he that is entered into his rest, he also hath ceased from his own works, as God did from his.

1. This reasoning from the time of David's speaking, showeth, how infallibly they were led that wrote the Scripture; that they could not fail in setting down a word, nor speak one word that could cross any other word spoken by any other prophet, before or after.

2. David taught of the spiritual rest in his time and so did Moses. Then, 1. The old church was not straitened with earthly promises so, but that they had heavenly and spiritual promises given them also, as signified by the earthly and typical promises. Their types had some star-light of interpretation, and they were taught to look through the veil of ceremonies and types.

3. He saith, he that is entered into his rest, ceaseth from his own works. Then, 1. Before a man be reconciled to God by faith in Christ, he is working his own works, doing his own will, and not God's. 2. He is working, without ceasing, his own unrest, and his own torment, which he procureth by working his own will. 3. The man that thinketh he is entered into God's rest, must be God's workman, and no more work what pleaseth himself, but what pleaseth God; ceasing from sinful works, and doing what is lawful and good, in way of obedience unto him.

VER. 11. Let us labour therefore, to enter into that rest, lest any man fall, after the same example of unbelief.

1. In the third verse he said, the believers entered into God's rest; here he exhorteth the believer to labour to enter into it.

Then, 1. The rest of God is entered into by degrees. 2. They who have entered, must study to enter yet more; going on from faith to faith, and from obedience to further obedience, and from grace to grace, till they have gone all the way that leadeth unto glory.

2. He requireth labour and diligence to enter in.

Then, 1. God's rest is no rest to the flesh, but rest to the soul, as Christ promiseth, Matt. xi. 29. 2. Without care and diligence a man cannot promise to himself to enter in; for the way is called strait which leadeth unto heaven.

3. He requireth this diligence, lest a man fall, as the Israelites did. Then, as some of the Israelites fell in a temporal misbelief, and drew on temporal judgments upon themselves, as Moses and Aaron, so many professors now also do, even elect. Again, as some fell in unbelief, with hardened hearts, yea in obstinate mischief, and perished in their sin, so yet among professors, some may fall into obstinate misbelief, and perish, except they give diligence to make progress towards their rest.

VER. 12. For the word of God is quick and powerful, and sharper than any two-edged sword, piercing even to the dividing asunder of soul and spirit, and of the joints and marrow, and is a discerner of the thoughts and intents of the heart.

1. Lest any one should shift off this threatening, as expired with those to whom it was first spoken; or cloak and dissemble their sins, and purpose of defection, when they should see their time, he letteth them know the power of the word, and of God, their adversary.

Then, the use, extent, and nature of God's word must be well studied, lest through mistaking or ignorance hereof, a man should misapply, or misregard it.

2. The first property of the word, it is quick: That is, dieth not when those die to whom it was first directed; but endureth, speaking on with that same authority to all that hear it, in all times after.

Then, the word is not a dead letter, nor expired with former ages; but the same to us that it was before to others, fit for operation, and working the work for which it is sent, for convincing or converting the hearer alway.

3. Again, it is powerful. That is, not fit to work only, but active and operative in effect, actually binding the conscience to obedience, or judgment, make the sinner what opposition he will. Yea, it falleth a-working on the hearer, if he believe it, presently to clear his mind, rectify his will, and reform his life, and to bring about his good and safety. If a man believe it not, it falleth a-working also, presently to bind him guilty unto judgment, and to augment his natural blindness, and his heart's hardness, and to bring on some degree of the deserved punishment upon himself; albeit not of its own nature, but by the disposition of the object whereupon it worketh.

Then, 1. The word wanteth not the own [proper] effect, whensoever it is preached, but always helpeth or hurteth the hearer, as he yieldeth to it, or rejecteth or neglecteth it. 2. We shall do well to observe what sort of operation it hath upon us, seeing it must have some, that we may be framed to the better by it.

4. Another property of the word: it is "sharper than any two-edged sword," because it pierceth speedily through a brazen brow, and dissembling countenance, and a lying mouth, and thrusteth itself without suffering resistance, into the conscience of the most obstinate, with a secret blow, and maketh him guilty within his own breast.

Then, 1. Let not preachers think their labour lost, when they have to do with obstinate sinners. The stroke is given at the hearing of the word, which will be found uncured after. 2. Neither let dissemblers please themselves with a fair countenance put upon the matter; as if the word did not touch them: but rather give glory to God in time, when they are pricked at the heart. For if they dissemble the wound received of this sword, the wound will prove deadly.

5. Piercing even to the dividing asunder of the soul and the spirit; that is, those most secret devices and plots of the mind or spirit, and those closest affections of the heart or soul towards any forbidden evil, this word will find out; yea, it

can divide asunder the soul and the spirit, the heart and the mind, and tell the man how his soul or heart cleaveth to the sin, and how his mind plotteth pretences to hide the evil of it from himself and others, even in those sins which have not broken forth, but lie as deep in the mind as the marrow in the bones. And it can put difference betwixt the purposes of the heart and the thoughts, how to compass the design, and how to hide the convoy [conveyance]. Or those ways how the sinner doth beguile himself, and seeketh to blind the eyes of others; the word doth decypher and distinguish all these things which self-deceiving sophistry confoundeth.

Then, 1. Secret purposes fall under the judicatory of the word, as well as practices accomplished. 2. Pretences and excuses will not put off the challenge of it. 3. Nothing remaineth but that we give up ourselves to the word's government, flying what it dischargeth, and following what it commandeth.

VER. 13. Neither is there any creature that is not manifest in his sight; but all things are naked and opened unto the eyes of him with whom we have to do.

To clear the power of the word, he bringeth in the property of God, whose word it is, and setteth up the sinner's secret thought, in the sight of the all-seeing God, with whom he hath to do.

Then, 1. God is the party with whom the hearer of the word hath to do, and hath his reckoning to make, and not the preacher. 2. God joineth with his word, and giveth it that searching and discovering and piercing virtue. 3. God's omniscience, and all-seeing sight, should make us look to our inward disposition; so shall this and other like exhortations and threatenings have better effect and fruit in us.

VER. 14. Seeing then, that we have a great high priest, that is passed into the heavens, Jesus, the Son of God, let us hold fast our profession.

1. He giveth them a direction for entering into their rest: to hold fast their profession; that is, in faith and love to avow the doctrine of Christ.

Then he that would enter into rest, must be stedfast in maintaining and avowing the true religion of Christ. 2. He who quitteth the profession of the truth of Christ, taketh courses to cut off himself from God's rest. For if we deny Christ he will deny us.

2. He commandeth to hold fast our profession. Then, 1. God will not be pleased with backsliding or coldness, or indifferency in matters of religion, because this is not to hold it fast; but to take a loose hold, which is the ready way to defection. 2. There is danger, lest our adversaries pull the truth from us. 3. The more danger we foresee, the more strongly must we hold the truth.

3. The encouragement which he giveth to hold fast is, We have Christ a great high priest, &c. Then, 1. As we have need of threatening, to drive us to enter into God's rest; so have we need of encouragements to draw us thereunto. 2. All our encouragement is from the help which

we shall have in Christ, and that is sufficient. 3. Christ is always for us in his office, albeit we do not always feel him sensibly in us.

4. He calleth Christ a great high priest, to put difference betwixt the typical high priest, and him in whom the truth of the priesthood is found. Then what the typical high priest did in show for the people, that the great high priest doth in substance for us: that is, reconcileth us to God perfectly, blesseth us with all blessings solidly, and intercedeth for us perpetually.

5. He affirmeth of Christ, that he is passed into the heaven; to wit, in regard of his manhead, to take possession thereof in our name.

Then, 1. Christ's corporal presence is in heaven only, and not on earth, from whence he is passed. 2. Christ's corporal presence in heaven, and absence from us in that respect, hindereth not our right unto him, and spiritual having or possessing of him. 3. Yea, it is our encouragement, to seek entry into heaven, that he is there before us.

6. He calleth him Jesus the Son of God; to lead us through his humanity unto his Godhead. Then no rest on the Mediator, till we go to the rock of h's Godhead, where is strength, and satisfaction to faith.

VER. 15. For we have not an high priest which cannot be touched with the feeling of our infirmities: but was in all points tempted like as we are, yet without sin.

1. Another encouragement is from the merciful and compassionate disposition of our high priest, whose nature, and office, and experience maketh him, that he cannot be but touched with our infirmities, both sinful and sinless infirmities of body, estate, or mind.

Then, 1. He presupposeth that the faithful are subject to infirmities, both of sin and misery, and by reason thereof to discouragements and dashing of their spirit. 2. Christ doth pity the infirmities of the faithful, their poverty, banishment, sickness, grief; yea, their sinful passions and perturbations, and short-coming in holy duties; he is compassionate in all these. Therefore may our faith gather strength from his pity, to bear these the better; and strive against our sinfulness with the greater courage. And in the sense of our infirmities, we should not stand back from Christ; but go to him the rather as to a compassionate physician, who can and will help us.

2. To give us assurance of his compassion, he showeth us, that he was in all points tempted like as we are, yet without sin.

Then, 1. Christ hath experience of all trials wherein any of his servants can fall; of poverty, contempt of the world, of being forsaken by friends, of exile, imprisonment, hunger, nakedness, watching, weariness, pain of body, dashing of mind, heaviness of heart, dolour, anguish, and perplexity of spirit; yea, of desertion to sense; yea, of the wrath and curse of God; the feeling whereof may justly be called " a descending to hell;" Christ in his own experience knoweth what all such exercises are. 2. These his experiences and sufferings are pawns to us of his compassion on us in such cases; so that we may as certainly believe the compassion as the passion.

3. He maketh exception of sin, whereof he was free, but not of his being tempted to sin. Then, 1. Albeit our Lord was free from committing sin, yet he was not free from being tempted to sin : and so can pity our weakness, when we are overcome of it. 2. His being free of sin, is our comfort against sin ; for if our Mediator had been defiled with sin, he could not have washed us ; but now he is able to justify us, and set us free of sin also.

VER. 16. Let us therefore come boldly unto the throne of grace, that we may obtain mercy, and find grace to help in time of need.

1. From these encouragements, he draweth another direction, to come boldly to God in prayer for every thing whereof we stand in need.

Then the apostle alloweth unto the believer, 1. Certain persuasion of the acceptation of his person, he biddeth him come boldly. 2. He alloweth certain persuasions of the granting of his prayers in the matter, namely, of grace and mercy, which includeth the remission of sins.

2. The throne of grace or the mercy seat, was above the ark, within the sanctuary, and represented God in Christ reconciled to his people, gracious and merciful unto them. To this he alludeth, and by this means teacheth us,

1. That the substance of that typical mercy seat, is to be found in Christ under the gospel. In him God is ever to be found, on his throne of grace. 2. That the veil of the ceremonial sanctuary is rent in Christ's suffering, and an open door made unto the holiest, unto every believer, and not for the highest alone to enter in. 3. That God layeth aside his terror and rigour of justice, when his own come to him in Christ, and offereth access unto the throne of grace unto them.

3. He will have us coming with boldness to obtain mercy, including himself with the faithful, and joining the meanest of the faithful, to whom he writeth, in the same privilege with himself. Then, 1. Free liberty to expound all our mind to God, as the word importeth, without employing the mediation of saint or angel, or any beside Christ, is one of the privileges of Christian religion. 2. This privilege is common to the meanest of the faithful, with the chiefest apostles. 3. There is mercy to be had for such as come for removing of every sin, and remedy of every misery.

4. He setteth before them the hope of grace to help in time of need. Importing hereby, 1. That albeit for the present, possibly we be not touched with the sense of wants, straits, and difficulties ; yet we are to expect, that time of need will come. 2. That it is good to foresee this, and make provision in the time of grace, in this acceptable day, while God is on his throne of grace. 3. That our prayers, if they get not an answer presently, yet shall they get an answer in the time of need. When our need cometh, then shall our help come also.

THE SUM OF CHAP. V.

I have called Jesus the Son of God, a great high priest, because the levitical priests are but a

resemblance of him, and that in their imperfect measure. For look what office they had, ver. 1. What properties were required in them, ver. 2, 3. How they were called to their office, ver. 4. A fairer calling hath Christ, and to a higher priesthood, ver. 5, 6. I called him a compassionate high priest, because he took on our frail nature, and had experience of such troubles as ours, both outward and inward, ver. 7. For the measure of the Mediator's obedience, albeit he was the Son, required actual and experimental suffering ; else the price had not actually been paid for us, ver. 8. And now being throughly fitted for his office by suffering, he is become the cause of the salvation of all that follow him, ver. 9. Authorized for that end of God, after the order of Melchisedek ; which order is more perfect than Aaron's, ver. 10. Of which mystery I must speak with greater difficulty, for your incapacity, ver. 11. For ye have need yet more to be catechised in the rudiments of religion as babes, ver. 12. For such are they to whom easy doctrine must be propounded, ver. 13. But harder doctrines are for riper Christians, ver. 14.

THE DOCTRINE OF CHAP. V.

VER. 1. For every high priest taken from amongst men, is ordained for men in things pertaining to God ; that he may offer both gifts and sacrifices for sins.

1. He setteth down the properties of the high priest, that he might show the truth of them in Christ. First, the people's comfort did require, that the high priest should be a man. So is Christ a man, chosen out from amongst men. The flower of all the flock. Therefore we may come the more homely to him.

2. The high priest was ordained for men ; that is, was appointed to imply all his office for men's good. So doth Christ : therefore may we expect that he will do for us, as Mediator, what he can : and that is all that we need.

3. The high priest's office reached to all things pertaining to God ; to communicate God's will unto the people, and to lay before God the people's necessities. So doth Christ's office to all the business betwixt God and us, for working in us repentance and amendment, and making our persons and service acceptable to God : and therefore in nothing may we pass by him.

4. In special, the priest behoved to offer gifts and sacrifices for sin, for removing of wrath and obtaining of favour. So hath Christ done, and fulfilled the type in this point also ; therefore by him must we obtain the good which we crave, and have the evil removed which we fear.

VER. 2. Who can have compassion on the ignorant, and on them that are out of the way, for that he himself also is compassed with infirmity.

1. He goeth on in the comparison ; the typical high priest behoved to be compassionate on the sinner. So in truth is Christ, even as the misery requireth, proportionally, as the word importeth.

2. He maketh two sorts of sinners, ignorants,

and transgressors. Then though there be difference of sinners, yet no sinner that seeketh to Christ is secluded from his compassion.

3. Followeth a difference, serving to advance Christ above the typical priest. The high-priest typical was compassed with infirmities, not only sinless infirmities, but sinful also; and so behoved to pity others. Christ, though not compassed with sinful infirmities, but sinless only, yet doth pity sinners of all sorts.

Then, look what compassion one sinner might expect of another, as much may we expect of our sinless Saviour.

Ver. 3. And by reason hereof he ought, as for the people, so also for himself to offer for sins.

Another difference. The typical priest had need of remission of his own sins, and the benefit of the true sacrifice; but Christ, because without sin, offered sacrifice only for our sins, and not for his own.

Then, all the benefit of Christ's sacrifice cometh unto us.

Ver. 4. And no man taketh this honour unto himself, but he that is called of God, as was Aaron.

He proceedeth in the comparison. The typical priest entered by authority to his calling, and was honoured by his calling; so entered Christ. No man, saith he, taketh this honour unto himself, but he that is called, as was Aaron. Then, 1. It is an honour to be called to an office in the house of God. 2. The calling is null if it have not God for the author and caller. 3. If a man take an office, not appointed of God, or intrude himself into an office, without a lawful calling, it is no kind of honour unto him.

Ver. 5. So also Christ glorified not himself to be made a high-priest, but he that said unto him, Thou art my Son, to-day have I begotten thee.

1. Our Lord is commended for not glorifying himself, by intrusion in his office.

Then, 1. Such as pretend to be Christ's servants must beware to intrude themselves into any office, and must attend, as Christ did, God's calling, to God's employment. 2. He that usurpeth a calling doth glorify himself, and taketh the honour that is not given him; for which he must give a reckoning.

2. Thou art my Son, this day have I begotten thee, doth import, by the apostle's alleging, not only Christ's Godhead, and declaration to be God's Son; but also the declaration of him to be high-priest in his manhead, taken out from amongst men. So deep are the consequences of Scripture, when the Spirit bringeth forth his own mind from it.

Ver. 6. As he saith also in another place, Thou art a priest for ever, after the order of Melchisedek.

He allegeth another place more clear.

Then howbeit truth may be proved from one place, yet it is needful also, for the hearer's cause, to allege more places, till the hearer be convinced.

Ver. 7. Who in the days of his flesh, when he had offered up prayers and supplications, with strong crying and tears unto him that was able to save him from death, and was heard in that he feared.

Having proved Christ's office, he showeth his exercise of it in offering for our sins a more precious oblation than the typical; even himself, with tears, to death.

In these words, then, Christ is pointed out unto us: 1. A high-priest taken from amongst men, a very true man of our substance, flesh of our flesh. 2. A man subject to the sinless infirmities of our nature, as grief, fear, mourning, death. 3. Having a set time, during which he was to bear these our infirmities, in the days of his flesh. 4. Exercising his priestly office in these his days, and offering his precious tears and cries, yea, his life for us. 5. One who howsoever fear was upon his holy nature, yet knew he should be delivered from death. 6. Who, as a man, in confidence of delivery made prayers to the Father. 7. Whose prayers are not refused, but accepted, and heard on our behalf. 8. And that these his sufferings were ended with the days of his humiliation.

1. These acts of fear and tears, &c. are the proper acts of his human nature.

Then, 1. As the Divine nature had its own acts proper to itself, so had the human nature acts proper to itself also; and some acts were common to both the natures. So of Christ's acts, some are divine, some human; some are both divine and human. 2. As man he was unable to bear our burden, or to help himself, and therefore behoved to have the help of the Godhead. 3. Albeit he was God in his own person, yet as man he behoved to take our room and place, and pray for assistance, both as surety for us and teacher of us, to give us example how to behave ourselves in straits.

2. He feared death, and offered prayers and tears, and strong cries. Because not only death temporal presented itself before him; but, which was much more, the curse of the law, the Father's wrath for sin duly deserved by us, was set in a cup to his head, which should have swallowed him up for ever, if he had not, by the worthiness of his person, overcome it, and turned the eternal wrath and curse due unto us into a temporal equivalent to himself.

Then, 1. The sense of God's wrath, whom will it not terrify, since it wrought so on Christ? and nature cannot choose but fear when sense feeleth wrath. 2. Felt wrath seemeth to threaten yet more, and worse; and therefore beside feeling doth breed yet further fear. 3. The curse of God due to our sins, virtually implying the deserved pains of hell, is more terrible than can be told, and such as the creature cannot choose but fear and abhor. 4. Christ's sufferings were no phantasy, but very earnest, vehement, and terrible. 5. No weapon nor buckler against wrath, but flying to God by supplication and crying and tears.

3. He prayed to him that was able to save him, and was heard.

Then, 1. Albeit sense of wrath seeth no outgate, but black fears are always before it; yet faith, looking to God's omnipotence, seeth an outgate. 2. Christ's prayers in our behalf receive no repulse, but are heard. 3. Christ both died and was saved from death also, because it could not keep dominion over him. So shall we be saved from death though we die.

Ver. 8. Though he were a Son, yet learned he obedience by the things which he suffered.

He removeth the scandal of his cross by showing the necessity and use thereof. Albeit he was the Son, yet he learned obedience by those things which he suffered.

Then, 1. In the time of Christ's deepest humiliation, the union betwixt his Godhead and Manhead was not loosed; he remained the Són of God still. 2. The excellency of his person exempted him not from suffering, having once taken on our debt. 3. Christ knew what suffering was before he suffered; but he knew not by experience till he actually suffered. 4. Christ's holy life was a part of his obedience to the Father, but his obedience in suffering for our sins was obedience in a higher degree. 5. To obey God by way of action is a common lesson to every holy creature; but that a sinless and holy person should suffer for sin was a new lesson proper to Christ, a practice which never passed but in Christ's person only.

Ver. 9. And being made perfect, he became the author of eternal salvation unto all them that obey him.

1. The suffering of Christ is called his perfection.

Then, 1. Christ, though perfect in his person, yet he wanted something to make him perfect in his office till he suffered; for he could not satisfy the Father's justice till he suffered, nor yet could he have fellow-feeling from experience of the miseries of his members. 2. After suffering, Christ lacketh nothing that may pacify God, or comfort and save sinners.

2. The fruit followeth; being perfected, he is become the author of salvation to all that obey him.

Then, 1. The proper cause of our salvation is to be sought in Christ, perfected by suffering; not in any one part of his holiness or obedience in doing, or in any part of his suffering; but in him perfected by his obedience, even to the death of the cross. We may take comfort from and make use of his holy conception, life, and several virtues; but we must remember that his accomplished obedience, in doing and suffering, is our ransom, jointly considered, and not any particular act looked on alone. 2. None should stumble at Christ's sufferings, which perfected him in his office, and likewise perfected our ransom to the Father. 3. Christ felt the bitterness of his own sufferings himself; but we got the sweet fruit thereof, even eternal life. 4. Only they who obey Christ can claim title to the purchase of eternal life by him. Now these are they who obey him, who in uprightness of heart believe in his promises, and aim to draw strength out of him for new obedience.

Ver. 10. Called of God an high-priest, after the order of Melchisedek.

He proveth that Christ is author of eternal salvation to his followers, from the nature of his priesthood, which is eternal, not after Aaron's order, but Melchisedek's.

Then the nature of Christ's priesthood after Melchesidek's order, and the Father's authorizing him in the office, is the evidence of our eternal salvation to be had by him with the Father's approbation.

Ver. 11. Of whom we have many things to say, and hard to be uttered, seeing ye are dull of hearing.

Being to speak more of this mystery, he prepareth them by checking their dulness, and advertising them of the difficulty of expressing himself because of the same.

Then, 1. Even the children of God are not free of this disease, of slowness to conceive spiritual things aright. 2. The incapacity of auditors will breed even unto the best preachers difficulty of expressing their mind. 3. Preachers should rebuke the dulness of people, to stir them up the more.

Ver. 12. For when for the time ye ought to be teachers, ye have need that one teach you again which be the first principles of the oracles of God; and are become such as have need of milk, and not of strong meat.

1. He maketh their fault the more because by reason of time they ought to have been teachers, that is, both well grounded themselves, and labouring to inform others.

Then, 1. As we had longer time to learn, so should we make more progress in knowledge. 2. As we are rooted in knowledge ourselves, so ought we to communicate our knowledge and inform others.

2. He calleth the catechising of the ignorant the teaching the first principles of the oracles of God, and compareth it to the giving of milk.

Then, 1. Catechising of the rude and ignorant is the first thing must be done for making sound Christians. 2. There is an order to be kept in bringing men unto knowledge. The first principles and fundamental doctrines must first be taught. 3. Nothing is to be taught for grounding men in religion but God's oracles, that which is in God's word only. 4. The manner of teaching the principles of religion should be easy and plain as milk for children.

Ver. 13. For every one that useth milk is unskilful in the word of righteousness: for he is a babe.

He proveth them to be rude in knowledge, by the description of one weak in knowledge, whom he calleth a babe using milk and unskilful in the word of righteousness, so called because how to be righteous is the sum of the doctrine of it.

Then, 1. There are degrees in Christianity. Some are weak, like babes; some more instructed and of full age. 2. All knowledge in Christianity is to be reckoned by acquaintance with the Scripture and skill therein, not by human learning.

VER. 14. But strong meat belongeth to them that are of full age, even those who by reason of use have their senses exercised to discern both good and evil.

1. He describeth the well instructed Christian by his meat, and exercised senses. The meat that he is fit for is strong meat; that is, more profound doctrine.

Then, 1. All the Scripture and doctrine from it is either milk or strong meat; but whether this or that, yet always it is food, fit for nourishment of men's souls. 2. Discretion must be used by teachers, to fit their teaching, as their people are advanced for milk, or stronger meat, so as they may best be fed.

2. For the exercise of his senses or wits to discern good or evil, he hath it by use, habit, and frequent acquainting himself with Scripture.

Then, 1. The use of the Scripture, and knowledge gotten thereby, is to discern by it what is good, what is evil, what is truth, what is error, what is right, what is wrong. 2. Though Scripture be the rule, yet not every one can take it up or make right application of the rule to the point in hand. 3. To get a man's wits exercised requireth frequent use of and acquaintance with the Scripture. And without this haunting our mind in the Scriptures, and observing the Lord's counsel therein, a man cannot be able, albeit he were versed in human writs, to discern false doctrine from true.

THE SUM OF CHAP. VI.

Therefore, albeit you be rude, yet presupposing you are so settled in the grounds of faith, repentance, baptism, &c. that you shall not renounce them again, I will lead you on a little further if God please, ver. 1—3. For if after clear conviction of the truth a man voluntarily revolt and fall away from the grounds of true religion, there is neither repentance nor mercy for such a man; because he maliciously doth what he can to put Christ to as great a shame as those who first crucified him, ver. 4—6. And, as God blesseth those who bring forth fruits by his manuring of them, ver. 7; so it is justice that he curse such as grew worse after manuring, ver. 8. But I hope better of you, ver. 9; as the fruits of your faith give me warrant, ver. 10. Only that you may be more and more assured, continue diligent, ver. 11. And follow the example of the faithful before you in the hope of inheritance, ver. 12. For the promise made to Abraham and the faithful his children is very sure confirmed by an oath, ver. 13, 14. And Abraham at last obtained it, ver. 15. For as an oath endeth strife among men, ver. 16, so to end our strife with God, in misbelieving of him, he sware the promise to Abraham and to his seed, ver. 17. That upon so solid grounds, as are God's promise and God's oath, we might have comfort, who have fled to Christ, and hope for his help, ver. 18. Which hope is as an anchor, which will not suffer us to be driven from heaven, where Christ is es-

tablished eternal priest, after the order of Melchisedek, ver. 19, 20.

THE DOCTRINE OF CHAP. VI.

VER. 1. Therefore leaving the principles of the doctrine of Christ, let us go on unto perfection; not laying again the foundation of repentance from dead works, and of faith towards God.

1. From the reproof of their dulness he draweth an exhortation to amend their pace and go forwards. Which teacheth us that the conscience of our bye-gone slips and slothfulness should be a sharp spur to drive us at a swifter pace for overtaking of our task.

2. He calleth the principles of religion the principles of the doctrine of Christ.

Then, 1. The doctrine of Christ is the sum of religion. He that hath learned Christ well hath learned all. 2. Nothing to be taught in Christ's house but his doctrine, which cometh from him, and tendeth to him.

3. He leaveth the principles and goeth on to perfection. Then, 1. There are two parts of Christian doctrine; one of the principles of religion, another of the perfection thereof. 2. The principles must first be learned, and the foundation laid. 3. When people have learned the principles, their teachers must advance them farther towards perfection.

4. He saith he will not lay again the foundation; presupposing it is so laid as it needeth not to be laid again; or if they make apostasy after once laying, cannot be laid the second time.

Then, the grounds of religion must be so solidly learned, as they may well be bettered afterwards by addition of farther knowledge, but never raised again; and must be so soundly believed as they never be renounced again.

5. He reckoneth a number of fundamental points of doctrine, and first of repentance from dead works; so he calleth our works before conversion.

Then, 1. It is a main point of the catechism to believe that all our works before repentance and conversion are but dead works; that is, sins making us liable to death. 2. If repentance be not learned from these works the rest of the building wanteth so much of the foundation.

6. In joining the doctrine of faith as the next point, he giveth us to understand that it is as necessary a ground of religion to teach a penitent to believe in God as to teach the believer to repent.

VER. 2. Of the doctrine of baptisms, and of laying on of hands, and of resurrection of the dead, and of eternal judgment.

1. The doctrine of baptisms in the plural number he maketh a third fundamental doctrine, and so maketh it necessary that the significations of baptism be taught, that the people may learn to put difference betwixt outward baptism by the minister, which a hypocrite may have, and the baptism by the Spirit which Christ bestoweth upon his own elect, and that they be instructed in the nature of this sacrament and the signification thereof; yea, and of the baptism of suffering

affliction for the gospel, whereunto the outward sacrament of baptism obligeth.

2. The fourth fundamental point of the doctrine of the catechism he maketh the doctrine of the laying on of hands. Now hands were in a special manner imposed. First, in the bestowing of spiritual and miraculous gifts for the confirmation of new converts in the primitive church, Acts viii. 17, 18. Which endured until Christian religion was sufficiently confirmed unto the world to be divine. Next, imposition of hands was used in the ordination of office-bearers in the church, both extraordinary and ordinary, 1 Tim. iv. 14, and chap. v. 22 ; Acts vi. 6.

Then, in the apostle's estimation, it is necessary for grounding of people in religion that they be instructed not only how the Lord founded the Christian religion, and confirmed it by extraordinary gifts of the Holy Spirit in the primitive church ; but also what offices and office-bearers he hath ordained for ordinary edification and ruling and maintaining of his church unto the end of the world, that they may acknowledge such as are sent of God, and submit themselves unto them.

3. The doctrine of resurrection of the dead he maketh the fifth point of the catechism ; and of the last judgment the sixth ; under which six the sum of Christian religion may be comprised, and in this order wherein they are set down may be best learned, believed, and made use of.

VER. 3. And this will we do, if God permit.

By this manner of speech, "if God permit," he teacheth us,

1. That a preacher's endeavour to instruct a people can have no success except God make way unto him and concur with him. 2. That he who is busied in the most necessary part of God's service, suppose it were in writing Scripture, or in ordinary preaching and writings, must do it with submission to God, to be stopped in the midst of his work and cut short, yea, and that in the midst of a meditated speech, if it so please God.

VER. 4. For it is impossible for those who were once enlightened, and have tasted of the heavenly gift, and were made partakers of the Holy Ghost,

VER. 5. And have tasted the good word of God, and the powers of the world to come,

VER. 6. If they shall fall away, to renew them again unto repentance ; seeing they crucify to themselves the Son of God afresh, and put him to an open shame.

1. Minding to stir them up to make progress in knowledge, he setteth before them the danger of apostasy.

Then, 1. He presupposeth except they study to make progress they shall go backwards, and that going backwards tendeth to apostasy, and that voluntary and complete apostasy from known truth doth harden the heart from repentance, and cutteth off a man from mercy. 2. He accounteth our natural security so great that there is need of

most fearful threatenings to awake us out of it. 3. That the only way to be freed from apostasy is to be aiming at a progress.

Next observe, 1. That he doth not speak here of every sin against knowledge, albeit indeed those be fearful and dangerous, but of apostasy from religion and the doctrine of Christ. 2. Not of the apostasy of ignorants who never were informed in the matter of religion, but lightly came and lightly went away (albeit the shame done to Christ by them is great and grievous); but of such who, after illumination and feeling somewhat of the power of truth, do revolt. 3. He speaketh not here of apostasy of infirmity, for fear in a fit of passion or hasty passage of one's life : but of a voluntary and deliberate falling away after clear conviction of the truth. This is that sin against the Holy Ghost which he here speaketh of. 4. He doth not presuppose here that an elect child of God, and renewed, may fall into this sin ; but that a professor, and some in the visible church, may fall away and die in this sin. Now a professor may be endued with many gifts and yet be a temporizer, and remain unrenewed inwardly and so may possibly fall into this ill. And therefore every professor should be the more circumspect, because of the possibility of some men's apostasy ; and the more diligent to attain to that faith which purifieth the heart and worketh by love which faileth not. 5. In telling what is the danger of a professor's apostasy, the apostle mindeth not to weaken any man's faith, or discourage him from progress making ; but by the contrary his intention is that men strengthen themselves so much the more in the faith. And therefore such as have felt no more in their own estimation but these tastings should be so far from discouragement and fainting that rather they must look to a necessity laid upon them to make progress in faith and the fruits thereof, and to draw near to God, who can preserve them from falling away.

But because some do trouble themselves and other some do harden themselves in error, by this place (as our intended brevity will suffer) let us study to give some light to both. Compare this place with verses 9, 10, &c. of this chapter, to the end. First in these verses, the 4th, 5th, and 6th, he is speaking of professors in general, conditionally ; but verses 9, 10, &c. he is speaking to the true believers amongst these Hebrews particularly.

2. Here in these verses are glorious gifts, illumination and tasting of spiritual things ; there, in those verses, is faith working by love, to the glory of Jesus and weal of his saints. 3. Here are men enrolled amongst Christians, so holden and esteemed both of themselves and others; there are sensible souls in the feeling of sin and fear of wrath and hope of mercy, flying to Jesus as to a refuge, and casting the anchor of their tossed souls within the veil where Jesus is in heaven. 4. Here men receiving from the Holy Ghost good things ; there men receiving from him, beside these good things, better things also. 5. Here things glorious indeed, yet not always accompanying salvation, but in some going before saving grace ; in others, possibly alone, without saving grace ; but there are saving graces always joined with salvation. 6. Here in these

verses the apostle is not confident, but such as have received these things here mentioned may fall away, except they go forward and study to make progress. But there in those verses the apostle is persuaded that they shall not fall away, but be saved, and thereupon encourageth them to go forwards.

From this comparison it is clear then,

1. That there is a possibility of the apostasy of professors and titular saints, but not of the apostasy of renewed souls and true Christians, true saints. 2. There is a ground of fear from these words to such as are secure and puffed up with the conceit of their spiritual gifts, but not of those who in fear have fled to Christ. 3. That in this place carnal confidence only is shaken in such who, as if they had done well enough, study not to make progress; but faith no ways weakened in such who still study to advance and make more and more progress. That here fruitless light and fruitless feeling is called in question, but not faith and laborious love, bringing out fruits to Christ's glory, and good of his saints.

Again from this comparison it is evident,

That the Holy Ghost is author both of these common spiritual gifts, and of these special saving graces also. Of these common gifts he is Author, as dwelling amongst professors, and distributing good things unto all professors that are in the visible house of his church. But he is author of those saving graces, as dwelling in true professors, who are his own house: bringing with himself better things than these gifts, and salvation unto them infallibly.

Thirdly, from this comparison it is clear,

1. That there are some converts, external from the world to the church, who yet stick in their naturals, and are not in the sense of sin, fled unto Christ for refuge, nor converted from nature to saving grace; to whom the apostle will not deny room in the church, if they will study to make progress. And 2. That illumination and tasting of spiritual things, may be given as well to such who are not renewed in their heart, as unto sound converts.

For, 1. The natural man may be convinced that the church is a blessed society, and join himself unto it. 2. Yea, change his outward conversation, and cast off his pollutions which are in the world through lust, and take himself to be ruled outwardly by Christ's discipline, and call him Lord, Lord. 3. And be so blameless before men that he may look with his lamp like a wise virgin waiting for the wedding, and yet be a graceless fool inwardly. 4. Yea, he may be illuminated, not only by learning the literal knowledge of the Gospel, as men do their philosophy; but also may be illuminated supernaturally, with insight in many profound things in the Scripture. For supernatural gifts may be in a natural and unrenewed man, so as he may say to Christ, I have prophesied in thy name, and yet be unrenewed in Christ's estimation. 5. He may taste of the heavenly gift, partly by historical believing the truth of the Gospel, partly by contemplation of the truth credited. Now historical faith, is a taste of that heavenly gift of justifying faith, because it is a good degree towards it: and contemplation of this truth bringeth a taste of the thing credited; and so of the heavenly gift revealed in the Gospel. For the contemplation of every truth bringeth with it, naturally, a delectation, such as philosophers do find in their studies. And the more eminent the truth be, no wonder the delectation be the greater. For many heard Christ's gracious sermons, and wondered and believed his words to be true: but Christ did not commit himself unto them; for he knew what was in them. 6. He may be made partaker of the Holy Ghost, and have his share of church gifts, distributed by the Holy Ghost; so as he can, from the light which the Holy Ghost giveth him, answer other men's doubts, comfort the feeble minded, and edify others in their faith by his speeches; yea, have the gift of expressing his brain light, both in conference to man, and in formal prayer to God, if he be a private man only: and if he be in public office, may have the gift of formal preaching and praying in public: yea, in those days of the apostle, might have had the extraordinary gifts of tongues, prophesying, and miracles' working. Therefore saith Christ, Many will say to me in that day, Lord, Lord, have we not prophesied in thy name? and in thy name have cast out devils; and in thy name have done many wonderful works? To whom Christ will answer, I never knew you, depart from me, ye that work iniquity, Matt. vii. 22, 23. Now this knowledge, convincing light, and gifts of utterance, &c. are from the Holy Ghost; or else, how could such apostates, as here are described, sin against the Holy Ghost? 7. He may taste of the good word of God: that is, find sweetness in the doctrine of the gospel, and be convinced of the goodness and mercy of God toward sinners, shining therein: yea, and by beholding the possibility of his own salvation, upon this condition, If he will sell all, and buy the pearl, he may taste of God's merchandise, in the blocking for them; beside all the false joys, and delusions, which he may get by presuming of the certainty of his own salvation: and yet in the mean time, as a fool, will not lay down the price; will not renounce his earthly and beastly affections: will not deny himself and his own corruptions: the care of this world, and the deceitfulness of riches, choking the fruits of the word heard, as they who receive the seed amongst thorns; wherefore in time of persecution for the word, he may by and by be offended, and quit the truth, albeit with the stony-hearted hearers, in time of prosperity, he heard the word, and anon with joy received it, Matt. xiii. 20—22. 8. Lastly, he may taste of the power of the world to come: that is, in contemplation of the blessedness promised to the saints in heaven, be taken with admiration of it, yea, and have a natural desire of it; as Balaam did, when upon such a speculation, he did wish to die the death of the righteous, and to have his last end as his: and yet love the wages of iniquity so well, as he forsook not his covetousness, for all his wish of heaven. In a word, It is possible that a man impenitent, and unrenewed in his heart, may be a glorious professor, for his outward behaviour, and have fair gifts; and yet make apostasy from the truth, when he getteth a fit temptation: or else, how should it be possible that the devil should make glorious professors, and churchmen in all ages, apostates, persecutors, betrayers of the truth to the adversary, underminers of the church of Christ : except they, under all their show, did lodge in their heart, the love of money, and worldly riches more than the love of heaven ? the love of the praise of men, rather than God's approbation ? the lust of their fleshly ease, and pleasure more than the pleasure of God ? the fleshly fear of those that can kill the body, more than of God, who can cast both soul and body into hell ? And therefore no wonder, if for satisfaction of their ambition, avarice, lusts, and earthly affections, they become ready to sell Christ and his truth, and his church, and their country and all, when they find their merchant, and the beloved price offered unto them.

4. Observe here ; how glorious soever these illuminations, and gifts, and tastings seem, yet there is no farther here granted, but tastings, to such rotten professors. That which they get, is either only in the brain, by knowledge ; or, if there be any feelings, they are but fleeting motions, flowing from temporary grounds, which proceed not from any spiritual life in the man, nor from a root in himself : that is, not from the Spirit dwelling in him. Such feelings do neither foster nor strengthen him for any spiritual obedience ; but vanish without changing the heart. It is true, all that the godly get in comparison of what he shall get, is but tastings : yet in comparison of these fruitless tastings of the unsound professors, that which he getteth is true eating and drinking, a real feeding ; holding his soul in life, and enabling him to work the work of God ; to mortify his lusts, and serve God in his spirit.

5. Observe, That here he doth not challenge those who have felt these tastings for unsound, nor threaten them, if they hold on, and make progress. Then, 1. The having of illumination, and spiritual gifts, and tastings of heavenly things is not to be lightly esteemed of ; but accounted as steps and degrees, unto a farther progress : wherefore as it is possible some fall away, so is it a piece of advancement, to encourage men to go on, that they fall not away. 2. There is no danger in having this illumination, or these light tastings : but all the hazard is, to rest upon them, and not to tend towards perfection ; or to fall away after receiving so much encouragement. 3. And therefore we must not rest on illumination, or common gifts, how glorious soever ; nor tastings and feelings how sweet soever : but seek still into a more near communion with Christ, and still more to mortify our lusts, and still to abound in the fruits of love to Christ and his church.

Ver. 6. If they shall fall away, to renew them again unto repentance ; seeing they crucify to themselves the Son of God afresh, and put him to an open shame.

1. He saith not, It is impossible they should be saved ; but that they shall be renewed by repentance.

Then apostates' salvation is not impossible, but because their repentance is impossible : and where repentance is, there is no impossibility of salvation, but a certainty of salvation rather.

For he that giveth the repentance, he declareth his purpose, to give remission also.

2. He giveth a reason why they cannot get repentance ; because they maliciously renounce Christ, and crucify him afresh unto themselves. That is, draw on the guiltiness of his enemies who crucified him did lie under, by apostasy, allowing their crucifying of him.

Then, 1. An apostate from Christ's doctrine, doth Christ as open shame as he can ; and saith in effect of Christ, that his doctrine is false, and not to be maintained. 2. An apostate alloweth Judas and the Jews, for crucifying of Christ ; and accounteth Christ no more worthy, than so to be dealt withal. 3. Renouncing of Christ, maketh repentance impossible. For he is a prince, to give repentance unto Israel. And therefore he who will not quit Christ, nor his true doctrine, is not debarred from having repentance, nor from salvation.

Ver. 7. For the earth which drinketh in the rain that cometh oft upon it, and bringeth forth herbs, meet for them by whom it is dressed, receiveth blessing from God :

Ver. 8. But that which beareth thorns and briers, is rejected, and is nigh unto cursing ; whose end is to be burned.

He giveth a reason of the punishment of apostates from the less to the more, under a similitude from land-labouring thus : as God blesseth such men, who after pains taken on them, bring forth the fruits of good works, so doth he curse those, who after pains taken on them, do bring forth but evil works. And if it be but equity, that God curse professors, who bring forth but evil fruits in their life ; much more equity he curse apostates, who profess open hostility against him.

The similitude showeth, 1. That men are like unmanured land, before they be brought within the church ; but after they are made partakers of the gospel, then are they like manured land within hedges, God's husbandry. 2. That such as begin to bring forth fruit worthy of repentance, God blesseth, and maketh more fruitful. 3. That the means of grace under the Gospel, are to our souls as rain, and labouring, and other husbandry is to the ground.

Ver. 8. But that which beareth thorns and briers is rejected, and is nigh unto cursing ; whose end is to be burned.

The similitude showeth, 1. That a man may perish for not bringing forth the fruits of the Gospel, albeit he fall not into the sin against the Holy Ghost. 2. That there is a great reason why God should cast away a man, who amendeth not his life by the Gospel, as that an husbandman should give over labouring of a piece of evil ground. 3. And by this means also showeth that God's most severe judgments, have all of them most equitable reasons. 4. That there is a necessity of bringing forth the fruits of welldoing, if a man would be free of the curse, either of apostates, or of the barren land.

VER. 9. But beloved, we are persuaded better things of you, and things that accompany salvation, though we thus speak.

1. He mitigateth his threatening of them, for fear of hurting their faith : Beloved, saith he, we are persuaded better things of you, though we thus speak. Then, 1. A preacher may threaten fearfully those of whom he hath good hopes : yet with prudency, lest he harm them. 2. And people threatened, must beware of weakening their own faith; knowing that threatenings are not used to weaken faith, but to put away security and slothfulness. 2. He taketh his assurance of them, from such things as accompany salvation.

Then in the fruits of faith, there are marks and evidences of a man's salvation to be found, which may give a charitable persuasion of their blessed estate, to such as know them.

VER. 10. For God is not unrighteous to forget your work and labour of love which you have showed towards his name, in that ye have ministered to the saints, and do minister.

1. The reason of his good hopes of them, is their bygone, and present fruits of love towards Christ's name, and his saints. Then, 1. The works of love, done for the glory of Christ, or to the saints for Christ's sake, from time to time, as God giveth occasion, are evident marks of a man's salvation; and more sure tokens of saving grace given, than illumination and tastings, spoken of before. 2. No love is to be reckoned for love, but working love. 3. No works are right works, which flow not from love to Christ. 2. Of such works he saith that God is not unrighteous to forget them, and so proveth their salvation, because such fruits accompany salvation. Then, 1. With the grace of laborious love towards Christ's name the grace of salvation doth go in company. 2. Justice doth agree with grace in the reward of well-doing; because the reward is graciously promised, and righteousness maketh promises to be . performed. 3. The man that loveth Christ in deed and in truth hath that which is most terrible in God for the pawn of his salvation, even his justice.

These are they whom he reproved for weakness of knowledge, chap. v. ver. 12, whom now he commendeth for their good affection and fruits. Then, 1. Mean knowledge, if it be sanctified and sound, will be fruitful in the works of love. 2. This virtue of love is no excuse for slothful following of the means of knowledge; we must grow in love and grow in knowledge also.

VER. 11. And we desire that every one of you do show the same diligence, to the full assurance of hope, unto the end.

1. He exhorteth to continue diligent unto the end. Then, 1. The diligent have need of exhortation to go on. 2. Exhortation to perseverance importeth not suspicion of falling away; but serveth to farther perseverance rather. 3. No other term-day is set to our diligence but the end. No license to slack, or give over.

2. The end of their going on in diligence is their full assurance of hope.

Then, 1. Whatsoever measure of assurance men have, they may yet obtain a fuller measure of it. Still we must study to grow. 2. Constant diligence in the works of love is the ready means to foster and augment our assurance. 3. Christian hope is not a conjecture or probability, but an assurance.

VER. 12. That ye be not slothful, but followers of them who through faith and patience inherit the promises.

1. He setteth the example of the fathers before them to be imitated.

Then, 1. So many examples as we have in Scripture of the godly gone before, as many leaders and encouragers must we reckon ourselves to have. 2. The painful and not the slothful are the true imitators of allowed examples. 3. In the way to heaven there are many things befalling us which make it unlikely we shall come there; for which cause there is need of faith. 4. A time must intervene, and troubles also, ere heaven be possessed. There is therefore need of patience also. 2. They inherit the promise, saith he.

Then, 1. The most patient and painful servants of God get not heaven by merit, but by inheritance. 2. They get not heaven by merit, but by promise. Now the promise is of grace.

VER. 13. For when God made promise to Abraham, because he could swear by no greater, he sware by himself,

VER. 14. Saying, Surely blessing I will bless thee, and multiplying I will multiply thee.

VER. 15. And so, after he had patiently endured, he obtained the promise.

1. For many examples he bringeth one of father Abraham, from Gen. xxii. 16, 17, and maketh use of it by application.

Then, because we cannot have all examples at once before our eyes, we shall do well for several duties to have some select examples singled out for our own more ready use.

2. He doth not bring forth all Abraham's virtues, but such as made for his purpose.

Then, when fit examples are found out, those points which most serve for our edification must be most in our eyes.

3. He marketh first the promise made, next the confirmation of it by an oath, then the fast and constant hold laid on it by Abraham, last, the fruit of the holding fast. He obtained the promise. Then, 1. In the example of believers the nature of the promise, and how they came by it, must especially be marked for helping of our faith. 2. Preachers have Paul's example here how to handle a text.

4. He setteth Abraham's obtaining for a pawn of their obtaining; albeit he knew their faith should be weaker, in degree, than Abraham's. Then, 1. In making use of examples, it must

be held for a ground that the honest and upright imitators, albeit weak, shall find the same success that the stronger, gone before them, have found.

Ver. 16. For men verily swear by the greater, and an oath for confirmation is to them an end of all strife.

1. The apostle being about to commence upon this oath, first he showeth the end of an oath amongst men, ver. 16, and then the use of the oath made to Abraham thereafter. 1. Men swear by a greater, saith he, that the authority of him by whom they swear may ratify the oath one way or other. But God hath not a greater, and therefore himself and all his, is laid in pawn to make his oath good. 2. He who is the greatest, and giveth authority and weight to all oaths among men, must be esteemed worthy to give weight and authority to his own oath; this is the force of his reasoning.

2. The end of an oath is to end controversy. Then, this similitude importeth that as long as we are in misbelief there is a controversy betwixt God and us; we testifying that we are in suspicion of his good affection towards us, and of his promise keeping unto us; and God is offended with us for our wicked thoughts entertained of him.

3. God hath sworn his promise to us to take away the controversy.

Then, 1. A man could condescend no farther to give his party satisfaction than God hath condescended to satisfy us. 2. Except we will deny God the honour which we cannot deny unto an honest man, we must believe the sworn covenant of God, and particular articles thereof. 3. Except we believe, the controversy remaineth; yea, and is doubled after the oath.

Ver. 17. Wherein God, willing more abundantly to show unto the heirs of promise the immutability of his conusel, confirmed it by an oath.

One of the ends of God's swearing to Abraham is the confirmation of the faithful, or the heirs of promise, concerning the unchangeableness of God's counsel in making the promise. Then, every believer hath the same ground of certainty with Abraham, seeing the oath sworn to Abraham is sworn for their confirmation.

2. He calleth believers by Isaac's style, heirs of the promise.

Then, believers are all reckoned by God as so many Isaacs, and entitled with Isaac to be heirs of Abraham with him, and heirs of the good promised to him, and heirs begotten by the force of God's promise and word, and not by the force of nature.

And certainly, albeit the law serve for a preparation, yet it is the gospel and the word of promise which pulleth in the heart of a man to God in love, as a reconciled father, and converteth him. Wherefore, even because of the believer's begetting to God by the immortal seed of the word of promise, he may be called the heir of promise also.

3. By the oath God declareth himself willing to show the immutability of his counsel concerning the salvation of believers.

Then, 1. As many as believe in Jesus and are begotten by the promise are fore-ordained in God's counsel for salvation. 2. The purpose and counsel of God concerning such men's salvation is immutable. 3. God will have believers knowing this his counsel concerning themselves and their salvation, and assured of the immutability thereof. 4. He will have the sworn promise made to Abraham and his seed, serving in particular to the heirs of promise, or believers, to make evident this his counsel to them in particular, as well as to Abraham, because he sware to Abraham to show them this purpose.

4. By the oath he saith, God is willing more abundantly to show the immutability of his counsél.

Then, 1. Till the immutability of the Lord's counsel concerning our salvation be laid hold upon, faith cannot be stedfast, as the Lord would have it. 2. God is willing that we should look in upon his counsel by the eye of faith, and read our names written in heaven in his decree, and so be made sure. 3. The promise of salvation, or of the blessing to believers, is of itself sufficient enough for assurance, albeit it were not sworn; and the oath is added, not of necessity for any weakness of the truth of the promise; but out of superabundant good will to have us made sure. 4. It behoveth to be most pleasant to God that believers have full assurance of faith, and overcome all doubting, seeing he sweareth the promise only for this end.

Ver. 18. That by two immutable things in which it was impossible for God to lie, we might have a strong consolation, who have fled for refuge to lay hold upon the hope set before us:

Another end of the oath is, that with assurance the believer may have strong consolation upon solid grounds.

1. But how describeth he the believers, to whom this comfort is allowed? We, saith he, who have fled for refuge to lay hold upon the hope set before us; that is, we, who to flee from deserved wrath, have taken our course towards Jesus, in hope to get the salvation offered unto us in him. Fleeing for refuge, a similitude, whether from nature, or from the ordinance of Moses's law, Numb. xxxv. 6, giveth us to understand, 1. That every true believer, of necessity, must be sensible of his own sins, and the deserved wrath of God pursuing him for sin. 2. Must have this estimation of Jesus, that he is both a ready and sufficiently strong refuge to save a man from sin and wrath when he runneth towards him. 3. That in this sense of sin and wrath and good estimation of Christ he set his face towards him only, avoiding all by-ways, leading elsewhere than to this refuge, and running for death and life to be found in him.

2. Again, while he saith, To lay hold upon the hope set before us, he giveth us to understand, 1. That in Christ, our refuge, not only is there deliverance from pursuing wrath, but also eternal life to be found, as it is set before us in the gospel. 2. That the believer must have hope to obtain this offer. 3. And as he is driven by fear of the law unto Christ, so must he also be drawn and allured by this salvation set before

him, griping undeserved grace, as well as fleeing deserved wrath.

3. While he describeth the believer after this manner, as the man to whom all these things appertain, he teacheth us,

That, whosoever findeth himself in any truth to be such a one as is here described, so driven and so drawn to Christ, fleeing from sin and wrath, and running on to Christ, in him alone to be saved, may be well assured he is a man endued with saving faith, one of Abraham's children, an heir of promise, one of the society of the saints and fellowship of the apostles, whom the apostle here taketh in with himself in this text, a man in God's counsel, fore-known, elected, predestinated, a man to whom God intended both to speak and swear, in Abraham's person, to whom God alloweth both strong consolation here and the possession hereafter of whatsoever is set before him in the offer of the gospel.

4. The end of the oath: That we might have strong consolation by two immutable things, that is God's promise and God's oath, in which it is impossible that God should lie.

Then, 1. The consolation which God alloweth upon the faithful is strong, able to overcome the challenge of sin, fear of judgment, death and hell, and feeling or fearing of any misery whatever. Other consolations are but weak in comparison hereof, and can overcome none of these. 2. God hath laid immutable grounds for this consolation; his unchangeable promise and his unchangeable oath. 3. God cannot lie nor deceive, whether he say or swear. 4. His nature maketh this impossibility of lying and immutability in promising and swearing. 5. God alloweth this strong consolation to come by faith's resting on these two immutable things, his promise and oath. So that the less a man apprehend the grounds of his faith to be solid the less he shall be comforted; and the more he apply the promise to himself, and apprehend the unchangeableness of the promise and oath of God, the more strong shall his consolation be.

VER. 19. Which hope we have as an anchor of the soul, both sure and stedfast, and which entereth into that within the veil;

VER. 20. Whither the forerunner is for us entered, even Jesus, made an high priest for ever after the order of Melchisedek.

1. He hath told the solidity of the ground whereupon the believer doth rest; and now he showeth the stability of the gripe which the believer taketh of these grounds, in the similitude of the gripe which a ship's anchor taketh, being cast on good ground. In the former verse, by Hope, was meant the thing hoped for, and laid hold on by Hope. In the relative, which, in this verse he understandeth the Hope which doth lay hold. In the similitude of an anchor cast out of a ship, he giveth us to understand, 1. That albeit we have not gotten full possession of the promises in this life, yet we get a gripe of them by faith and hope. 2. That hope's gripe is not a slender imagination, but solid and strong, like the gripe of an anchor. 3. That the believer is not exempted from some tossing of trouble and temptations while he is in this world, yea, subject rather to the same, as a ship upon the sea. 4. That whatever tossing there be, yet all is safe; the soul's anchor is cast within the heaven; the soul is sure.

2. He giveth the anchor all good properties: it is weighty, solid, and firm: it will not drive, nor bow, nor break, it is so sure and stedfast. Again, it is sharp and piercing: it is entered into that within the veil, that is, into heaven, represented by the sanctuary beyond the veil. And so the ground is good, as well as the anchor, to hold all fast.

VER. 20. Whither the forerunner is for us entered, even Jesus, made an high priest for ever after the order of Melchisedek.

2. He commendeth our anchor-ground for this, that Christ is there, where our anchor is cast, as our forerunner. In continuing the comparison, and calling Christ our forerunner, he bringeth to mind,

1. Christ being once in the ship of the militant church, tossed and tempted as others, albeit without sin. 2. That he is now gone ashore to heaven, where the ship of the church is seeking to land. 3. That his going ashore is as our forerunner; and so his landing is an evidence of our landing also, who are to follow after him. 4. That his going before is to make easy our entry: he is forerunner for us for our behoof, to prepare a place for us. 5. That our anchor is where Christ is, and so must be the surer for his being there, to hold all fast, till he draw the ship to the shore.

2. Christ is entered into heaven, and made an high priest for ever.

Then, 1. Christ in heaven is invested in an office for us. 2. His office is the high priesthood: the truth and substance of the typical priesthood. 3. His office is for ever, and so for the benefit of all ages, that we now, as well as others before us, may have the benefit of his intercession.

3. He is said to be made an high priest after his entry in heaven. Then, albeit Christ was priest for his church from the beginning, yet was it never so declared, as after his ascension, when he sent down blessings sensibly upon his church, since which time he doth so still.

THE SUM OF CHAP. VII.

I brake off my speech of Melchisedek, (will the apostle say), now I return to him again, and in his excellency will show you Christ's excellency, who is priest after his order. We have no more of him in Scripture but what we find Gen. xiv. 19, 20, and there he is king and priest both, ver. 1, bearing a mystery in his name and office, ver. 2, without father or mother, or end of life, as he standeth in Scripture, that he might resemble Christ, ver. 3. Acknowledged to be superior to Abraham, by his paying of tithes unto them, ver. 4, even as Levi for that same cause is superior to the brethren, ver. 5; superior also because he blessed Abraham, ver. 6, 7; superior to Levi for his typical immortality, ver. 8, and for his taking tithes of Levi, in Abraham's loins, ver. 9, 10. Yea, the priesthood of

Levi, because imperfect, calleth for a priest of another order, to give perfection, which is Christ, ver. 11, 12. And so both the priesthood, and all the ordinances thereof, are abolished by the Messias, who behoved to be of another tribe than Levi, ver. 13, 14, and of another order also, ver. 15. Bodily shadows were in the priesthood of Levi, but endless truth in Christ, ver. 16, as David's words do prove, ver. 17; by which also it is prophesied, that Aaron's priesthood shall be disannulled, when Christ's priesthood is come, because it was not able to do men's turn under the law, as Christ's doth under the gospel, ver. 18, 19. And God obliged not himself to make Aaron's priesthood stand, as he sware to establish Christ's, ver. 20, 21. And so the covenant under Messias is declared to be better than under Levi, ver. 22. Again, the priesthood of Levi had sundry office-bearers, but Christ hath none in his priesthood with himself, nor none after himself, ver. 23, 24; therefore he is able alone to work out our salvation throughly, ver. 25. For such a priest have we need of, who needeth not offer up daily his sacrifice, for he hath offered one, and never more, ver. 26, 27. And no wonder; for under the law mortal men might be priests, but under the gospel only the Son of God is priest, and that for evermore, ver. 28.

THE DOCTRINE OF CHAP. VII.

VER. 1. For this Melchisedek, king of Salem, priest of the most high God, who met Abraham returning from the slaughter of the kings, and blessed him;

By saying "for," he giveth a reason why he calleth Christ a priest after the order of Melchisedek; because such a one was Melchisedek, his type; therefore such a one it behoved Christ in truth and substance to be, as the type imported he should be.

1. He repeateth from Gen. xiv. 18—20, as much as served to resemble any thing in Christ, but never a word toucheth he of Melchisedek's bringing forth of bread and wine to Abraham. Therefore he did not account this any typical action, having any resemblance of that which was to be done of Christ his anti-type; for then should he not have failed to mark it, seeing he observeth the mystery of his name and place of dwelling, which is les .

2. Melchisedek, and the church in Salem, where Melchisedek was priest, were not of Abraham's family. Therefore albeit God did choose Abraham's family, as the race wherein he was to continue the ordinary race of his church, yet had he churches and saints besides.

3. This meeting of Abraham, and entertaining him and his company with bread and drink, being the exercise of an ordinary virtue, showeth that it is the duty of all men, and namely of kings, great men, and churchmen, to countenance and encourage, according to their place and power, those who hazard themselves in God's service and good causes.

4. To come to a particular comparison of the type and the truth. 1. As Melchisedek was king and priest in his kingdom, so is Christ king

and priest in his kingdom, both to care for the religion and outward conversation of his subjects, to the weal of their souls and bodies, both amongst men and towards God, in this life and hereafter. 2. As Melchisedek is the blesser of Abraham, the father of the faithful, in the type, so is Christ in truth the blesser of Abraham and all the faithful, the fountain of all blessing, in whom alone every one is blessed who getteth blessing.

VER. 2. To whom also Abraham gave a tenth part of all: first being by interpretation King of righteousness, and after that also King of Salem, which is, King of peace;

1. To go on in the comparison. As Melchisedek, the type, was honoured by Abraham's paying of tithes unto him, so is Christ to be honoured by all Abraham's children, by giving of their substance and worldly goods what is sufficient to maintain the honour of his kingdom amongst them.

2. Presuppose the type were laid aside, yet this thankful meeting that Abraham gave to the man whose office was to bless him in the name of the Lord, doth teach all the faithful, Abraham's true seed, a duty of thankfulness to God's servants set over them, to bless them in the name of the Lord; even to honour them, by giving of their goods for their sufficient maintenance.

3. As Melchisedek, the type, is, by interpretation, King of righteousness, so is Christ in truth King of righteousness. 1. For the personal righteousness in himself. 2. Because he is the righteousness of his subjects, made of God unto us righteousness by imputation. 3. Because he frameth his subjects, piece and piece, unto a righteous disposition, by sanctifying them.

4. As Melchisedek, the type, is king of Salem, that is, King of peace, so is Christ in truth King of peace to his subjects, by reconciling them to the Father, by giving peace of conscience within themselves, by making all the creatures at peace with them, and all things turn together for their good, and by working still on their eternal welfare and blessedness, until he perfect it.

5. As Melchisedek was first King of righteousness, and then King of peace in the type, so is Christ in truth, in this order, first, king of righteousness to his subjects, to take away their sins, and to give them righteousness. And then, King of peace, because he giveth them his peace, as the fruit of righteousness. This is the order of his kingdom, righteousness, and peace, and joy in the Holy Ghost.

VER. 3. Without father, without mother, without descent, having neither beginning of days, nor end of life; but made like unto the Son of God, abideth a priest continually.

Melchisedek certainly was a very man, king, and priest in such a city, if we consider him in his natural being; but if we consider him in his spiritual being, as he standeth in Scripture, under this name, he hath neither father nor mother, beginning nor end. There is no more mention of him, what he was, or of whom he came, or of his death, but these three verses of Genesis xiv.

c

As then he is in a typical being in Scripture, so is Christ in truth in his personal being, as God, without mother; as man, without father; as God, without beginning; as God and man, without ending of life.

2. As Melchisedek, looking how he standeth in his spiritual being, abideth a priest continually, so that wheresoever he is named in Scripture, there he is ever found a priest also, and never a word of his laying down the priesthood; even so is Christ's priesthood inseparable from his person; he abideth a priest continually in real accomplishment.

3. By saying, he is made like unto the Son of God, he giveth us to understand that God's purpose was, in those particulars, so to describe him, as he might resemble the person and offices of the Son of God; and so is a type of God's own appointment.

4. And if he was made a likely type of Christ in his office of priesthood, then it followeth, as Melchisedek had neither any joined with him in his priesthood, nor deputy, nor vicar under him in it, nor successor to his office; so neither hath Christ any joined with him, or substitute or successor to him in his priesthood.

VER. 4. Now consider how great this man was, unto whom even the patriarch Abraham gave the tenth of the spoils.

To show Christ's excellency, he draweth them to consider Melchisedek's excellency above Abraham's, that so they might see Christ's excellency to be far more. The reason in force goeth thus: 1. If Melchisedek, the type, be more excellent than Abraham, much more must Christ, of whom he is a type. 2. And if Melchisedek's greatness be not easily perceived, except there be a due consideration of it; much more Christ's greatness requireth consideration, and is worthy of contemplation. 3. If Abraham, by paying of tithes, acknowledged Melchisedek's superiority, much more should all Abraham's offspring acknowledge Christ's superiority, whom Melchisedek typically represented, by paying of what is due for the maintenance of his service, and bestowing on his ministers, who are appointed to bless in his name (whether it be less or more which they bestow) in such a manner as it vilify not nor disgrace their high employment, which Christ hath put upon them, and so dishonour him whose servants they are.

VER. 5. And verily they that are of the sons of Levi, who receive the office of the priesthood, have a commandment to take tithes of the people, according to the law; that is, of their brethren, though they come out of the loins of Abraham:

He proveth that in tithes-taking, Melchisedek was greater than Abraham, who did pay tithes; because, for the same respect, the Levites, by taking tithes of their brethren, as priests, had a superiority over them, for their office sake, who otherwise were their equals.

Then, 1. The priestly office lifted up the Levites above their brethren, who were sprung of Abraham as well as they. 2. The command of taking tithes was annexed to the office of the priesthood, in token of their superiority by office over them who by nature were at least their equals.

VER. 6. But he whose descent is not counted from them received tithes of Abraham, and blessed him that had the promises.

VER. 7. And without all contradiction the less is blessed of the greater.

He proveth again Melchisedek to be greater than Abraham, and so greater than Levi, because he blessed him, and therefore behoved to be greater.

Then, 1. Abraham, notwithstanding he had the promises, yet got he the blessing by Melchisedek in type; and from Christ, represented by him, in truth. 2. If Melchisedek was greater because he blessed him as type, then Christ far more, who blesseth in effect.

Now, there are sundry sorts of blessings. 1. There is a blessing of reverence and worship: so men bless God. This sort importeth no greatness in the blesser, but subjection. 2. There is a blessing of charity: so men bless one another by mutual prayer. This sort implies no superiority neither. 3. There is a blessing of authority ordinary: so do God's ministers bless the people in the Lord's name. 4. A blessing of authority extraordinary: so Melchisedek blessed Abraham, and the prophets and patriarchs such as by inspiration they were directed to bless. And this official blessing, with authority, proveth superiority, whether it be ordinary or extraordinary. 5. There is a blessing of power, of itself effectual: so blesseth Christ, and so God blesseth men.

From this: 1. The excellency of the office of God's ministers is evident, who are appointed to bless the people in God's name. 2. And how they should be respected in love for their work's sake. 3. And how they should walk worthy of that high and holy employment, lest their sins make them vile and contemptible before the people, as in Malachi's time, Mal. ii. 9.

VER. 8. And here men that die receive tithes; but there he receiveth them, of whom it is witnessed that he liveth.

Another point of comparison, tending to this end: the Levites, in their tithing, were mortal men, one succeeding another, but Melchisedek, in type of his priesthood and scriptural being, and Christ, in the truth of his priesthood, are immortal; and therefore Melchisedek, as the typical priest, and Christ as the true priest, are greater than Levitical priests, by as much as immortality is above mortality.

Then, every age hath Christ for a priest, living in their own time, to deal for them with God; and what benefit they get by him in their own time, he can make forthcoming unto them, even for ever.

VER. 9. And as I may so say, Levi also, who receiveth tithes, payed tithes in Abraham.

VER. 10. For he was yet in the loins of his father, when Melchisedek met him.

Another reason to this same purpose. Levi paid tithes to Melchisedek in Abraham's loins, therefore Melchisedek is greater in his priesthood than the Levitical priests. So was Christ in Abraham's loins, will you say. I answer, Christ was the true represented priest, even when Melchisedek met Abraham: and in Melchisedek's person, as type, the honour was done to Christ, in truth, and to his priesthood, by Abraham. And again, Christ was in Abraham's loins only in regard of the matter of human nature; not for the manner of propagation; and so is exempted from the law of natural posterity.

1. Always from this reasoning we learn, that as receiving tithes proveth superiority in office, so paying of tithes, or maintenance in room of tithes, proveth subjection to that office, and office-bearers which receive the same. And so, maintenance of ministers should be a matter of honouring of them, or rather of him that sent them, of its own proper institution, though men turn it into a beggarly stipend, and count the more basely of the office because of the manner of maintenance.

2. From the reason of Levi's paying of tithes in Abraham's loins, we learn,

That there is ground in nature for imputation of the father's deed unto the children descended of him by natural propagation, so that as justly may God impute unto us Adam's sins, as to Levi Abraham's tithes-paying.

VER. 11. If therefore perfection were by the Levitical priesthood, (for under it the people received the law,) what farther need was there that another priest should rise after the order of Melchisedek, and not be called after the order of Aaron?

To the end of the chapter he showeth a necessity of the abolishing of the Levitical priesthood, and establishing of Christ's. One reason is in this verse; because perfection was not to be had by the Levitical priesthood. By perfection, is understood a perfect satisfaction for our sins, and a perfect purchase of all that we have need of unto eternal life. He proveth that such perfection could not be had by Aaron's priesthood, because then there had been no need of another priesthood after Aaron's, if perfection could have been by his priesthood. But the Scripture showeth that there behoved to arise a priest after Melchisedek's order, by whom perfection was to be gotten, Psalm cx.

1. Therefore, perfection could not be by Aaron's priesthood. From this we learn, that under the law remission of sins and eternal life was not obtained by virtue of any sacrifice then offered, but by the virtue of Christ's sacrifice, and Christ's priesthood represented thereby.

2. But why could not perfection be by that priesthood? He giveth a reason, saying, For under it the people received the law. The word importeth as much, as the people were then legalised, disciplined, after a legal manner; that is, the law was still urged upon them; still they were pressed to give perfect obedience, under pain of the curse; still God dealt in the external form of handling them; as one not satisfied for

any thing that was offered, as yet, in their name. Therefore, perfection could not be had by that service; for it was evident that neither God was pacified, nor their consciences quieted, by any thing in that priesthood; but all were sent to the thing signified, and to the time which was to come, in the Messiah's manifestation.

Then, comparing their time, and ours, for outward manner of handling, as they were legalized, that is, straitly urged, by the yoke of the law; we were evangelised; that is, smoothly entreated, under the gospel; God, laying aside terror, entreating us to be reconciled, and to come and receive grace for grace.

VER. 12. For the priesthood being changed, there is made, of necessity, a change also of the law.

From the change of the Levitical priesthood he inferreth, of necessity, the abolishing of the Levitical law, and of our obligation thereunto.

Then, 1. The Levitical priesthood and the Levitical law do stand and fall together. 2. The Levitical law cannot stand with any other priesthood than Aaron's: it cannot stand with Christ's under the gospel. 3. Christ's priesthood, seeing it is another than Aaron's, must have another law, other ordinances, and statutes, than Aaron's; a law and ordinances suitable unto itself. 4. To use Levitical ceremonies under the gospel, is to confound the priesthood of Aaron and Christ.

VER. 13. For he of whom these things are spoken pertaineth to another tribe, of which no man gave attendance at the altar.

VER. 14. For it is evident that our Lord sprang out of Judah; of which tribe Moses spake concerning priesthood.

VER. 15. And it is yet far more evident: for that after the similitude of Melchisedek, there ariseth another priest.

1. He proveth that Aaron's priesthood is changed and the ordinance thereof; because Psal. cx. speaketh of Christ's priesthood: that is, freed from the service of the altar. By the altar he meaneth the material altar, commanded in the law; another altar he knoweth not. And Christ's priesthood he declareth to be freed from the service of this altar; beside this, no law could tie it to any other altar.

Then Christ's priesthood is freed from the altar which God commandeth, and all the service there. And whosoever will erect another material altar in Christ's priesthood, and tie his Church unto it, must look by what law they do it.

2. From ver. 14, we learn, That Christ's genealogy was well known in the apostles' times, and no controversy about it. And it sufficeth us that we know this by the apostles' testimony; albeit we could not lineally deduce the same.

3. Observe how he reasoneth, That none of the tribe of Judah attended the altar, because Moses spake nothing of that tribe, concerning the priesthood.

Then negative conclusions, in matters of faith,

and duties, follow well upon the Scriptures' silence. It is not warranted from Scripture; therefore I am not bound to believe it. The Scripture doth not require any such thing of me; therefore God accounteth it not service to him to do it; is good reasoning.

4. From ver. 15, the apostle comparing the proofs of his argument, calleth this last in plain terms, Far more evident.

Then of reasons drawn from Scripture, by consequence some will be less evident, some more evident; and yet all be good reasons, and prove the purpose strongly.

VER. 16. Who is made, not after the law of a carnal commandment; but after the power of an endless life.

He entereth into a more particular comparison of the Levitical priesthood, and Christ's; to show the weakness of the one, in comparison of the other. The Levitical priests in their consecration, got a commandment, for the exercise of bodily and carnal rites, some few years of their mortal life; without power to convey the grace signified by those bodily rites. But Christ in consecration, is endued with power to confer grace and life eternal, from generation to generation, to all that seek the benefit of his priesthood.

Then we may be assured of Christ's power, to make the means which he useth for our salvation effectual; as we may be assured of his endless life.

VER. 17. For he testifieth, Thou art a priest for ever, after the order of Melchisedek.

He proveth this by Scripture, because God calleth him a priest for ever; therefore he hath power for ever, as living for ever, to make his own priesthood effectual. So the eternity of Christ's priesthood proveth it to be forcible, to give eternal life. For if it did not endure in his person, it could not give eternal life; and people's hearts would not rest upon it, with any ground: and so it behoved to be renounced, and another priesthood sought. But seeing it is not to be changed, but shall endure; then of necessity, it hath the thing to give us, which we are seeking, that is, eternal life.

Then as long as Christ endureth, we want not a priest, to hear confession of sin, to give absolution, to bless us, and give us eternal life.

VER. 18. For there is verily a disannulling of the commandment going before, for the weakness and unprofitableness thereof.

1. By the same words of establishing Christ's priesthood, Psal. cx. he proveth that the Levitical law was to be abolished, when Christ came: because the establishing of Christ's priesthood, and bringing it to light, is the disannulling of the Levitical.

Then there needeth no more to declare, that the Levitical priesthood and law is abolished, and we freed from the ceremonies thereof, but the coming of Christ, and his entering to his office of priesthood.

2. He giveth a reason of the abolishing of this priesthood; because it was weak and unprofitable.

Quest. How can that be, seeing it was ordained to strengthen the believers then, and was profitable for that end?

I answer, It is called weak and unprofitable, in regard of any power, to make satisfaction to God's justice for our sins, or to purchase any salvation unto us: for other ways as a mean to lead men for that time, unto the Messias, who should satisfy for us, it was not weak, nor unprofitable: but to pacify God, and purchase salvation, as the misbelieving Jews did use it, it was weak and unprofitable altogether. Again being considered as a mean, to prefigure Christ, it was profitable still till Christ came; namely, for that end and use. But when he is come, no end nor use more for it; but that it should be abolished, having served the turn whereunto it was ordained.

Then, 1. Levitical ceremonies, whatsoever use they might have had before Christ, are weak and unprofitable, after his coming. 2. It is evil reasoning to say such rites and ceremonies were used before Christ came; therefore they may be used now also.

VER. 19. For the law made nothing perfect; but the bringing in of a better hope did; by the which we draw nigh unto God.

He proveth, that those rites were weak: because the law, whether moral or ceremonial, could not perfect any thing; that is, justify, sanctify, and save any man.

1. They served as a pedagogue, to lead a man to Christ, for expiation of sin, and purchase of salvation, but could not effectuate this by themselves. And this maketh good the answer to the question in the former verse.

Then to seek to be perfected, justified, and saved by works, is to seek that by the law, which could never be brought to pass by it.

2. What, then, doth perfect all? He answereth, the bringing in a better hope, perfecteth all. That is, Christ then hoped for, and looked unto who is that better end, and the signification of those legal ordinances, being brought in unto believers, he doth perfect all.

Then, 1. What the believers could not get under the law, by their outward service, they got it by Christ, hopes for and believed into. 2. The believers of old rested not on the shadows; but had the eye of their hope on Christ.

3. He commendeth his better hope: that is, Christ's priesthood hoped for under the law; because by it we draw nigh unto God. Now drawing nigh, importeth a distance before drawing nigh; and again drawing nigh, was the priest's prerogative under the law.

Then by nature, and without Christ, we are aliens from God, and far away from him: but by Christ we get liberty to come nigh, not only as God's people, but as priests through Christ, to offer our spiritual oblations. The priest's privilege of old, is common to believers now.

VER. 20. And inasmuch, as not without an oath, he was made priest:

Ver. 21. (For those priests were made without an oath; but this, with an oath, by him that said unto him, The Lord sware, and will not repent, Thou art a priest for ever, after the order of Melchisedek.)

Ver. 22. By so much was Jesus made a surety of a better testament.

1. He goeth on to compare the Levitical priesthood with Christ's. Two comparisons are here conjoined: first Levitical priests were made without an oath, only by way of simple ordinance and direction; God leaving room to himself, how long he pleased to hold on the direction; and when he pleased to change it. But Christ was made priest with an oath, that he should never be changed.

Then, 1. When God gave forth the ceremonial law, he reserved room to himself, to change it; yea, gave evidence that he was to change it; for he obliged the people, during his will, but not himself. 2. But for Christ's priesthood, God is bound with an oath, never to change it: and it leaneth on his nature which cannot alter, nor repent; and upon his oath, which cannot be violated.

2. Another comparison between the Levitical covenant, and the evangelical covenant. As far as the oath is above the changeable commandment, by so much is the new covenant better than the covenant under the law.

Then, 1. There was a covenant or testament, whereby believers were saved as well under the law, as under the gospel. 2. The covenant now, though, in substance of salvation, one with the former; yet, in the manner of down-setting the articles and the form of it, is better than the covenant then, more clear, more free, more full, more largely extended, and more firm.

3. Christ is here called Surety of this covenant. Then, 1. Christ must see the covenant kept, and be good for it. 2. God hath Christ to crave for our performance of the covenant; and we have Christ to crave, for God's part of the covenant: yea, and Christ to crave, to give us grace to perform that which God requireth of us in his covenant. 3. Jesus is content to be surety; and the Father hath consented, and ordained, and made him surety. So it resteth only, that we be content also, and make much of Christ, that he may do all our work for us, and all God's work in us.

Ver. 23. And they, truly, were many priests; because they were not suffered to continue, by reason of death.

Ver. 24. But this man, because he continueth ever, hath an unchangeable priesthood.

The excellency of Christ's priesthood, above the Levitical; which may be branched out in these particulars following,

1. The Levitical priests were many, both at one time, and one after another: by reason whereof that priesthood was weakened, while one part of the office, for such a time, was in the hands of this man; and another part for another time, was in the hands of that man. And because one man could not be ready to take the sacrifices from all the people, therefore, several men behoved to take several parts of the burden. But in Christ's priesthood, there is but one man, even himself; his priesthood is undivided; no man beareth a part of the burden with him; he alone attendeth all men's sacrifices by himself; he is at leisure, for every man's employment, at all times, in the greatest throng of sacrifices. Then as long as Christ is at leisure, no reason to employ another to carry our prayers.

2. The Levitical priesthood did pass from one person to another; death made interruption. But Christ's priesthood cannot pass from his own person to any other; neither death, nor any other infirmity, can interrupt his office.

Then, 1. To make any priest by special office in the New Testament, beside Christ, is to rent the priesthood of Christ, and make it imperfect, like Aaron's; which for the same reason, that it had many priests, was weak and imperfect, and inferior to Christ's. 2. To make priests by office in the New Testament, to offer up any corporal sacrifice, is to make Christ's priesthood separable from his own person: which is against the nature of Christ's priesthood, which cannot pass from one to another: for so importeth the word. 3. To make plurality of priests in Christ's priesthood, vicars, or substitutes, or in any respect partaker of the office with him, is to presuppose that Christ is not able to do that office alone; but is either dead or weak, that he cannot fulfil that office: contrary to the text here, which saith, "Because he continueth ever, he hath an unchangeable priesthood," or a priesthood which cannot pass from one to another.

Ver. 25. Wherefore he is able also to save them to the uttermost, which come unto God by him; seeing he ever liveth to make intercession for them.

1. He showeth the fruit of Christ's keeping still the priesthood, altogether in his own person, to be the perfect salvation of all believers for ever: he is able to save to the uttermost, them that come unto God through him.

Then, 1. Whosoever communicateth Christ's priesthood, with any other beside his own person, maketh Christ not able, alone, to save to the uttermost those that come unto God through him. 2. From this ground also, it doth follow, that Christ not only beginneth the believer's salvation, but perfecteth it also. He doth not work a part of a man's salvation, and leave the rest to his own merits, (or the merits of others,) but perfecteth it himself, even to the uttermost. 3. And if a man join any thing meritorious unto Christ's priesthood, or any mediator, for intercession beside him, or seeketh by his own works to purchase salvation, he denieth Christ to be able to save him to the uttermost.

2. He describeth believers, to be those that come to God, through Christ. Then, 1. Christ is the door, and the way through which only access is gotten to God. By saints or angels there is not a way to come to God; but by Christ only. 2. They that come not through him alone to God, seclude themselves from the sufficiency of salvation to be had in him. 3. The nature of

believing, is to make a man come towards God, to get communion with him through Christ. 4. And none but such as come in faith to God through Christ, can take comfort from his priesthood or look for salvation.

3. He giveth a reason, why perfect salvation is to be had for such as come to God, through Christ: because he liveth for ever, to make intercession for them. He saith not, to offer, or cause offer up, the sacrifice of his body for them; but he liveth, and is not to be offered any more, and liveth to make intercession.

Then, 1. The sacrificing part is done and ended: his intercession hath now the place; and by his intercession, we get the merit of his death and passion applied unto us: and not by any new oblation. 2. If he brook his life, he will not fail to intercede for us, who come unto God through him; and not through saint, or angel, or any person beside; for he liveth for ever, to make intercession for us.

VER. 26. For such a high priest became us, who is holy, harmless, undefiled, separate from sinners, and made higher than the heavens.

To the end he may force the Hebrews to forsake the priesthood of Levi, he draweth a strong reason, from the nature of our estate under the gospel.

Whereby he proveth, not only that the priests of Aaron's order are abolished, but also every son of Adam is excluded from the office of the priesthood, except Jesus Christ in his own person only. Because every priest that wanteth the properties of Jesus Christ, is unbeseeming for us under the gospel. A sinful man might have been a priest under the law, to prefigure Christ before he came: but now no sinful man may be a priest by office, but Christ only, in whom there is no sin. When the sacrifice was a beast, then a sinful man might be a priest: but now when the Son of God is the sacrifice, and hath offered up himself already, and is gone in, into the sanctuary, with his own blood, to make intercession; there must be no more any sacrificing till he come out of the sanctuary again, at the day of judgment; nor any priest but he, till he have ended his intercession. "For such a high priest became us, who is holy, harmless," &c. Question. But why is it unbeseeming us under the Gospel, to have a priest without these properties? I answer. The sacrifice of the New Testament, is the unspotted Lamb of God, Jesus Christ, holy, harmless, &c. Therefore it becometh us to have such a priest, who is holy, harmless, and undefiled. For, it were unseemly that the priest should be worse than the sacrifice. Next, our priest hath our sins, original and actual, to remove, and heaven to open unto us; and therefore it were unbeseeming that any should be our priest, who hath not his own sins altogether removed, nor yet hath gotten entry, as yet, into heaven himself.

1. In that he draweth them, of necessity, to quit all men's priesthood, and betake them unto Christ, as priest only, we learn, That our necessities being well weighed, with the insufficiency of any beside Christ to do our turn, we shall be forced to quit all priests but Christ only: for what priest can know all our needs, all our sins, all our thoughts, all our desires, all our prayers, all our purposes, and wait on upon our business, with God, night and day, to see that no wrath break out upon us? Who can do this, but Christ only? What man? what saint? what angel?

2. In that he reckoneth a number of perfections necessary to be in a priest in the time of the gospel, all of them in Christ, and all such as we stand in need of, we learn, that all the perfections whereof we have need in a priest are all in Christ; and the perfections which are in Christ, we have need of them all, and should make use of them all.

3. The first property of a priest under the gospel is this, he must be holy, that is, of his own nature holy, in his original, holy.

Then no sinful man can be a sufficient priest in the New Testament to do for us, who wants holiness by nature.

4. The next property: Our priest must be harmless, ill-less, free from any original guiltiness.

Then, no man, come of Adam by natural propagation, can be a priest for us now, to satisfy our necessities, who have sin original in us.

5. The third property: We have need of a priest undefiled, that is, free from actual sin.

Then, no priests can suffice us who are defiled with actual sin but Christ, who never sinned.

6. The fourth property: A priest meet for us must be free from the pollution of those amongst whom he converseth.

Then, we who are of polluted lips and lives, and dwell among such a people, communicating many ways of their guiltiness, cannot have sufficient comfort through any priest who can be infected with sin. And he who is a man of polluted lips is not meet to be a priest for us.

The fifth property: A priest meet for us, behoved to have his residence in heaven, and have commandment over heaven to open it unto us, and give us entry.

Then, none other, but Christ, could suffice us on whom by nature the doors of heaven are closed. No priest out of heaven is meet for us.

VER. 27. Who needeth not daily, as those high priests, to offer up sacrifice first for his own sins, and then for the people's; for this he did once when he offered up himself.

1. The sixth property of a fit priest for us: He must have no need to offer sacrifice for his own sins.

Then, neither Levi, nor any sinful man after him, can be a priest under the New Testament; but Christ only, who never sinned, and so had never need to offer for himself.

2. The seventh property: He must not have need to offer daily for the people's sins who must be our priest; for if he should offer the second day, then the first day's sacrifice should be declared insufficient; or else why offereth he again after that which is sufficient?

Then, 1. The priest of the New Testament needeth not to offer oftener than once 2. And if Christ's sacrifice were offered oftener than once, or daily, he could not be a fit priest for us, nor offer a perfect sacrifice for us, for the oft offering should declare the former offerings insufficient and imperfect.

3. He giveth a reason why Christ needed not to offer up oftener, because he hath offered up himself once for the sins of the people.

Then, 1. Christ was both the priest and the sacrifice in his own offering. 2. Christ's sacrifice cannot be offered up by any but himself; another than Christ's self cannot offer up Christ. 3. Betwixt the coming of Christ and the writing of this epistle, which was sundry years after Christ's ascension, the apostle knew no offering of Christ, but that only once upon the cross, and yet times out of number was the sacrament of the Lord's supper celebrated before this time.

4. In that he maketh that once offering the reason of his not offering daily, it ·teacheth us, that the perfection of that once offered sacrifice, maketh the repetition needless; and whosoever maketh it needful that Christ be offered daily maketh both Christ an imperfect priest, and his sacrifice imperfect also.

Ver. 28. For the law maketh men high priests which have infirmity, but the word of the oath, which was since the law, maketh the Son, who is consecrated for evermore.

He giveth a special reason why it beseemeth not us under the gospel to have a sinful man for our priest, because this is the very difference betwixt the law and the gospel.

1. The law maketh men which have infirmities high priests; but the word of the oath, which was since the law, maketh the Son, and none but the Son, who is consecrated for evermore.

Then, the Scripture knoweth no priest but the Levitical priests of Aaron's posterity for the time of the law; or else that one priest which was made by an oath for the time of the gospel. Beside these the apostle acknowledgeth none, nor were there any other in his time in the church.

2. He maketh the difference of the law and the gospel to stand amongst other things in the difference of priests, so as the gospel cannot admit such priests as the law admitted.

Then, to have priests now after the similitude of the priests under the law, were to remove the difference which God hath made betwixt the law and the gospel.

3. The differences, as the apostle setteth them down here, are, 1. The course taken about priests under the law was alterable, they were made without an oath, the lawgiver declaring it to be his will to change that course when he saw fit; but the course taken about the priests of the New Testament is with an oath, and so cannot be changed.

Then, to make a priest in the gospel, who is not consecrated by an oath to abide for evermore in the office, but may be changed, and another come in in his place, is contrary to the institution of the evangelical priesthood.

The next difference, he maketh this: The law admitteth men in the plural number, a plurality of priests; but the gospel admitteth no plurality of priests, but the Son only to be priest. Mel-

chisedek's order in the type hath no priest but one in it, without a suffragan or substituted priest. Therefore Christ, the true Melchisedek, is alone in his priesthood, without partner or deputy or suffragan.

Then, to make plurality of priests in the gospel is to alter the order of Melchisedek, sworn with an oath, and to renounce the mark set betwixt the law and the gospel.

3. The third difference: The law maketh men priests; but the evangelical oath maketh the Son of God priest for the gospel.

Then, to make a man priest now is to mar the Son of God's privilege, to whom the privilege only belongeth.

4. The fourth difference: The law maketh such priests as have infirmity; that is, sinful men who cannot make the sacrifice which they offer, effectually to pacify, not the blessing which they pronounce to come, nor the instruction which they give forcibly to open the eyes. But the evangelical oath maketh the Son, who is able to save to the uttermost all that come to God, through him.

Then, to make a sinful and weak man a priest now is to weaken the priesthood of the gospel, and make it like the law.

5. The fifth difference: The law maketh men priests which have infirmities over whom death had power, that they could not be consecrated but for their short life-time. But the evangelical oath maketh the Son, whom the sorrows of death could not hold, and hath consecrated him for evermore.

Then as long as Christ's consecration lasteth, none must meddle with his office.

6. The last difference: The law instituting priests was not God's last will, but might suffer addition. But the evangelical oath is since the law, and God's last and unchangeable will.

Therefore to add unto it and bring in as many priests now as did serve in the temple of old, is to provoke God to add as many plagues as are written in God's book upon themselves and their priests also.

THE SUM OF CHAP. VIII.

This is the sum of all that I have spoken: We have no priest now but Christ, who is equal in glory to his Father in heaven, ver. 1. The offerer of his own body, signified by the tabernacle, ver. 2. For every priest must offer something, therefore so must Christ, ver. 3. But the typical sacrifice he could not offer by the law, albeit he were on earth, ver. 4. Because he is not of the tribe of Levi, whose proper office was to meddle with the shadows. Therefore he must be the offerer of the substance; that is of his own body, signified by the shadows, ver. 5. And so, now, he hath taken the office over the Levites' head, and hath an office more excellent than they, and is Mediator of a better covenant than the covenant which was in their time, ver. 6. For if that covenant had been perfect, another had been needless, ver. 7. But another covenant was needful, and God promised to make a new one, ver. 8. A better covenant than that old, which the people brake, ver. 9. For in this covenant God undertaketh to make us keep our part of it, ver.

10, 11. And to pardon where we fail, ver. 12. Now when God promised a new covenant he declared the other to be old, and to be abolished when the new one came, ver. 13.

THE DOCTRINE OF CHAP. VIII.

VER. 1. Now, of the things which we have spoken, this is the sum: We have such a high priest, who is set on the right hand of the throne of the majesty in the heavens.

1. The apostle, accommodating himself to help the capacity and memory of the Hebrews, and urging the special point of his discourse, is worthy of imitation.

2. In saying, "We have such a high priest, who is set down on the right hand," &c., he setteth forth the glory of Christ's person, that he may commend his priesthood.

Then, 1. The glory of Christ's office is not seen till the glory of his person be seen. 2. The glory of his person is not seen till his glorious sovereignty and government of the world be seen. 3. Yea, the glory of Christ is not rightly seen till his equality with the Father, in glory, be seen and acknowledged.

3. In saying that Christ as high priest is set down on the right hand of the throne, he giveth us to understand, that Christ, as in his divine nature, he is undivided from the Father in glory and dominion, so in his human nature he is exalted to the fellowship of divine glory with the Father; because of the union of the human nature with the divine, in one person of the Mediator. The two natures still remaining distinguished, but not divided, nor separated, the one from the other.

4. He noteth the place of this glory to be in the heavens, wherein he preferreth Christ above the Levitical priests; for, their priesthood is only exercised on earth, but Christ's in heaven.

And therefore when we will employ our high priest, we have no earthly city to seek him in; but in the heaven, the only place and palace of his residence.

VER. 2. A minister of the sanctuary, and of the true tabernacle, which the Lord pitched, and not man.

1. For all this glory, yet Christ is still called a minister, to show us,

That this high honour hindereth him not to do his office for our good.

2. He is called a minister of the sanctuary, or of the holy things; for the word will agree with both, and both tend to one purpose; for the holy things were all tied to the sanctuary, and he that was minister of the sanctuary was minister of the holy things also, and that in the name of the saints. Now, the sanctuary, or the holy things, which is here spoken of, is the thing signified by the sanctuary and by the holy things; and so taking all the significations of the word together, we are taught,

That Christ, in his glory, is not idle, but as a faithful agent, in the heavenly sanctuary, taking the care of all the holy things which his saints and people are commanded to present, procuring and giving forth all holy and spiritual things from heaven, to his saints, which their estate requireth.

3. He is called a minister of the true tabernacle, which God pitched, and not man; that is, the minister of his own body, miraculously formed by God, not after the ordinary manner of other men, signified and represented by the typical tabernacle.

Then, the tabernacle and temple under the law was but the shadow, and Christ's body was the true tabernacle. For, 1. As the symbols of God's presence was in the typical tabernacle, so the fulness of the Godhead dwelleth bodily in Christ. 2. As the typical tabernacle had inclosed in it all the holy things, the candlestick, table of shew-bread, laver, altar, &c., so hath the humanity of Christ, or Christ the man, all holiness and perfection, the fulness of all good, and all holy things in him, light, food, washing, and reconciliation, and all in himself, that out of his fulness we may all receive grace for grace. 3. As the tabernacle in the outmost coverings seemed but base, yet had better stuff within, so our Lord, when he dwelt in the tabernacle of his flesh amongst us, was found in form as a man, and in the shape of a servant, but inwardly was full of grace and truth.

4. In calling Christ's body the true tabernacle which God builded, and not man, he teacheth us to make use of Christ in truth, as the church of old made use of the tabernacle in the type; that is, in him seek God, towards him turn the eye of our soul, when we seem to ourselves to be far removed to the end of the earth. In him offer all our spiritual sacrifices; in him seek our washing, our food, our light, our comfort; in him, as his priests, make our abode and daily dwelling; in him let us live and breathe.

5. In so calling Christ, he appropriateth the sacrificing of his body to himself in his own person, as the personal and proper act of his priesthood; for the offering of the which sacrifice once, and never oftener, (as Heb. vii. 27. showeth,) he keepeth still the style of the only minister of the true tabernacle, as his own incommunicable prerogative.

And therefore whosoever presumeth to offer his body, presumeth also to take his place.

VER. 3. For every high priest is ordained to offer gifts and sacrifices; wherefore it is of necessity that this man have somewhat also to offer.

He proveth that Christ is the minister of the tabernacle of his own body, by offering it up; because it behoved him, seeing he is a priest, to offer up something, either the typical oblations, or else his own body, represented by them. But the typical oblations he could not offer, according to the law, not being a Levite; therefore he behoved to offer up himself, represented by the typical oblations.

Then, the apostle acknowledgeth no priest, but either the Levitical priest, or the priest that offereth up his own body. And whosoever pretendeth to have the office of a priest now, usurpeth either the office of the Levite, or Christ's office.

Ver. 4. For if he were on earth, he should not be a priest, seeing that there are priests which offer gifts according to the law.

1. He proveth that Christ cannot offer up the typical oblations, because he cannot be a priest on earth, albeit he were on earth, because priesthood on earth is proper to the Levites only ; for they are the only priests by law on earth, and have prescribed to them by law what they should offer.

Quest. You will ask me here, Was not Christ a priest when he was on earth?

I answer, Yes.

Quest. How then, saith the apostle here, if he were on earth, he should not be a priest?

I answer, Because albeit he began his priest-hood upon earth, yet he could not brook his office of priesthood on the earth ; for as the high priest, who was the type, carried the sacrifice once a year through the court, and before the sanctuary killed the sacrifice, and then took the blood thereof in unto the holiest of all, and presented himself there before the Lord with the blood, to intercede for the people, and there remained during the time of intercession appointed to him ; so Christ, carrying his sacrifice out of the city, offered up his body on the altar of his Godhead to his Father, and by his own blood entered into the heavenly sanctuary, and sat down on the right hand of the Majesty on high, and there he liveth for ever to intercede for us. Having thus ended his sacrifice, as this apostle proveth, chap. vii. 27, and chap. ix. 25, 26, and having no sacrifice now to offer on earth, it is with reason that the apostle saith, If he were on earth, he should not be a priest.

Whence we learn, 1. That Christ is not now on the earth, nor in any place thereof ; and therefore if any man say to us, " Lo, here he is ; lo, there he is," we must not believe him : it is a false Christ he showeth us, and not the true, as Christ himself forewarneth, Matt. xxiv. 23. 2. That it is impossible that Christ should now be on the earth, for then should he lose his priesthood, which is impossible. For if he were on earth, he should not be a priest, saith the apostle here. 3. That Christ's priesthood is only discharged now in heaven, seeing he cannot be a priest on earth.

2. His reason is, they are priests which offer gifts according to the law. Then every priest who brooketh [holdeth] his priesthood on earth must offer gifts, according to the law, as the apostle here reasoneth ; and such priests as those Christ hath abolished, having changed the priesthood, and the law also.

Therefore there can be no priest by office on earth at all with God's allowance.

Ver. 5. Who serve unto the example and shadow of heavenly things ; as Moses was admonished of God, when he was about to make the tabernacle. For, See, saith he, that thou make all things according to the pattern showed unto thee in the Mount.

He describeth the proper use of the Levitical priests, to serve unto the example of heavenly things.

Then, 1. The incarnation of Christ, his death, and the benefits thereof, signified by Levitical shadows, are heavenly things in regard of their heavenly fruits and effects, and other heavenly respects, and are with a heavenly mind to be looked upon. 2. The ceremonies of the law were not idle rites, but examples and figures of Christ and his graces, by the which men were led then, as by the hand, to Christ, who was to come.

2. From Exod. xxv. 40, he proveth they were shadows of heavenly things, because the pattern in the Mount represented the heavenly things, and Moses' tabernacle represented the pattern in the Mount ; therefore it represented heavenly things. And unto this pattern was Moses tied.

Then, 1. God would not, no, not in the time of types, suffer any device of man to come in for representing any thing heavenly ; much less will he now. 2. Those which himself ordaineth he will have observed, and none omitted.

Ver. 6. But now hath he ordained a more excellent ministry : by how much also he is the mediator of a better covenant, which was established upon better promises.

1. The offering of the typical oblations he hath made proper to the Levites. Now, the offering of the true sacrifices, and service belonging thereunto, he appropriateth to Christ, and calleth it a more excellent ministry.

Then, 1. The offering of the thing signified by the Levitical types, is more excellent than all their offerings. 2. This ministry is proper unto Christ only, in his own person.

2. From this he preferreth the mediatorship of Christ to the typical ; the promises, and the covenant now, to the covenant then. His reasoning is, as the ministry is, so is the mediator. The ministry is more excellent, in offering up himself, than the shadows. Therefore the mediator is more excellent now than the typical of old.

Then, the offering of Christ's body, which is the more excellent ministry, is still annexed to the person of the Mediator only. And whosoever intrudeth himself in that excellent ministry of offering up Christ's body, intrudeth himself also into the office of the Mediator.

3. In comparing the covenant then and now, he maketh this the better, because the promises are better.

Whence we learn, 1. That there was a covenant between God and his church of old, under the law, and so reconciliation to be had with God then. 2. That howsoever in substance of grace, both the covenants agreed, yet the form of this covenant under the gospel is better, because the express conditions are better, the promises are more spiritual, and more free of strait conditions.

Ver. 7. For if that first covenant had been faultless, then should no place have been sought for the second.

To clear the abolishing of the old covenant, he proveth it not to be faultless, because a new covenant was promised in place thereof. Not that any thing was wrong in that covenant, but because it was imperfect, and all things needful not expressed in it clearly.

Whence we learn, 1. That the Lord's proceeding with his church hath ever been from the less perfect to the more perfect, till Christ came. 2. That wherever God addeth or altereth what he once did institute, by so doing he showeth, that before his addition he had not expressed all his mind, as in the time of the Old Testament. 3. When once he hath perfected his course taken with his church, as now he hath done under the New Testament, he altereth the matter no more.

VER. 8. For, finding fault with them, he saith, Behold, the days come, saith the Lord, when I will make a new covenant with the house of Israel, and the house of Judah.

1. He proveth that there was an imperfection in the old covenant, because God found fault with the people under it.

Then, the imperfection of the covenant of old was specially in default of the parties with whom it was made, who by their inability to fulfil it, or behold the drift of it, made it unable to save themselves. 2. In the words of Jeremiah, xxxi. 31, the Lord promiseth to make a covenant afterwards with the house of Israel and Judah.

Then, 1. The party in the new covenant is not all mankind, but the church of the New Testament, the spiritual Israel and Judah. 2. This covenant was not brought to light of old, but had its own time of manifestation. 3. Even then the church was made wise of the imperfection of the old covenant, that they might learn to look through the outward form of it to a better. 4. The hope and too-look [expectation] which they had towards the new covenant held up their heart, that they, without us and our privileges, should not be perfected.

VER. 9. Not according to the covenant that I made with their fathers, in the day when I took them by the hand to lead them out of the land of Egypt, because they continued not in my covenant, and I regarded them not, saith the Lord.

1. The prophet distinguisheth the old covenant from the new, by describing the old, what it was, how broken, and how punished. For the first, the ten commandments, and the rest of the law delivered unto them when they came out of Egypt, was the covenant of old, wherein God promised to be their God, upon condition that they did all that he commanded them; and they accepted the condition. So, albeit there was grace here, in sundry articles covenanted, yet the form of the covenant was like the covenant of works. Compare Jer. xvii. 23, with Jer. xxxi. 31—33, &c.

2. For the next, they continued not in it, through leaning to their own strength, and seeking to establish their own righteousness, being ignorant of the righteousness of God. They dealt deceitfully in the covenant, and fell to open idolatry from time to time. So, by the covenant of works, no man will be found stedfast.

3. For the punishment of it, I regarded them not. In the Hebrew, it is as much as, I lorded it over them; that is, used my husbandly and lordly authority over them, and so misregarded them.

Whereof we have to learn, 1. That as God's lordship and husbandship is an obligation of doing well to the covenant keeper, so is it a declaration of his just freedom and authority to punish the covenant breaker. 2. That when God is pleased to exercise his dominion and authority over covenant breakers, the transgressor falleth in misregard with God; that is, as little account is made of his life as of one without the covenant. 3. That to be misregarded of God is the sum of all judgment. 4. That the impotency of the people to keep the old covenant did not exempt them from the punishment due to the breaking of it.

4. The Lord maketh their instability in the old covenant the reason of his making of a new one, wherein the Lord's bounty is very remarkable; who out of our evil taketh occasion to do us so much more good; and because of men's instability in the old covenant, maketh another covenant, whereby he maketh us to persevere in obedience.

VER. 10. For this is the covenant that I will make with the house of Israel, After those days, saith the Lord: I will put my laws into their mind, and write them in their hearts; and I will be to them a God, and they shall be to me a people.

This is the better covenant, containing better promises, whereof Christ is Mediator and Surety, unto all them that believe in him.

Wherein consider, 1. That all the articles are promises, and so do require, in the party that will join in the covenant, faith to embrace the promises, that the covenant may be agreed unto on both sides; God promising, and the needy sinner heartily accepting. 2. That what is required in the old covenant as a condition, is here turned into a promise by God in the new. In the old covenant he required obedience to his commandments; and here he promiseth to write his laws in our hearts. God undertaketh to do our part in us, if we will believe in him. 3. That the sense of wants, and the feeling of our imperfections, yea, of our heart's wickedness and carefulness, both of heart and mind, yea, the feeling of the inlacks or defects of repentance and faith, are not just hinderances to make a soul that gladly would be reconciled with God in Christ, stand back from embracing this covenant: but, by the contrary, the feeling of sinfulness in mind and heart are preparations to fit us and set us on to join in this covenant, wherein God undertaketh to help and remedy all these felt evils, through his Christ, by putting his laws in our mind, and writing them in our hearts. For what is this else but to illuminate our mind more and more with the understanding of his will, and to frame our heart and affections to the obedience of the same? 4. That by the covenant, comfort is provided for sinners, who are humbled in the sense of their sins, and no door opened for presumption, nor room given to profane persons to go on their ways blessing themselves. For the maker of the new covenant presupposeth two things: first, that his party renounce his own righteousness, which he might seem able to have by the old covenant. Next that he flee for relief to God in Christ, to have the benefits promised in this new covenant, which if he do, it is impossible that he can either lean to his own merits, or live in the love of his sinful lusts. 5. That by this covenant such an union is made betwixt God and the believer, that the believer is the Lord's adopted child, and the Lord is the believer's God, all-sufficient for ever, promising to be all to the believer, which, to be our God, may import, and to make the believer all that one of his people should be.

VER. 11. And they shall not teach every man his neighbour, and every man his brother, saying, Know the Lord; for all shall know me, from the least to the greatest.

1. While he saith, "They shall not teach every man his neighbour," he doth not mean that his word and ordinances, and ministry appointed by him, or brotherly communion for mutual edification, shall be misregarded or not made use of, but, by the contrary, that he will himself be their teacher, in these his own means, first giving his children a greater measure of the Spirit, and a more near communion with himself than of old. 2. Making his children so wise unto salvation, as they shall not hang their faith upon man's authority, but search by all means till they understand the mind of God, the infallible Teacher, as he hath revealed himself in his word. 3. So clearing the truth, which is outwardly taught unto them by his own instruments, after so sure and persuasive a manner, by his Spirit inwardly, that the outward teaching shall be no teaching, in comparison of the inward concurrence; according as we hear those Samaritans were taught, who believed indeed the woman's report, that they might go to Christ; but when they were come to him, got so great satisfaction from himself, that they said unto her, "Now we believe, not because of thy saying, for we have heard him ourselves, and know that this is indeed the Christ," John iv. 42. So will the Lord inwardly make his truth powerful unto salvation to his own, that they may say to those that are his instruments, "Now we believe, not because of your saying, but because we have heard him ourselves."

Then, 1. It is not God's will that other men's belief should be the rule of our belief; but that we all search to understand the Scriptures, and God's will revealed therein. 2. It is easy from this ground to answer that famous question, How know you such and such grounds of salvation? We answer, It is an article of the new covenant, They shall be all taught of God.

2. He saith, "They shall all know me, from the least to the greatest."

Then, 1. The new covenant admitteth all ranks and degrees of persons, and excludeth none, high nor low, that love to embrace it. 2. It may be, in sundry points of truth, some of them be ignorant and mistaken, more nor other some; but of the saving knowledge of God in Christ, they shall all have light in a saving measure. 3. The greatest as well as the meanest, in whatsoever respect of place or gifts, must be God's disciples in the study of saving knowledge and hearty obedience.

VER. 12. For I will be merciful to their unrighteousness, and their sins and their iniquities will I remember no more.

1. To make us believe the former promises, he addeth to a new article of remission of sins, because from the conscience of those ordinarily do arise our doubts and difficulty of drawing near to God.

Then, 1. The conscience of sin must not drive us away from God, but rather force us to run unto God more humbly, because only to such as come unto him in his Christ, is remission of sin promised. 2. Whatsoever sort of sins they be, unrighteousness, or sin, or iniquity, they shall not hinder God to be gracious to the penitent fleeing to this covenant for refuge.

2. In saying, "For I will be merciful," 1. He maketh his mercy, pardoning sin, the reason of his bestowing the former good things; his giving of one grace, the reason of giving another, even grace for grace. 2. He maketh his mercy the ground of all this favour, and nothing in the man's person, or works, or worthiness of his faith. 3. The word "merciful" is in the original "pacified," and doth import both God's respect to the propitiatory sacrifice of Christ, which pacifieth him towards us, and also our duty in looking towards it as the price of our reconciliation.

3. In that the Lord joineth the promise of putting his law in the mind, and writing it in our heart, with the promise of remission of sins, he teacheth us, that he will have every confederate soul that seeketh the benefit of this covenant, to join all these benefits together in their claim, with remission of sin, seeking to join the illumination of their mind, renovation of their heart and life, at least in their desires and endeavours, and not to sever one of them from another, but study in uprightness to have them all.

4. While he saith, he will remember their sins no more, he teacheth, 1. That he will never forgive sin nor forget it, but set it ever in his sight, till a man enter into this covenant with him through Christ. 2. That when he hath forgiven sin, he forgetteth sin also: whatsoever he remitteth, he removeth from his remembrance.

VER. 13. In that he saith, A new covenant, he hath made the first old. Now that which decayeth and waxeth old, is ready to vanish away.

From the name that the Lord giveth this covenant, in calling it new, he draweth two consequences: the first, that the former covenant, by this word, was declared old. Next, that as it was declared old, so was it declared shortly after to be abolished.

Then, 1. The least word that proceedeth out of God's mouth is weighty and worthy of consideration. 2. Whatsoever God's word doth import, by due consequence, must be taken for God's truth and God's mind, as if it were expressed. 3. Seeing Christ is come, and the time is now of this new covenant, we know that by God's authority the Levitical ordinances and whole form of the legal covenant and ceremonial forms of worship are abrogated.

THE SUM OF CHAP. IX.

Then that you may see this more clearly, let us take a view of the typical ordinances in the old covenant, and of their accomplishment in Christ. Under the old covenant, and typical tabernacle, there were sundry shadows, ver. 1, 2 : the tabernacle divided in two rooms, and their furniture within them both, ver. 3—5 : in the outer room the priests resorted daily, ver. 6 : in the inner room, only the high priest once a year, ver. 7 ; the close keeping of which room signified that the way to heaven was not to be fully clear during the time of those shadows, ver. 8. Nothing done then externally could quiet the conscience, ver. 9 : all being but temporary shadows, imposed till Christ came to reform all, ver. 10. But when Christ came, he gave to those shadows, accomplishment; for he was priest of the true tabernacle of his own body, signified by the typical tabernacle, ver. 11, and by his own blood entered into heaven, for our eternal redemption, ver. 12. For if the types procured a ceremonial cleansing, ver. 13, how much more shall his blood truly and in effect procure our justification and sanctification? ver. 14. And therefore that remission of sins and eternal life might be given to the faithful, both then of old and now, he behoved by his office to make his testament and die, ver. 15, for so requireth the nature of a testament, ver. 16, 17. Wherefore the typical testament of old also behoved to have a typical death, as Levit. xvi. maketh plain, ver. 18—21. Yea, every cleansing of the types, and every remission, behoved to be with blood, ver. 22. Therefore the things represented by the types, behoved to be cleansed by better blood, even the blood of the Messias, ver. 23, for Christ entered not into the typical sanctuary, but into heaven itself, ver. 24, and offered not himself often, as the imperfect Levitical sacrifice was offered, ver. 25, for then should he have often died ; but his once offering was sufficient for ever, ver. 26. And as God appointed men but once to die, ver. 27, so Christ was but once offered, till the time he come to judgment, for the salvation of the faithful, ver. 28.

THE DOCTRINE OF CHAP. IX.

VER. 1. Then verily the first covenant had also ordinances of divine service, and a worldly sanctuary.

The word [ordinances] in the original, is also justifications, in the plural number; so called, because they represented our justification.

Whereof we learn, 1. That as other things were typed under the law, so also was our justification, and the manner of obtaining the same shadowed forth. 2. That those things which were then called justifications, were so called only because they were the representations of the way of obtaining justification; for they did not justify. 3. That albeit justification be only one, yet the types thereof were many ; no one of them being able to express the truth but in part.

2. By calling them ordinances of divine service, he teacheth us, that some time those ceremonies which are now abolished, were during their own time parts of God's external worship, in regard of the commandment of God enjoining them.

3. By calling the sanctuary worldly, he teacheth us to think of all the external glory of the Levitical service, only as the earthly representation of heavenly things ; and under all these earthly shadows to seek in to [for] a heavenly signification.

VER. 2. For there was a tabernacle made ; the first, wherein was the candlestick, and the table, and the shewbread ; which is called the sanctuary.

VER. 3. And after the second veil, the tabernacle which is called the holiest of all ;

VER. 4. Which had the golden censer, and the ark of the covenant overlaid round about with gold, wherein was the golden pot that had manna, and Aaron's rod that budded, and the tables of the covenant ;

VER. 5. And over it the cherubims of glory shadowing the mercy-seat; of which we cannot now speak particularly.

VER. 6. Now when these things were thus ordained, the priests went always into the first tabernacle, accomplishing the service of God.

VER. 7. But into the second went the high priest alone once every year, not without blood, which he offered for himself, and for the errors of the people.

He setteth before our eyes the pleasant face of God's outward worship ; that, in the wise appointing of everything, for place, for division of rooms, for furniture, for ornaments, for materials, for persons, for actions, for order of doing, we may behold the glory, not only of the appointer of them, but also the glory of the church, and of heaven, and of Christ, and of his saints represented thereby ; as far above the glory of those outward things, as heavenly and spiritual things are above earthly ; as the particular exposition of the meaning of the types, in their own proper place, will make plain, which we cannot meddle with here, seeing the apostle judgeth it not pertinent.

VER. 8. The Holy Ghost this signifying, that the way into the holiest of all was not yet made manifest, while as the first tabernacle was yet standing.

He expoundeth what the high priest's going through the veil but once a year did mean, saying the Holy Ghost signified something thereby. Then, 1. The Holy Ghost is the author of these ordinances of Levi, and of matters appointed about that old tabernacle, as of the expressions of his own mind to the church, and so he is very God. 2. The Holy Ghost is a distinct person of the Godhead, exercising the proper actions of a person, subsisting by himself; directing the ordinances of the church, teaching the church, and interpreting the meaning of the types unto the church. 3. The church under the law was not altogether ignorant of the spiritual signification of the Levitical ordinances, because the Holy Ghost was then teaching them the meaning. 4. Those rites and ceremonies were not so dark in themselves, as they could not be in any sort understood, but were expressions of the mind of God to the church of that time.

2. That which the Holy Ghost did signify was this : that the way unto the holiest of all was not yet made manifest, while as the first tabernacle was yet standing.

Then, that the holiest of all represented heaven, the old church did know.

3. He saith not that the way to heaven was closed, but not clearly manifested.

Then, they knew the way to heaven, darkly, through the veil of types. 2. They knew there was a time of clearer light coming.

4. The time of the endurance of this not clear manifestation of the way to heaven is set down to be, while the first tabernacle was standing.

Then, the old church was taught, 1. That the clear light of the way to heaven was not to be revealed while those shadows and that tabernacle endured. 2. That when the clear manifestation of that way should come by the Messias, that tabernacle was not to stand. 3. That when God should cause that first tabernacle to be removed, the true light was at hand. 4. That none should receive the clear light of the way to heaven, but such as should renounce the ordinances of the first tabernacle.

And so the apostle, by the authority of the Holy Ghost, enforceth these Hebrews either to renounce the Levitical ordinances or to be deprived of the true light of the way to heaven now revealed.

5. While he calleth this typical tabernacle the first tabernacle, he importeth, 1. That Christ's body was the next tabernacle. 2. That the temple is comprehended under the name of the tabernacle, in this dispute.

VER. 9. Which was a figure, for the time then present, in which were offered both gifts and sacrifices, that could not make him that did the service perfect, as pertaining to the conscience.

He showeth the use of the tabernacle, and the imperfection of the service thereof, saying, The tabernacle was a figure for the time then present. Whereby he giveth us to understand, 1. That the tabernacle was a type and figure of Christ. 2. That it was not appointed for all time to come, but for that present time of the church's non-age. 3. That howsoever it was an obscure figure, yet having some resemblance of the thing signified, it was fit for those of that time.

2. Next, he showeth the weakness of the offerings offered in the tabernacle, that they could not make the man that did the service perfect, as concerning the conscience ; that is, they could not perfectly satisfy the conscience that sin was forgiven, and life granted, for any worthiness of those offerings ; they could not furnish the conscience with a good answer towards God, for saving of them who did that service, 1 Pet. iii. 21, because the conscience could not have sound ground of satisfaction how God's justice would be made quiet by those offerings. And that which doth not satisfy God's justice cannot satisfy the conscience, because the conscience is God's deputy, and will not be quiet, if it be well informed, till it see God pacified.

Then, it followeth from this ground, seeing those offerings could not perfect a man in his conscience, 1. That Christ's sacrifice, signified by them, must perfectly satisfy God's justice, and the conscience also, and purge the filthiness of it, and heal its wounds. 2. That as many as were justified before God, and in their consciences truly quieted under the law, behoved, of necessity, to see through these offerings, and flee into the offering of the sacrifice represented by them, as Psal. li. 7. For, otherwise, the apostle testifieth here the outward offerings could not perfect them in the conscience. 3. That when remission of sin, and atonement, is promised in the law, upon the offering of these gifts, as Levit. xiv. 9, xvii. 11; the form of speech is sacramental, joining the virtue of the sacrifice of Christ, signified with the offering of the figurative sacrifices, unto the believer. 4. That true believers, notwithstanding many imperfections of their life, may be perfected, as concerning their conscience, by flying to the mediation and sacrifice of Christ, which washeth the conscience throughly.

VER. 10. Which stood only in meats and drinks, and divers washings, and carnal ordinances, imposed on them, until the time of reformation.

He giveth a reason why those ceremonies should not perfect the conscience, because they stood in meats, and drinks, and divers washings, and carnal ordinances ; to wit, if they be considered by themselves, separate from their signification, as many of the Jews took them.

Then, there is a twofold consideration to be had of the Levitical ceremonies ; one, as they are joined with the significations, and so promises were made of atonement by them in the law. Another, as they were looked upon, by themselves, separate from their signification, as the carnal Jews took them, and rested on them, and so they could not perfect the conscience.

2. He showeth their endurance, saying, They were imposed on them until the time of reformation ; that is, till the time of the gospel, that Christ came with clear light to perfect matters.

Then, 1. These ceremonies were by God imposed upon no people but them; that is, the Jews only. 2. Neither were they imposed on the Jews for ever, but for a time only, until the time of reformation. 3. Seeing the time of reformation by Christ is come, these ceremonies are expired and abolished.

3. Seeing the time of the gospel is the time of reformation, or correction,

Then, 1. The shadows are fulfilled, and the substance is come. 2. The darkness of teaching is removed, and the time of clearness is come. 3. The price of redemption, promised to be laid down, is now paid. 4. The difficulty, and impossibility, of bearing the yoke of God's external worship is removed, and Christ's easy yoke, in place thereof, is come. In a word, whatsoever was then wanting under the law, of the measure of the Spirit, or the means to get the Spirit, and fruits thereof, is now helped, in the frame of the gospel.

VER. 11. But Christ being come, a high priest of good things to come, by a greater and more perfect tabernacle, not made with hands; that is to say, not of this building.

To show the accomplishment of these things in Christ's priesthood, he opposeth his excellency to the imperfection of the Levitical high priest's service, thus : 1. The Levitical priest was priest of the shadows of good things; but Christ, priest of the good things themselves; keeping the dispensation of them proper to his own person, such as are reconciliation, redemption, righteousness, and life, &c.

2. The Levitical high priest had a tabernacle builded with hands, wherein he served; but Christ served in a greater and more perfect tabernacle, not made with hands; that is, in the precious tabernacle of his own body, wherein he dwelt amongst us, John i. 14, represented by the material tabernacle.

3. He expoundeth how the tabernacle of Christ's body is not made with hands, by this, that it is not of this building. First, because it was not formed by the art of any Bezaleel, or Aholiab, but by the Holy Ghost. 2. Albeit the tabernacle of his body was like ours, in substance; yet, for the manner of his holy conception, he is of another building than ours; for our tabernacles are builded by natural generation of man and woman, with propagation of original sin : but Christ's body, in a singular manner, even by the special operation of the Holy Ghost, in the womb of the virgin; and so without original sin.

VER. 12. Neither by the blood of goats and calves, but by his own blood, he entered in once into the holy place, having obtained eternal redemption for us.

The opposition goeth on. 1. The Levitical high priest entered into the typical holy place; but Christ entered into the holy place properly so called, that is, into heaven. 2. The Levitical priest entered often into the holy place; Christ entered but once into heaven.

Hereby the Levitical priest's entry was declared to be imperfect, because it behoved to be repeated : but Christ's entry into heaven, to be perfect, because but once, not to be repeated.

3. The Levitical priest entered by the blood of goats and calves; but Christ entered by his own blood.

1. And if Christ entered but once into heaven, after his suffering, Then, we must not think that his body is anywhere else, but in heaven only, wherein it is once only entered.

2. If the blood whereby Christ entered into heaven was his own blood, then, 1. Verily Christ's body was like ours, in substance, having blood in it, as ours; and we must not conceive otherwise of his body than to be of the same substance and substantial properties with ours. 2. The blood belonged to the same person, to whom the properties of God belongeth, so often in this epistle attributed unto Christ. His blood was the blood of God, Acts xx. 28. That is, the same Jesus was God and man, with flesh and blood, in one person.

3. The fruit of Christ's bloody sacrifice he maketh the eternal redemption of those for whom he offered it; and to the typical sacrifice he ascribeth no redemption at all in the comparison, thereby giving us to understand,

1. That from the world's beginning to the end thereof, salvation of sinners is by way of Christ's redemption; that is, by his loosing them through payment of a price. 2. That the redemption was manifested to have force when after his bloody sacrifice, he entered into heaven. 3. That such as are once redeemed by Christ are eternally redeemed, not for a time, to fall away again; but eternally to be saved, most certainly.

VER. 13. For if the blood of bulls and of goats, and the ashes of an heifer, sprinkling the unclean, sanctifieth to the purifying of the flesh,

VER. 14. How much more shall the blood of Christ, who, through the eternal Spirit, offered himself without spot to God, purge your consciences from dead works to serve the living God?

To prove that eternal redemption is the fruit of Christ's sacrifice, he reasoneth thus : If the typical sacrifices and rites of old were able to work that for which they were ordained, that is, external sanctification, much more shall Christ's true sacrifice be able to work that for which it was appointed, that is, eternal remission of sins, and inward sanctification unto eternal life.

Then, there are two sorts of sanctification, one external of the flesh, which maketh a man holy to the church, whatsoever he be within. Another, internal of the conscience and inner man, which maketh a man holy before God.

2. The purifying of the flesh he maketh to be by the exercise of such and such ordinances of divine service for the time.

Then, external or church holiness of the outward man is procured by such and such exercises of divine ordinances in the church as serve to make a man to be reputed and holden for clean, before men, and so to be received for. a member of the church, as is to be seen, Numb. xix.

3. From his form of reasoning we learn that whatsoever liberty and access of coming to the church was made to the Jews of old by these ceremonies of the law, as much and more liberty is made to the Christian to come in to God, by the blood of Christ.

4. In describing Christ's sacrifice he saith, Christ, through the eternal Spirit, offered himself without spot to God.

Then, 1. Christ is both the sacrifice and the priest in one person. He offered himself as man through the eternal Spirit, that is by the virtue and power of his own Godhead, by which he preached before his incarnation to sinners, 1 Pet. iii. 19. 2. His sacrifice was without spot. He was that spotless lamb in whom was no sin, nor imperfection, nor defect of any thing that the sacrifice required. 3. The virtue of the sacrifice which made it to purchase eternal redemption unto us, floweth from the infinite worth of his eternal Godhead. 4. Albeit Christ's two natures have their distinct respects in the actions of his office, yet Christ is one, and undivided in the execution of his office.

5. The fruit and force of the sacrifice is set down in this, that this blood shall purge our conscience from dead works to serve the living God. That is, shall both absolve a man from his foregone sin, and also enable him to serve God for time to come.

Then, 1. Sins are but dead works flowing from nature dead in sin; and not only deserving, but also drawing on death upon the sinner. 2. The conscience lieth polluted with the filthiness of dead works till the virtue of the blood of Jesus applied bring intimation of absolution. 3. Christ's blood doth not purge the conscience from dead works that a man should go wallow in them again, but that he may serve the living God more acceptably. 4. The purging virtue of Christ's blood is joined with the sanctifying and renewing of the absolved sinner; and what God hath conjoined let no man put asunder.

Ver. 15. And for this cause, he is the Mediator of the New Testament, that, by means of death, for the redemption of the transgressions which were under the first Testament, they which are called might receive the promise of eternal inheritance.

Now, lest any man should stumble at Christ's death, he showeth a necessity thereof, in respect of his office of mediation, and the purchase to be made by his redemption. The force of the reason is this: Remission of sins could not have been given under the law, except the Mediator had been to pay the price of the same under the gospel; nor could the faithful and called ones either then or now obtain eternal life for an inheritance otherwise than by the Mediator's death. Therefore it behoved the true Mediator, by means of death, to pay the promised price of the purchase of remission of sins and eternal life.

Then, 1. The remission of transgressions and the inheritance of eternal life are both fruits of Christ's passion. 2. The fruits of his passion

extended themselves unto them who were under the Old Testament as well as unto us under the New. 3. The way of purchase of these benefits was by redemption; that is to say, by lawful purchase, such as might satisfy justice. 4. The way in special was by means of the Mediator's death; his life was laid down to redeem ours; his one life, as good as all ours. 5. For this cause, Christ took the office of a Mediator unto himself, that he might have right and interest by death to make this purchase. 6. And therefore except he had really died, the purchase could not have been lawfully made.

Ver. 16. For where a testament is, there must also of necessity be the death of the testator.

Another reason to prove the necessity of Christ's death, from the force of the word covenant, which signifieth also a Testament. The force of the reason is this: Christ, Jer. xxxi. 31, promised to make a new covenant, and therefore a New Testament; then also, he promised to die. The articles of the covenant also evinceth it to be a Testament, and the promiser bound to make his word good and so to die. For Jer. xxxi. the Lord Christ promiseth to reconcile his people to God, to take away their sins, and to be their God. Justice required satisfaction of them before they could be reconciled; satisfaction they could not make themselves; therefore he who promised to make the reconciliation with God was bound to make the satisfaction for them to God, and if satisfaction for them, then to undergo the curse of the law for them, and so to die.

The new covenant is of the nature of a Testament; and the benefits promised therein, to wit, remission of sins, reconciliation, sanctification, and life eternal, are legacies freely left unto us by our defunct Lord, who was dead and is alive to execute his own will for evermore. The Scripture is the instrument and evidence; the apostles, notaries; the sacraments are seals; witnesses from heaven, the Father, the Word, and the Spirit; witnesses on earth, the water, the blood, and the Spirit. 2. Christ Jesus is both the maker of the covenant which is in Jeremiah xxxi. and the Mediator thereof also; the testator and executor of that blessed Testament. 3. Christ's death was concluded and resolved upon and intimated before he came into the world.

Ver. 17. For a testament is of force after men are dead; otherwise it is of no strength at all, whilst the testator liveth.

He cleareth his reasoning from that nature of Testaments amongst men, which, not before, but after a man's death, have force. But here it may be objected, how can this be, seeing by virtue of the Testament of Christ, benefits not a few were bestowed upon the church before his death from the beginning of the world; not only remission of sins and eternal life, but also many graces and blessings in this life, both bodily and spiritual? I answer, albeit Christ's death was not accomplished in act till of late, yet for the certainty of his death to follow, and the unchangeableness of his mind towards his church before his death, he was reckoned both with God and the church for dead; and the promise of laying down his life for his people accepted for the time, as if it had been performed, for which cause he is called, Rev. xiii. 8, the lamb slain from the beginning of the world. And Christ was still represented as a slain man in all these sacrifices, which the apostle pointeth at, as meeting this doubt, in the next words, which follow hereafter, ver. 18.

VER. 18. Whereupon, neither the first Testament was dedicated without blood.

He proveth the necessity of Christ's death yet further. Under the law his bloodshed was represented by types of bloody sacrifices; therefore it behoved those types to be answered by his real bloodshed and death.

Then, 1. What the types of the law did signify, Christ behoved to accomplish in verity. 2. The old church was taught that, by virtue of the blood signified by these types, the covenant stood betwixt God and them.

VER. 19. For when Moses had spoken every precept to all the people, according to the law, he took the blood of calves, and of goats, with water and scarlet wool and hyssop, and sprinkled both the book and all the people,

VER. 20. Saying, This is the blood of the Testament, which God hath enjoined unto you.

VER. 21. Moreover, he sprinkled with blood, both the tabernacle, and all the vessels of the ministry.

From Moses's example we learn, 1. That the Lord's word should be manifested to all the people; and none of them debarred from taking knowledge thereof. 2. That the word must be spoken plainly, with a distinct voice in the common language, and not muttered in an unknown tongue. 3. That with the use of holy rites, appointed of God, the preaching of God's word should be joined to show the institution and force of God's ordinances to his people.

2. In that the book and the people and instruments of service were all to be sprinkled, we learn that every thing which we touch or meddle with or make use of is unclean unto us, were it never so holy in itself, except the blood of Jesus make it clean unto us, and cleanse us in the using of it.

VER. 22. And almost all things are by the law purged with blood, and without shedding of blood is no remission.

He saith, "almost" because of some purging which was done by washing, and yet even that washing also, drew the virtue of ceremonial purging from the sacrifice whereunto the washing was annexed.

2. In saying, "without shedding of blood there is no remission" of sins, he teacheth us that whatsoever a sacrifice is offered for obtaining a remission of sin there shedding of blood must really be; and where an unbloody sacrifice is pretended to be offered for obtaining remission it serveth not the purpose, because without shedding of blood there is no remission. Either therefore must such as pretend to offer Christ for obtaining the remission of sin grant that Christ is daily murdered by them, and his blood shed of new in their pretended offering, or else, that by their offering no new remission is purchased. But the truth is, Christ's blood is once shed, and never to be shed again; and that once offering and bloodshedding is sufficient for everlasting remission, without any new offering of him again.

VER. 23. It was therefore necessary that the patterns of things in the heavens should be purified with these; but the heavenly things themselves with better sacrifices than these.

Another reason of the necessity of Christ's death: inforce thus much: if things figuratively holy, behoved to be cleansed, with the typical blood of beasts, then things truly holy, behoved to be cleansed with better blood, even the blood of the Messias.

Hence we learn, 1. That for the signification's cause, God would not have the tabernacle, nor any instrument of service about it, to be esteemed holy, till blood was shed, to sprinkle it: that it might be known thereby, that without the shedding of Christ's blood, he would not accept of any thing from us as holy. 2. That the blood of beasts was sufficient, to make representation: but better blood, even the blood of the Messiah, behoved to be shed, to give the truth of the signification. For as far as heaven is above the earthly sanctuary, and men's souls above the vessels thereof; as far better behoved to be that blood, which made souls acceptable to God, and to get entrance into heaven, than the blood of Levitical sacrifices was.

VER. 24. For Christ is not entered into the holy places made with hands, which are the figures of the true; but into heaven itself, now to appear in the presence of God for us.

He cleareth the matter, how Christ hath offered a better sacrifice than the Levitical, yea, and behoved to offer a better, because he is entered into a better sanctuary; another man, in another manner, and to another end, than the high priest under the law entered, the comparison goeth thus.

1. The Levitical high priest entered into the material and artificial sanctuary; and a typical sacrifice became him: but Christ entered not into that typical sanctuary; therefore a typical sacrifice became not him.

2. The Levitical high priest entered bodily into the figurative sanctuary: but Christ did enter bodily into the true sanctuary in heaven itself.

3. The high priest entered in behalf of the people, with the names of the twelve tribes upon his breast and shoulders: but Christ is entered in, in behalf of us all his people, to appear for us, bearing the particular memory of every saint in his memory.

4. The high priest entered in, to appear for a short time; and stayed not within the sanctuary:

but Christ is entered in, to appear now all the time from his ascension unto this day, and constantly still while it is called now.

VER. 25. Nor yet that he should offer himself often, as the high priest entereth into the holy place every year, with blood of others.

He proveth that he had offered a better sacrifice than the Levitical, because he behoveth to offer an offering, not to be repeated as the Levitical: and so a more perfect offering. The comparison goeth in dissimilitudes.
1. The high priest entered in, with the blood of others: but Christ entered in with his own blood.
2. The high priest made an offering of other things than himself: but Christ did offer himself. Then the offering of Christ is the personal action of Christ himself. None can, nor may offer him, but himself. For the priest must be either better than the sacrifice, or as good, at least, as the sacrifice; but none can be so good as Christ, nor be more excellent, or better; therefore none can offer Christ but himself.
3. The high priest offered his sacrifice oftener: but Christ offered not himself oftener than once.
Then to imagine an offering of Christ often, is both to give the lie to this text, and to make Christ's offering by repeating of it imperfect, and like to the Levitical; for if once offering of Christ be sufficient, often offering is superfluous. And if often offering be needful, then that once offering was not sufficient; and so, was not perfect; which were blasphemy to say. 2. If any man pretend to offer Christ often, it is not Christ that giveth him warrant so to do: for here it is declared, that he hath no hand in offering himself often.

VER. 26. For then must he often have suffered, since the foundation of the world: but now once in the end of the world, hath he appeared, to put away sin, by the sacrifice of himself.

He proveth that Christ cannot be often offered, because then, saith he, must he often have suffered. Then,
1. No offering of Christ, without the suffering of Christ: his passion and death, is inseparable from his sacrifice. If Christ were often offered, he behoved to be often slain and put to death. But that cannot be, that he should suffer, and be slain oftener; therefore he cannot be offered up in a sacrifice oftener. And they who will take upon them to offer Christ again and again, take upon them to slay him, and put him to new suffering again and again. 2. The offering of Christ in an unbloody sacrifice, is a vain imagination, which the apostle acknowledgeth not: for if that were possible, then were the apostle's words here false, and his reasoning ridiculous; which were blasphemy to say.
2. He saith, he behoved to have suffered often, since the beginning of the world; because as often as new sins were committed, and new remission was to be bestowed; as often behoved he to have suffered to expiate these sins, and to

purchase the new remission, since the beginning of the world: but this is impossible, therefore his offering often is impossible. Then,
1. They who make it needful to offer Christ often, make it needful also, that he should have taken on flesh sooner than he did, and been slain sooner than he was, and slain as often as new sins were to be expiated, and forgiven, from the beginning of the world. And so by this vain conceit, they do ranverse [oppose] all the wisdom of God about Christ, and set to him an order, and course of their own; making themselves wiser than God. 2. It is by the apostle's estimation, as vain a conceit, and as impossible to offer Christ oftener than once, now in the end of the world, as to have offered him before he came in the flesh, since the beginning of the world.
3. But now, saith he, once in the end of the world, he hath appeared, to put away sin, by the sacrifice of himself. Then,
1. No sacrifice of Christ, doth the apostle acknowledge but such as is joined with his bodily appearance in the world for that end. Once hath he appeared, and once only hath he sacrificed himself, saith the apostle. 2. The apostle understood no offering of Christ, but only one; and once to be offered, for time foregone, or time to come, from the beginning of the world, unto the end thereof. 3. This one offering once offered was sufficient to expiate the sins of the saved, before it was offered: and therefore must have force also, to expiate the sins of the saved without repetition now, after it is once offered.
4. Whose sins Christ doth take away, for those he appeared, for those he made a sacrifice of himself: and whose sins he doth not put away, for those he appeared not, he sacrificed not.
4. In calling the time of Christ's suffering, The end of the world, he giveth us to understand That there cannot be so much time betwixt Christ's first and second coming, as was betwixt the world's beginning, and his first coming: but a great deal of less time, need force [necessarily]: else, were not that time the end of the world.

VER. 27. And as it is appointed unto men, once to die; but after this the judgment,

Another reason to prove that Christ neither could nor should, offer oftener than one, from the common law laid upon man, of once dying. Which law Christ having once satisfied, by dying when he offered up himself; there is no reason he should offer himself again; and so die again.
1. It is appointed, saith he, for men once to die. Then, 1. It is come by God's just appointment, that men should die, since his law is broken by men. 2. The common law of nature appointeth but one death, once to be suffered. And though God by singularity of miracles, make some exceptions, yet the common law standeth for a rule; beyond which no reason Christ should be tied, since his once dying is sufficient. 3. Every man must take death to him, and prepare himself to obey the appointment.
2. He saith, after death cometh judgment. Then, 1. Every man's particular judgment day followeth his departure out of this life; and

D

general judgment, abideth all, at length. 2. The time of grace and mercy getting, is only in this life : nothing but justice remaineth ; either to absolve the reconciled, or to condemn the unreconciled sinner. Men's devices, for the relief of the dead, are but delusions of the living.

VER. 28. So Christ was once offered to bear the sins of many : and unto them that look for him, shall he appear the second time, without sin unto salvation.

He applieth the common law of dying once to Christ, saying, Christ was once offered to bear the sins of many.

Then, 1. It is as unreasonable, that Christ should offer himself oftener than once, as it is to exact of him, the laying down of his life oftener than once ; for that is to exact more than the severity of God's justice requireth of him. 2. Christ's death was not for any sin in him ; but for our sins. 3. He took not away the sins of every man in particular, (for many die in their sins, and bear their own judgment) but the sins of many : the sins of his own elect people, Matt. i. 21. He shall save his people from their sins.

2. He saith, That unto them that look for him he shall appear the second time.

Then, 1. After that once offering of Christ, and ascending to heaven, he is not to be corporally present on earth again, till the day of judgment. The apostle acknowledgeth corporal presence no oftener. 2. To look for Christ's corporal presence upon earth then, and not till then, is the property of true believers. 3. Corporal presence is joined with appearance ; the one is put here for the other.

3. He will appear the second time without sin.

Then in his first coming, he was not without our sin, yet lying upon him by imputation ; as his baseness and misery declared. But the glorious manner of his second coming, shall make evident, that he is without sin ; that is, fully exonored [disburdened] by that one offering of the debt thereof which he took upon him.

4. Instead of saying, that those who look for him, shall be without sin, he saith, That Christ shall appear without sin,

To teach us, 1. That the defraying the debt of the sins of such, for whom Christ hath undertaken, lieth upon Christ, and not upon the believers, for whom he undertook. 2. And that if his once sacrificing himself for them, did not expiate their sins sufficiently, then sin should cleave unto Christ, until his second coming. 3. That Christ's freedom from sin shall evidence our freedom from sin, for whom he became surety.

5. He will appear unto them who look for him unto salvation.

Then, 1. The full accomplishment of the salvation of the believers, shall not be until Christ's second coming : though their souls be blessed before, yet the full blessedness of soul and body is deferred till then. 2. As Christ's glory shall testify then, that his once offering freed him of the suretiship for our sins : so our salvation shall testify that his offering was sufficient to exonor [disburden, or free] us. 3. They that love not his coming, cannot look for salvation.

THE SUM OF CHAP. X.

This once offering of Christ, putteth the main difference betwixt this sacrifice, and those offerings of the law : which because they were repeated, could never perfect the worshipper, ver. 1. For if they could have perfected the worshipper, they should have ceased to be repeated, ver. 2. Now cease they did not, but were repeated, ver. 3. Because they could not take away sin, ver. 4. Wherefore as the Scripture doth witness, Psal. xl., sacrifices of the law were to be abolished, and Christ's sacrifice to come in their room, ver. 5—9. By which sacrifice once offered we are for ever sanctified. ver. 10. And as their sacrifice was imperfect, so was their priesthood also, ever repeating the same sacrifices, which could not (because they were repeated) abolish sin, ver. 11. But Christ hath ended his sacrificing in his once offering ; and entered to his glory, to subdue his enemies, ver. 12, 13. Having by that once offering, done all to his followers that was needful to perfect them, ver. 14. As the word of the new covenant, Jer. xxxi. proveth, ver. 15—18. Having spoken then of Christ's divine excellency, and of the privileges which the faithful have in him, I exhort you to make use of it : in special seeing we have by Christ's blood, access unto heaven, ver. 19. By so perfect a way as is Christ's fellowship of our nature, ver. 20. And so great moyen [benefited] by Christ before us there, ver. 21. Let us strengthen our faith, for the better holding of our justification, and sanctification through him, ver. 22. And let us avow our religion constantly, ver. 23. And help forwards one another, ver. 24. Neglecting no means, public nor private, for that end, as some apostates have done, ver. 25. For if we make wilful apostasy from his known truth, no mercy to be looked for, ver. 26, but certain damnation of us, as of his enemies, ver. 27 ; for if the despisers of the law were damned to death, without mercy, ver. 28, what judgment abideth those, who so abuse Jesus, his grace, and Spirit, as wilful apostates do? ver. 29. For God's threatening in the law is not in vain, ver. 30, and it is a fearful thing to fall as a foe, in God's hand, ver. 31. but rather, prepare you for such sufferings, as you began to feel at your conversion, ver. 32, partly in your own persons, and partly by your fellowship with sufferers, ver. 33, which you did joyfully bear in hope of a reward, ver. 34 ; therefore retain your confidence, ver. 35, and be patient, ver. 36. God will come and help shortly, ver. 37, and till he come you must live by faith, and not by sense ; but if you will not, you shall be rejected, ver. 38. But I and you are not of that sort that shall make apostasy ; but of the number of true believers, who shall persevere and be saved, ver. 39.

THE DOCTRINE OF CHAP. X.

That he may yet farther show the impossibility of offering Christ oftener, he giveth the often repetition of Levitical sacrifices, year by year, for a reason of their imperfection, and inability to perfect the worshipper ; and therefore, of necessity, Christ's sacrifice could not be repeated, except we should make it imperfect, like the Levitical, and unable to perfect the worshipper, as the legal sacrifice was.

The force of his reasoning is this: the most solemn sacrifice offered by the high priest himself, Lev. xvi., and least subject to repetition of all the sacrifices, being offered not so often as each month, or each week, or each day, as some sacrifices were, but once a-year only; yet because they were repeated year by year, they were declared, by this means, unable ever to make the comers thereunto perfect. Therefore, Christ's sacrifice could not be often offered, lest, for that same reason, it should be found imperfect also. And this is his drift in ver. 1.

He proveth his reason to be good, thus: if they could have perfected the comer, then they should not have been repeated, but ceased from being offered, because they should have delivered the worshipper perfectly from sin: and having done that, the repetition was to no purpose, ver. 2. But they did not free the worshipper from sin; for still after offering he professed himself guilty, (for any thing these sacrifices could do) by offering of a new offering, ver. 3. And no wonder, because such sacrifices were not worthy to expiate sin; and so unable to take away sin; and so, also, unable to quiet the conscience.

Ver. 1. For the law having a shadow of good things to come, and not the very image of the things, can never with those sacrifices which they offered year by year continually make the comers thereunto perfect.

The old covenant is called the law, because it was drawn up in a legal form, upon conditions of obedience to the law; and grace and life in Jesus Christ to come, were set before them in shadows, not in a clear manner as in the gospel. Then, 1. In the old covenant the law was expressly urged, and grace in the Messias covered and hid under veils. 2. Christ and his grace, and the good things which come by him, were not so hid, but they might have been seen, albeit but darkly, being, as by their shadows, represented. 3. The revealing of Christ, and his benefits, under the gospel, and under the law, differ as far in measure of light, as the shadow of a thing, and the lively image thereof, drawn with all the lineaments. For they saw Christ, and righteousness, and eternal life through him, as those which are in the house see the shadow of a man coming, before he enter within the doors; but we, with open face, behold in the gospel, as in a mirror, Christ's glory shining; Christ, in the preaching of his word, crucified before our eyes, as it were, and bringing with him life and immortality to light.

2. He maketh the repeating of the sacrifices a reason of their inability to perfect the comers thereunto. That is, perfectly to satisfy for those who came to the sacrifice, and to sanctify and save them in whose name it was offered.

Then, 1. A sacrifice that perfectly satisfieth God's justice for sin, cannot be repeated; and a sacrifice which hath need to be repeated hath not perfectly satisfied God's justice for the sinner, nor perfected the sinner for whom it is offered, by doing all that justice required to purchase

justification, sanctification, and salvation to him. 2. Whosoever will have Christ offered up in a sacrifice oftener than once, whether by himself or by another, denieth the perfection of that sacrifice on the cross, denieth that by tnat one sacrifice purchase is made of all that is required to perfect sinners, which is fearful blasphemy.

Ver. 2. For then would they not have ceased to be offered; because that the worshippers once purged should have had no more conscience of sins.

By way of question he asketh, Would not those sacrifices have ceased to be offered, if they could have made the comers thereunto perfect?

Then, the apostle esteemeth this reason so clear, that any man of sound judgment being asked the question, must of necessity grant it. For nature's light doth teach thus much, that if a sacrifice do all that is to be done for the sinner, it standeth there, because there is nothing more to do. If it pay the full price of the sinner's expiation, at once offering, what need can there be to offer it over again? And, therefore, if Christ's one sacrifice, once offered, perfect the comers thereunto, must it not cease to be offered any more, by this reasoning of the apostle? For if he have made a perfect purchase of whatsoever is required to perfect us, by once offering, wisdom and justice will not suffer the price of the purchase to be offered again. And if he must be offered again, he hath not perfected the purchase for us, by any offering going before.

2. The apostle's reason why a sacrifice which perfecteth the worshipper must cease to be offered, is, because that the worshipper once purged should have no more conscience of sins. By which he meaneth not that the purged worshipper may do hereafter what he listeth, and make no conscience to sin; nor yet, that after he is purged, and falleth into a new sin, he should not take with his guiltiness, and repent, and run again to the benefit of that sacrifice; but this he meaneth, that the purging of his conscience, by virtue of a perfect sacrifice, is such, that he is freed from the just challenge, and condemnatory sentence of the conscience, for that sin wherefrom he is purged.

Question. How is it, then, will you say, that many of God's children are often times troubled with the guiltiness of their conscience for those same sins which they have repented and sought pardon for, through Christ's sacrifice, and found remission intimated, and peace granted?

I answer, Not for any imperfection of the sacrifice, or of their remission; but for the weakness of their holding of the ever-flowing virtue of that once offered sacrifice, and the remission granted there-through.

Then, 1. He that is purged by virtue of the sacrifice of Christ, hath God's warrant to have a quiet and peaceable conscience. 2. And if he have a challenge, after he is fled to this sacrifice, he may, by God's approbation, stop the same, by opposing the virtue of that perfect sacrifice to the challenge.

3. The comers unto the sacrifice, to have benefit thereby, ver. 1, are here called worshippers, ver. 2.

Then, the Lord reckoneth it a part of Divine service, and worship done unto him, to come and seek the benefit of that sacrifice whereby he is pacified and we ransomed.

4. To make the worshipper perfect, ver. 1, is expounded, by purging them, and delivering them from the conscience of sin, ver. 2.

Then, that sacrifice which purgeth the conscience from sin, doth also perfect the man. Neither needeth he any thing unto salvation, which such a sacrifice doth not purchase. And such is that once-offered sacrifice of Christ.

VER. 3. But in those sacrifices there is a remembrance again made of sins every year.

He proveth that the Levitical sacrifices took not away the conscience of sins, because there was a yearly commemoration made of the same sins, not only of that year, but also of former; yea, beside the commemoration expressly done by the priest, even in these repeated sacrifices, saith he, there was, in effect, a real taking up again of those sins for which sacrifice had been offered before; because the offering of sacrifice of new did plainly import, that by no preceding sacrifice was the ransom of the sinner paid. And so, in effect the sacrificers did profess, that for anything which the former sacrifices could merit, their sins remained unexpiated.

Quest. But you will ask, Were not believers, under the law, purged from their sins, and made clean, and white as snow? Psal. li. 7.

I answer, Yes, indeed, but not by virtue of those typical sacrifices, but by virtue of the sacrifice signified by them; to wit, the sacrifice of the true Lamb of God, which taketh away the sins of the world. And therefore, when atonement and expiation of sin is attributed to the Levitical sacrifices, as Lev. xvii. 11, the form of speech is sacramental, the property of the thing signified being ascribed to the sign, as was marked before.

Quest. But do not we Christians make a commemoration of our sins, year by year; yea, daily remembering even the sins of our youth, and deprecating the wrath which they deserve?

I answer, It is true we do: but not by way of offering a sacrifice, as they; for of them it is said here, "In those sacrifices there is a remembrance of sin."

Quest. What is the difference betwixt commemoration of sin, without renewed sacrifice, and commemoration of sin with renewed sacrifices? betwixt the Jews' commemoration of sins, year by year, spoken of in this place, and the commemoration which true Christians do make?

I answer, The Jew, in his solemn commemoration of sin, by renewed sacrifice, did really profess two things; one, that no sacrifice formerly offered was sufficient to expiate his sin, or cleanse his conscience; another, that he had not sufficiently holden, by faith, that signified sacrifice which was to come, but had need, through the spectacles, and transparencies of these typical sacrifices enjoined for his help, to take a new view of that true sacrifice which was to come; of both which, the repeated sacrifice did bear witness. But we, by commemoration of our sins, and not

sacrificing, profess, that by Christ's sacrifice, already past, God's justice is so well satisfied, as there is no need of new sacrifice, nor oftener offering of that one; and therefore that we desire no other ransom but Christ's, which is paid already on the cross, but only crave to have, by faith, a better hold of Christ, who hath paid the ransom for us, that we may find the virtue of his ransom yet more and more in ourselves.

Quest. But what if, with the commemoration of sins, year by year, and day by day, we should pretend to join a sacrifice, that new expiation might be made, by offering of Christ over again, as is pretended to be done now-a-days?

I answer, By so doing we should take away the difference which the apostle here putteth betwixt the Levitical sacrifices and Christ, and make Christ's no better than theirs; we should avow that Christ's sacrifice on the cross, done by himself, was not a full ransom for our sins, but that a man's offering were able to do that which Christ's sacrifice on the cross had not done. Finally, with the Jew we should avow, that the true and satisfactory sacrifice were not as yet come; nothing heretofore being done which were able to pacify God, or purge the worshippers from the conscience of sin. For if a man think that the price of expiation of sin be already paid, he doth but mock God's justice, and disgrace the price paid, if he presume to pay the price over again.

VER. 4. For it is not possible that the blood of bulls and of goats should take away sins.

He giveth a reason why these sacrifices could not pacify the conscience, even because it is not possible that they should take away sin.

Then, 1. The conscience can never be purged, except it see sin taken away by a perfect sacrifice, and a ransom so worthy, as justice may be satisfied. 2. It is impossible that atonement was properly made by the Levitical sacrifice, but only figuratively; because here it is said, It was impossible they could take away sins. 3. Sin is not wiped away by any unworthy mean; for sin being the breach of the law of nature, and of the written law, God's majesty so glorious, his justice so exact, his truth, in threatening death to the offender, so constant, no less worthy sacrifice can expiate sin than that which is of value to answer all these.

VER. 5. Wherefore when he cometh into the world, he saith, Sacrifice and offering thou wouldest not, but a body hast thou prepared me.

VER. 6. In burnt-offerings and sacrifices for sin thou hast had no pleasure.

He proveth, by testimony of Psal. xl. 6, 7, &c. that these sacrifices did never by themselves pacify God; and therefore, were not to endure longer than Christ should come to fulfil what they did signify, and so abolish them.

Then, of necessity the old church was not altogether ignorant of the imperfection of their legal service for removing of their sins, and that the true expiation of their sins signified by these sacrifices was to be sought in the Messias.

2. Christ is brought in by the prophet, coming into the world, that is, taking on our nature and manifesting himself in the flesh, because by the word he is set before the church of that time as incarnate, removing the Levitical sacrifices, and offering himself in their place.

Then, the word of God bringeth all divine truth to a present being unto faith; and so, by prophecy, made Christ incarnate present unto the faith of the fathers under the law.

3. Christ's words unto the Father are, sacrifice and oblation thou wouldest not, but a body hast thou prepared me. Which is in substance the same with, Mine ear hast thou opened or bored unto me, in the Hebrew, Psal. xl. 6. For if the Father open the ear of his Son by making him a wise servant for the work of redemption, if he bore his ear by making him a willing and obedient servant, then must he also prepare a body unto him, and bring him into the world by incarnation, that he may accomplish that service as became him.

Then, 1. Christ's body is of God's preparation, and fitting made of God, so holy and harmless, so free of sin as it should be fit to be joined with the Godhead of the Son, and fit to be an expiatory sacrifice for sin. 2. The sacrifice of Christ's body and the obedience done to God in it by him is the accomplishment and substance of these sacrifices. 3. God was never pleased nor pacified by these sacrifices in themselves, but by Christ's sacrifice signified by them. 4. God prepared a satisfaction to himself for us when we could not.

VER. 7. Then said I, Lo, I come (in the volume of the book it is written of me) to do thy will, O God.

Then said Christ, "Lo, I come to do thy will, O God:" That is, when the legal sacrifices are found and declared unable to pacify God, Christ then findeth it the fit time to come into the world, and to do that which the sacrifices did fore-signify, but could not effectuate.

Then, 1. Christ did not think it the due time for himself to come into the world till it should be found that without him neither God could be satisfied nor man saved by any other mean but by his obedience. 2. Christ assumed our nature and offered himself in our room to the Father willingly, ready to perform what the Father's will could exact of us, yea, earnestly desired he to discharge that service for us, blessed be his name for that willingness, even for evermore. 3. Speaking as in our nature, now incarnate, he calleth the Father his God. So Christ, as man, hath our God for his God.

2. One of the reasons of his offer-making is, "In the volume of thy book it is written of me:" That is, so is it decreed and fore-prophesied in the scripture of me, that I should satisfy thee, O Father, and do thy will for man.

Then, 1. Christ hath a great respect to the scripture, to have all things fulfilled which are there spoken, though it should cost him his life, he will have it done. 2. He desireth that before we look upon his manner of redeeming us, we should look to the prophecies which went before of him in the scripture. 3. The sum of God's

decree, and of his scripture, which revealeth his decree, is, that God will save man by Christ; or, that the Son shall be incarnate and do the Father's will for redemption of man, that the seed of the woman shall tread down the head of the serpent, is amongst the first oracles of God's good will to man.

VER. 8. Above when he said, Sacrifice and offering and burnt offerings and offering for sin thou wouldest not, neither hadst pleasure therein; which are offered by the law;

VER. 9. Then said he, Lo, I come to do thy will, O God. He taketh away the first, that he may establish the second.

Now, the apostle gathereth from the words of the Psalm set down, ver. 5, 6, that the Levitical sacrifices are abolished and taken away, because they could not please God; and from the words of the Psalm set down ver. 7, declareth that Christ's sacrifice is that only which pleaseth God, now come in the room of the Levitical.

Then, 1. Clear consequences drawn from the scripture are sound doctrine. 2. Collation of places doth yield both ground of good consequences and ground of clearness. 3. The abolition of Levitical sacrifices is necessary that Christ's sacrifice may have full place and room for pleasing of God and saving of us.

VER. 10. By the which will we are sanctified through the offering of the body of Jesus Christ once for all.

The apostle showeth what this will was, and how it is accepted by the Father. The will is, that Christ should offer up his own body in a sacrifice, once for all. If but once, then, 1. It is not the Father's will that Christ's body should be offered oftener than once. If but once for all, then these all for whom he offered, were condescended upon, betwixt the Father and the Mediator. God knew those whom he gave to the Son to be ransomed, and Christ knew those whom he bought. 3. If but once for those all, then, that once made a perfect purchase for all those. The Father craved no more for their ransom. Another offering for them is needless : for if it had been needful to offer again, once offering had not satisfied God's will for their ransom.

2. For the Father's acceptation and fruit of it, he saith, "by this will," to wit, being obeyed, "we are sanctified." That is, I and you, and the rest of our society, elect, are separated from the perishing world, and consecrated as devoted souls unto God's use, as holy vessels of honour, reconciled in due time, regenerate, and by degrees at length throughly made free of sin, and endued with God's image in holiness.

Then, 1. Those only who are of the apostle's society set apart for God's use by election before time and regeneration in time, those sanctified ones, are those all for whom Christ offered himself. 2. All those for whom Christ did offer himself are sanctified in God's decree, and in due time by virtue of Christ's offering. 3. Those who are never sanctified, the body of Christ was never offered for them.

VER. 11. And every priest standeth daily ministering and offering oftentimes the same sacrifices, which can never take away sins:

VER. 12. But this man, after he had offered one sacrifice for sins, for ever sat down on the right hand of God.

That he may end the comparison of Aaron's priesthood and Christ's, he heapeth together a number of the imperfections of the Levitical priesthood to show the reasons why it must be abolished, ver. 11. And in the verses following unto the 15th, he layeth open the perfection of Christ's priesthood, which is to endure for ever. Let the words of the text be observed.

1. In the Levitical priesthood there is a plurality of priests [every priest] importing many; but in Christ's priesthood not a priest but himself alone. This man, ver. 12, is opposed to their every priest, ver. 11.

Then, to make more priests under Christ's priesthood by special office to offer up Christ, is to make the priesthood of Christ imperfect, like that of Levi.

2. In the Levitical priesthood every priest standeth as a servant, moveable in his office; but Christ sat down, ver. 12, established with dignity in his priesthood, as Master and Lord.

3. In the Levitical priesthood every priest standeth daily offering oftentimes; but Christ, ver. 12, offered but one sacrifice for ever.

Then Christ's sacrifice never was offered, nor shall be for ever offered but once, say the contrary who will.

4. In the Levitical priesthood they offered the same sacrifice oftentimes, that is, multitudes of sacrifices of the same kind; but Christ offered one sacrifice for ever, ver. 12; that is, a sacrifice one in number and one in offering, one individual offering, one time only, offered he.

Then, no sort of plurality doth Christ's sacrifice admit, seeing it is one only, and only once offered. The apostle leaveth no room for an unbloody sacrifice beside the blood; nor another offerer but himself only; nor another time but that once on the cross.

5. In the Levitical priesthood many priests, many sacrifices oftentimes offered could never take away sin; but Christ, our priest, offered one offering; to wit, his own body, once, and not oftener; and this sufficeth for sin for ever, ver. 12, 14.

Then, that sacrifice which taketh away sins, must do it at once and for ever; and that sacrifice which doth not take away sins at once, and at one offering, shall never be able to take away sins by repetition, how often soever it be offered.

6. From the apostle's artifice we learn, 1. To gather together in our mind, in a heap, the evils and imperfections of every thing which is like to draw or divert us from Christ; and on the other hand, the properties and excellences of Christ, that we may be tied fast unto him. 2. In special when any mean or instrument appointed of God to bring us to Christ is like to come in more estimation than becometh, we are taught to ride marches betwixt the same and Christ, that the mean may have the mean's room, and Christ may have God's room.

VER. 13. From henceforth expecting till his enemies be made his footstool.

What is Christ doing now, then, seeing he hath no sacrifice to offer? He is sitting at the right hand of God, from henceforth expecting till his enemies be made his footstool; that is, his Man-head being no more on earth now subject unto suffering, is entered into the fellowship and fruition of the glory of his Godhead, to exercise his power and authority for the good of his church and overthrow of his enemies.

Then, 1. Albeit all Christ's personal sufferings are ended, yet the warfare of the subjects of his kingdom endureth still against enemies, such as are Satan and the wicked of the world, and sin and death. 2. That battle is Christ's, he is adversary to all the foes of his kingdom, they are his enemies. 3. He is not alone in the battle, the Father is joined with him, and set on work to subdue his enemies; as it is said, Psal. cx. 1, 2, whereunto this place hath reference, his enemies shall be made his footstool. 4. Albeit this victory be not completed for a time, yet it is in working, and shall surely be brought to pass. 5. As our Lord expecteth and waiteth on patiently till it be done, so must we his subjects do also. 6. At length the highest of his enemies shall be made lower than the basest of Christ's members. They shall be made his footstool, subdued under him, and trampled upon.

VER. 14. For by one offering he hath perfected for ever them that are sanctified.

He giveth a reason why Christ now hath no more offering to make, nor no more suffering to endure; but only to behold the fruit of his sufferings brought about by the Father, and to concur with the Father on his throne for that end; because by one offering he hath perfected for ever them that are sanctified. That is, by that one offering on the cross done and ended before he sat down on the right hand of God, he hath paid the full price for ever of the purchase of remission of sins and salvation to those that are consecrated to God in holiness.

Then, 1. Whosoever will have any more offering up of Christ than that one, once offered before his ascension, denieth that Christ by once offering hath perfected for ever them that are sanctified. 2. Howsoever you take the word sanctified, whether for those that are separated from the world and dedicated unto God in Christ, in God's purpose and decree, comprehending all those whom the Father hath given unto Christ out of the world, that is, the elect, or whether you take it for the renewed and sanctified in time, the offering of Christ is not but for the sanctified; that is, for such as are consecrated and separated out of the world, and dedicated to be vessels of honour unto God.

2. They for whom Christ hath made that offering once; those, saith he, he hath perfected for ever.

Then, 1. He hath not made purchase of a possibility of their salvation only, but he hath perfected them in making purchase of all that they need to have, even to their full perfection. 2. He hath not purchased unto them the remission of some sins, and left the satisfaction to be paid by themselves for other some ; but hath perfected them, perfectly satisfied for them, and perfectly expiated all their sins. 3. He hath not made purchase of some graces unto them only for a certain time, so as he will let them be taken out of his hand afterwards and perish, but he hath perfected them for ever. 4. He hath not appointed any offering for them to be made by any other after him ; but hath made one offering, himself, for them, which satisfieth for ever, so as the Father craveth no more offering for expiating their sin for ever. For God hath set forth Christ to be a propitiation through faith in his blood, Rom. iii. 25. That is, God maketh it manifest by his gospel that he is pacified in Christ towards them that believe in his blood, that believe in him crucified.

Ver. 15. Whereof the Holy Ghost also is a witness unto us : for after that he had said before,

Ver. 16. This is the covenant that I will make with them after those days, saith the Lord, I will put my laws into their hearts, and in their minds will I write them ;

Ver. 17. And their sins and iniquities will I remember no more.

He proveth that it is needless there should be any repetition of a sacrifice for sin in the New Testament, because remission of sins purchased by Christ's death, who is the testator, is still in force continually in Christ's kingdom, there being an article of the covenant for remission of sins to be consecrated ; and if remission of sins be, no oblation for sin can be, ver. 8.

1. He saith, that the Holy Ghost is witness unto us of this truth, that Christ cannot be offered again.

Then, 1. We who do teach this doctrine, and deny any more offering of Christ as a sacrifice, have the Holy Ghost testifying for us. 2. The Holy Ghost is author of the Scripture, and doth speak unto us thereby.

2. He declareth the new covenant to be of the Holy Ghost's making, and calleth him, The Lord. Wherein he teacheth us, 1. That the Holy Ghost is a distinct person of the Godhead, bearing witness by himself to the church of the truth. 2. And one in essence with the Father and the Son, even the Lord, Jehovah, author of the new covenant with the Father and the Son.

Ver. 18. Now where remission of these is, there is no more offering for sin.

From this article of remission of sins in the new covenant, he concludeth, no more offering for sin but once under this covenant, because sin is expiated.

Quest. How then could there be remission of sin under the law, where there was daily offering for sin ? Or, if there was remission, how could there be offering for sin ?

I answer, There is a remission granted upon surety given, for satisfaction to be made for the party remitted ; and there is a remission granted for satisfaction already made for the party remitted. The remission that the fathers under the law had, was of the first sort, upon promise of the Mediator to come, and to satisfy. And with remission of this sort a typical sacrifice might stand, for signifying that the true expiatory sacrifice was not yet paid, but was coming to be paid. But the remission that we get under the gospel, is upon satisfaction already made by the true expiatory and satisfactory sacrifice of Jesus Christ, done and ended with the personal suffering. And this sort of remission is it, whereof the apostle here speaketh ; and it admitteth no manner of offering for sin ; neither typical offering, because Christ is come, and hath fulfilled what the typical sacrifice did signify ; neither the repeating of true expiatory sacrifice of Christ's body, because then Christ behoved to suffer daily and die daily, after that he hath made satisfaction. And besides those two sorts of offering, the Jewish bloody sacrifices typical, and the true expiatory bloody sacrifice of Christ's body on the cross, the Scripture acknowledgeth none. So the meaning of the apostle in these words must be this : where remission of sins is already purchased, by offering of the true expiatory sacrifice, as now it is under the new covenant, there no more offering can be for sin any more.

Then, 1. The apostle acknowledgeth no use for any sacrifice under the New Testament, after Christ's ascension ; else his reason should [would] not hold. 2. The sacrifice which is offered, to wit, the body of Jesus, hath already suffered for sin, so that now the remission of those, that is, of sin and iniquity, all sort of the elects' sins, is obtained thereby already. 3. Not only no sacrifice is any more to be offered for sin under the new covenant, but also no offering, saith he, bloody or unbloody, is to be offered. 4. That church which pretendeth to offer any offering for sins of quick or dead, now under the gospel, professeth that no remission of sin is to be had in such a church, because where there is remission of sin, there is more offering for sin, saith the apostle expressly.

Ver. 19. Having therefore, brethren, boldness to enter into the holiest by the blood of Jesus,

From the by-past doctrine of Christ's excellency and riches of grace, which cometh unto us through him, he draweth exhortations for usemaking of this doctrine, in soundness of faith and the fruits thereof, unto the end of the epistle. And, first, he exhorteth to seek unto communion with God in heaven through Christ, using the terms of the ceremonial law, but mixed with words touching the excellency of the thing signified above those ceremonies ; to show the Hebrews that those ceremonies had nothing in themselves, but did serve to represent Christ and his benefits, and so to draw them from those shadows unto the truth of that which once being signified by them, is now manifested in Christ.

To make the exhortation to be the better received, he setteth down sundry privileges of the faithful, ver. 19—21, from which he inferreth his exhortation, ver. 22. For the first privilege he saith, We have liberty to enter into the holiest; that is, into heaven.

1. In that he maketh this privilege proper to the society of Christians, himself, and others, he teacheth us, 1. That so long as men are without Christ, they are debarred out of heaven; no door nor way open, but the flaming sword of God's justice to keep out every one that shall press to enter before Christ bring them. But such as come to Christ by faith, heaven is opened unto them, and the door cast up for them to enter in who were exiled before.

2. Next, he commendeth this privilege by calling the place, "the holiest," the place where God's holiness dwelleth, represented by the sanctuary, where nothing can enter but that which is holy. Teaching us thereby, that the faithful are so washed from their sins, through faith in Christ, that God will admit them into the place of his dwelling—into his heavenly sanctuary by faith now, and fruition hereafter.

3. He commendeth this privilege, by calling it a "liberty." The word properly signifieth, liberty to speak all our mind, as hath been marked before. Whereby he teacheth us, 1. How we do enter into the holiest; to wit, by prayer, sending up our supplications to heaven. And again, 2. That in our prayers to God we may use freedom of speech, telling him all our mind, all our griefs, all our fears, all our desires, and even pour out our hearts before him at all times.

4. He commendeth this privilege by the price of the purchase thereof, even the blood of Jesus. Whereby he teacheth us, 1. To have this privilege in high estimation. 2. To make good use of it. 3. To be confident of the standing of it; and all because it is so dearly bought.

5. Lastly, he commendeth this privilege by the common right which all believers have unto it, the apostle, and these Hebrews, as his brethren, and all other of that society. Whereby he teacheth, that albeit there be great difference in the measure of faith, and other graces, betwixt Christians; some being stronger, some weaker; some as apostles, some as these weak Hebrews, &c., yet all are the children of one Father, all are brethren, and all are admitted by prayer to come and enter heaven, freely to pour out their souls at all times unto God.

VER. 20. By a new and living way, which he hath consecrated for us, through the veil, that is to say, his flesh;

This is one privilege, that we have liberty to enter into heaven, followeth another. There is a way made to lead us on thereunto, which is Christ's flesh, compared to the veil of the sanctuary, which hath hid those things which were within the sanctuary, and yet yielded an entry through itself unto the sanctuary. So is Christ's flesh the veil of his Godhead, which did hide the glory of his deity from the carnal beholders who stumbled at his baseness, and yet opened a door for the spiritual man to look in upon him that was invisible, while as he observed the brightness of the glory of God breaking through the doctrine and works of the man Christ.

1. He maketh the way to be Christ's flesh, or Christ as incarnate, or Christ considered according to his humanity, because Christ's taking on our nature is the only mean of reconciling us unto God. No man ever came to the Father but by him. No other name whereby men are saved, but the name of Jesus Christ. And therefore as in the way a man must enter, and hold on still till he come to the end, to the place where he would be; even so must every man who would be at heaven, begin at Christ, and hold on, making progress in him still from faith to faith, from grace to grace, till he come to his rest.

2. This way of Christ's own making, he hath devised it and consecrated it. He who is the Father's wisdom hath thought it the best way to bring man to God, that God should become man, that the Word should be made flesh. The best way to bring men to heaven, that God should come down to the earth, to take on man's nature upon him, that he might make man partaker of the divine nature.

3. He hath consecrated and dedicated his flesh, his human nature, set apart and sanctified himself to this same end, that men might make their means with God by him, as man, and by the bands of nature with him, be helped up to the bands of grace with God, by coming to the man Christ, might find God in Christ.

4. He calleth it a "new way," 1. Because of the clear manifesting of the way to heaven under the gospel, in comparison of the time of the law. 2. Because a ready, plain, and safe way, without stumbling-blocks, pits or snares, dangers or inconveniences to such as keep themselves therein, such as new made ways use to be. 3. Because it waxeth never old, is now established, and never to be altered or abolished.

5. It is a "living way," 1. Because Christ liveth for ever to help them all to heaven who seek unto God through him only. 2. Because life is here in Christ, as in the fountain, that he may give life to whomsoever he will; that is, unto all that come unto him. 3. Because it giveth life and refreshment to the weary passenger, and quickeneth his dead and dumpish heart, when he considereth that his Saviour is a man indeed so earnest to have us saved, that he hath yoked himself in communion of nature with us, thereby to save us. It is meat indeed to his soul, that the Word is made flesh: it is drink indeed to consider that he hath suffered for our sins. As Elijah's chariot, so is Christ's manhead and sufferings. Get up here by faith in him, and thou shalt go up to God. This way is that of eagles' wings. Lay first hold upon Jesus Christ, God manifested in the flesh, and he will mount up with thee, and carry thee through the wilderness to Canaan, from the natural misery and sins which thou liest in, unto heaven.

6. This "way" leadeth through the veil, to teach us, that we coming to Christ's manhead, must not subsist there, but by this mean seeking to God, who dwelleth in him, that our faith and hope may be in God. We enter by the man Christ, and do rest on God in Christ, on the fulness of the Godhead, which dwelleth bodily in

Christ. This is to distinguish the natures of
Christ, and to keep the unity of his person
rightly.

VER. 21. And having a high priest over the
house of God;

For our further satisfaction, he giveth us
Christ over again, to make yet more use of him,
to direct, guide, and convoy us in the way, to
lead us to the Father in heaven, through the
courts of his dwelling, and to bring us in to him,
and make us welcome there.

1. We have Christ for a priest to us, whose
lips do always preserve knowledge, in whom are
hid all the treasures of wisdom and knowledge,
who will inform our minds, and persuade our
hearts to believe and obey; who will reconcile,
by his once offered sacrifice, the believer; will
intercede for the reconciled, to keep him still in
grace; will bless us with all spiritual blessings;
will take our prayers, thanksgivings, and the
spiritual sacrifice of all the good works of our
hands, and wash the pollutions from them; will
offer them in our name, with the incense and
perfume of his own merits; and lead ourselves
in, where our lamps shall be furnished, and our
table filled, till we go into heaven; and there he
will welcome us in a mansion prepared for us.

2. He is a high priest adorned with all authority and all perfections, having all in substance
which the types did signify; who beareth our
names, yea, ourselves, on the shoulders of his
power, and in the breast of his hearty love; who
beareth the iniquity of the holy things, and holiness in his forehead for us; in whom the Father is well pleased with us, and hath made us
acceptable, as in his well-beloved.

3. He is over the house of God: he hath
authority and power to bring in whom he pleaseth, and to give forth of the treasure as much as
he will: all the mansions in his Father's dwelling
house are his, and all at his disposing, to open so
as none shall shut: to him belongeth to give
forth the sentence of admission to heaven, and
to say, Come you blessed of the Father. Yea,
to make this his authority manifest, he will come
again, and take us unto himself, that where he is,
we may be there also.

4. We have his high priest: that is, he is ours,
because, 1. Taken out from amongst us, one of
our number, albeit not of our conditions; of our
nature, but separate from our sinful manners,
holy and harmless. 2. Because he is for us, in
things appertaining to God, to employ his means
and power for our behoof towards God. 3. Because bound in all bands with us, of nature, of
grace, and good will, of the Father's gift and appointment, and his own covenant and special
contract with us. So that albeit an uncouth man
may possibly leave a stranger in his journey alone,
yet Christ cannot choose to do so to us: but for
the bands betwixt him and us, he will never leave
us nor forsake us.

VER. 22. Let us draw near with a true heart in
full assurance of faith, having our hearts
sprinkled from an evil conscience, and our
bodies washed with pure water.

From these privileges he presseth an exhortation. To draw near to God, and prescribeth
the disposition required of us in our drawing
near.

1. This exhortation showeth, 1. That true
Christians are oftentimes so sensible of their own
unworthiness, that under that sense, they are
inclined of themselves to stand afar off; and
have need of encouragement and invitation to
draw near. 2. That such as are most sensible of
their own unworthiness, are most called to come
forwards unto God: for he giveth grace to the
humble.

2. He layeth down the privileges in the former
verses: and in this draweth on the exhortation:
To teach us, 1. That such privileges as are granted
unto us in Christ, must be received and believed
as truth. 2. That we must study to make use of
our privileges, and challenge them for our own.
3. That the weakest of true believers in Christ,
may thrust in themselves at the doors of grace,
amongst the holy apostles: for the apostle putteth the Hebrews with himself in the exhortation
for this end.

3. For our disposition, and fitting to draw
near, he requireth first, That we have a true heart.
He saith not, a senseless heart, but a true heart;
that is, such a heart, as in the matter of believing,
mindeth no confidence but in God's grace, through
Christ only: and in the matter of God's service
mindeth only his will in its aim, and alloweth
only that which is his will in its censure.

Then an honest heart, which honestly acknowledgeth its own sins, and fleeth to Christ's blood
for sprinkling, whose aim is upright, endeavours
upright, and censure of itself upright, allowing
in itself nothing but what God alloweth, and dis-
pleased with that which displeaseth God, albeit
many ways weak and imperfect, yet hath liberty
to draw near unto God.

4. The next thing he requireth, is full assurance of faith: that is, a settled and full persuasion
to be accepted, even through Jesus Christ.

Then albeit the Lord will not despise the
weakest measure of faith, and will not quench
the smoking flax; yet it pleaseth him better, yea,
it is his commandment, that men study unto the
full assurance of faith; for the more thou restest
on God's covenant with thee in Jesus Christ, the
more thou sealest his truth, glorifiest him, be-
comest the more like unto faithful Abraham, and
gettest the deeper rooting in Christ.

5. The third is, that the heart be sprinkled
from an evil conscience. The heart is sprinkled
when a sinner sensible of sin, maketh hearty
application to himself of the blood of Jesus for
remission of sins: after this hearty application of
Christ's blood, the conscience is furnished with
a good answer unto all challenges, and so is made
good, a comfortable conscience, absolving the
man through faith in Jesus, whom it tormented
with challenges, before it ran to the blood of
Jesus for sprinkling.

Then whensoever the conscience is evil, accus-
eth and vexeth, let the vexed heart run to
Christ's blood; and then shall it be free from an
evil conscience; for the blood of Jesus cleanseth
us from all sin. Let the heart be sprinkled, and
the conscience will be good.

6. The fourth thing required in him that draweth near as he should, is, That his body be washed with pure water; that is, that according to the signification of that legal right, their outward conversation be blameless and holy; sin being so curbed within, that it reign not in their mortal body; so foughten against within, as it break not forth in scandalous works of darkness in the actions of the body.

Then, 1. With a sprinkled conscience within, men must join a holy and blameless conversation without. 2. The washing of the conversation without, must proceed from a heart sensibly acquainted with the power of the blood of Jesus. 3. And this outward holiness of the body must be wrought with pure water, that is, by the spirit of sanctification; to distinguish the reformation of a believer from a counterfeit, who without may look like a righteous man, but within be as a whited tomb, full of rottenness.

Ver. 23. Let us hold fast the profession of our faith without wavering; (for he is faithful that promised;)

Another exhortation to avow the faith of Christ; that is, the doctrine of Christ, the truth received from Christ, and believed, and not to quit it in the time of trial, upon any condition.

1. The requiring to hold fast the confession of our faith, or hope, as the word importeth, teacheth,

1. That a true Christian must not only hold the truth of Christ secretly, but must confess it, profess and avow it openly, where God's glory and other's good requireth the same. 2. That he must look for adversary powers, and temptations, to take that truth, or at least the confession of it, from him. 3. That in these trials and essays he must hold the faster gripe, and avow it so much the more stedfastly, as he is tempted to quit it. 4. That when he is put to the trial of this confession of any point of his faith, he is also put to the trial of the confession of his hope; whether his hopes of the promised salvation in Jesus be stronger to keep him stedfast, or the terror and allurement from men, stronger to make him quit the point of truth controverted. 5. That nothing but this hope, is able to make a man stand out in trial, if he be hardly urged.

2. He will have the avowing of the truth of Christ, to be without wavering.

Then, 1. Men must so learn the truth, that they need not to change again: that is, must study to know the truth soundly, and solidly. 2. And having learned it, must not say and unsay; one day avow it, and another day quit it: for so God getteth not his due glory. Beholders are not edified, the man's testimony wanteth weight with the adversary. But he must be invincible in the truth, who will neither alter nor change or diminish any thing of it, for fear or favour.

3. He giveth this for a ground of constancy, for he is faithful who hath promised: that is, the promises which Jesus hath made to such as constantly believe in him, shall be surely performed, that no constant professor of his truth shall be ashamed.

Then, 1. Where we have a promise of any thing made unto us in Scripture, we may be confident to obtain it, and bold to avow our hope thereof, against such as would teach us the doctrine of doubting, whereunto we are of ourselves prone and inclined; and against such as shake the assurance of the saints' perseverance. 2. The ground of our confidence is not in ourselves, but in the faithfulness of Jesus Christ, who hath promised such graces to his children. 3. Our bold avowing of our hope, is not a bragging of our own strength, but a magnifying of Christ's faithfulness.

Ver. 24. And let us consider one another, to provoke unto love and to good works.

He strengtheneth his former exhortation by giving of directions, to further their obedience thereunto. And first for mutual upstirring one another. Whereof we learn,

1. That mutual edification of Christians amongst themselves, and sharpening one of another, is a special help to constancy in true religion, and a preservative against apostasy. 2. Prudence is required hereunto, that mutually we observe one another's disposition, gifts, experience, virtues, and faults; that we may the better fit ourselves to do good each one of us unto another; and to receive good each one of another, in our Christian conversing together. 3. A godly striving one with another, who shall be first in love, and well doing, is better than the ordinary strife, who shall exceed others in vanity and superfluity of apparel and fare.

Ver. 25. Not forsaking the assembling of ourselves together, as the manner of some is; but exhorting one another: and so much the more, as ye see the day approaching.

Another mean to this same end, is the frequenting of Christian assemblies and meetings, which may further this purpose of mutual edification. And therefore,

1. Church assemblies must be well kept, by such as do mind to prove constant in the true religion. 2. Christian meetings also of private Christians, for mutual conference, and exhorting one of another, is not to be neglected nor forsaken; but to be used for keeping unity in the church: and not to foster schism, or hinder the public assemblies.

2. He taxeth the fault of some amongst them, who in schism, or purpose of apostasy, withdrew themselves from all church assemblies, and Christian meetings, and fell back again, or were in the way of falling back to the denial of Christ openly.

Then, 1. Separation from the true church, and Christian society of the faithful, is a remarkable evil. 2. The schism or apostasy of others, should not weaken us in following any good mean of edification, but rather stir us up unto more diligence, best by negligence we fall piece and piece back after their example.

3. He maketh the approaching of the day, to wit, of God's judgment, a special motive to use the means diligently, and make us constant in the faith.

Then, 1. The day of God's judgment should still be looked unto, as a thing near hand, even at the doors; because it is but a very little, and our day shall come; yea, and but a little time, till our Lord shall come to judgment. 2. The consideration of the day of judgment, is a fit mean to sharpen us unto all good duties, which may make our reckoning to be furthered at that day, and to make us boldly maintain the truth against all fear of men.

VER. 26. For if we sin wilfully after that we have received the knowledge of the truth, there remaineth no more sacrifice for sins,

Another motive to constancy in the truth of religion, taken from the fearful case of wilful apostates, who sinning the sin against the Holy Ghost, are secluded for ever from mercy. I say, the sin against the Holy Ghost; because we shall find the sin here described, not to be any particular sin against the law, but against the gospel: not a sin against some point of truth, but against Christ's whole doctrine: not of infirmity but wilfulness; not of rashness but of deliberation, wittingly and willingly; not of ignorance but after illumination and profession; such as Jews turned Christians, revolting from Christianity, back again to their former hostility against Christ, did commit. It is true, many who commit lesser sins, get never grace to repent; and many who make defection, in some point of their profession, may be secluded from mercy thereafter: but this sin here described, is a wilful rejection of Christ, and the benefit of his sacrifice, after illumination, and profession of the faith of Christ.

Then, 1. As apostasy from the true religion lieth nearest unto this sin; so they who desire to be freed of this sin, must be the more careful to be constant in the profession of every point of the truth of the gospel. 2. If a man reject the benefit of that once offered sacrifice of Christ, there is no other sacrifice for sin after that, nor any other mean to help him. But if a man seek unto Jesus Christ, and will not quit him, whatsoever he may think of the heinousness of his own sins, the sacrifice which Jesus offered for sins, remaineth, whereby he may be saved.

VER. 27. But a certain fearful looking-for of judgment, and fiery indignation, which shall devour the adversaries.

Having secluded the apostate from mercy, he goeth on in these words, to show his miserable estate. Whereof we gather,

1. That the wilful apostate from the faith of Christ, is also a wilful adversary to Christ, of the highest sort, partaker of Satan's sin and Satan's profession. 2. That every apostate of this sort is destitute of God's peace, self-condemned, desperate of salvation, hopeless of relief, without all purpose of repentance, or using means of help, stricken with the foresight of the wrath coming upon him, and made to expect it, although he should dissemble it never so much. 3. The apostate's fear shall come upon him, judgment answerable to his sin, the indignation and wrath

of God, yea, fiery indignation, the most terrible that can be thought upon, which he shall not escape; but it shall devour him, swallow him up, and feed upon his body and soul, even for ever.

2. In that he maketh this the judgment of Christ's adversaries, we learn,

That the soul which loveth Christ, and cannot quit him, cannot endure to think of a separation, will not quit the true religion, nor any known point of Christ's truth, and is using the means to get God's peace: albeit it might seem to itself, because of the present sense of wrath, to be in the selfsame estate that is here described: yet is it free, as yet, of the sin against the Holy Ghost, and not to be reckoned amongst adversaries, but amongst the friends and lovers of Christ, how vehemently soever Satan's suggestions bear in the contrary.

3. In that by setting before them the fearful estate of apostates from the known truth of the true religion, he laboureth to strengthen them against the fear of persecution. Whence we learn,

That if apostates, before they make apostasy from the true religion, did foresee their own danger, as after apostasy they are made to foresee their own condemnation, all the terror of all the torment which man could put them unto, and all the allurements which this world could give them, would not move them to quit the least point of the truth of true religion.

VER. 28. He that despised Moses' law died without mercy under two or three witnesses:

VER. 29. Of how much sorer punishment, suppose ye, shall he be thought worthy, who hath trodden under foot the Son of God, and hath counted the blood of the covenant, wherewith he was sanctified, an unholy thing, and hath done despite unto the Spirit of grace?

He proveth the equity of their judgment by the proportion of their punishment who despised the law of Moses.

Then, as sins are greater, so must the punishment be greater: and the conscience being posed as here, cannot but subscribe to the proportion.

2. To make the sin appear the better, he pointeth out some particular sins, involved within this great sin. For clearing whereof it may be asked, How can the apostates tread the blood of the Son of God under foot? &c.

I answer, They cannot, indeed, by physical action; but by doing the equivalent sin they are accounted of God to do it, by judicial interpretation. Their apostasy importeth, their agreeing to do Christ as much indignity as if they did offer him this personal violence. Their deeds show, that they have this base estimation of Christ and his blood, and no better; for what saith the apostate of Christ, by his deed, but that he is not worthy to be professed, or avowed, or followed? And what is this in effect, but to tread him under all these base things which the apostate preferreth before him? And so is to be understood of the blood of Christ, and his Spirit.

Quest. But how can the reprobate be said to be sanctified by the blood of the covenant?

I answer, there is a sanctification to the purifying of the flesh, and a sanctification to the purifying of the conscience from dead works to serve the living God, Heb. ix. 13, 14.

The sanctification, external, to the purifying of the flesh, consisteth in the man's separation from the world, and dedication unto God's service, by calling and covenant, common to all the members of the visible church: and it is forcible thus far, as to bring a man into credit and estimation as a saint, before men, and unto the common privileges of the church; whereupon, as men, so God also speaketh unto him, and of him, as one of his people, and dealeth with him, in his external dispensation, as with one of his own people. In this sense all the congregation of Israel, and every one of them, is called holy, yea Cora also, and his followers, Numb. xvi. 3. The sanctification internal, by renovation, consisteth in a man's separation from the state of nature to the state of grace; and from his old condition to be a new creature indeed. By this latter sort, a reprobate cannot be called sanctified, but by the former he may be called sanctified, and that by virtue of the blood of the covenant, albeit he should not get any further good thereby. For as the blood of Christ hath virtue to cleanse the conscience, and renew the soul which cometh unto it truly and spiritually, so it must have force to do that which is less; that is, purify the flesh, and external condition, of the man who cometh unto it outwardly only, as the types did under the law; whereupon, a hypocrite in the Christian church must be accounted one of the congregation of the saints, as well as a hypocrite under the law was so called; because Christ's blood cannot be inferior to the types, which were of this force, to sanctify men to the purifying of the flesh. Or we may say more shortly, there is a sanctification by consecration, when any thing is devoted or dedicated unto God, and a sanctification by inhabitation of the Holy Spirit, 2 Cor. vi. 16—18. Of the former sort, the censers of Core, Dathan, and Abiram, are called holy. And the reason is given: "Because they offered them before the Lord, therefore they are hallowed," Numb. xvi. 38. And in this sense, all the members of the visible church, even such as afterwards do prove apostates, are sanctified, because they are offered, and offer themselves unto the Lord. But the inhabitation of the Holy Spirit is proper only to the elect, and God's children.

Hence learn, 1. That all the members of the visible church are so confederate unto God, that it is sacrilege for them not to seek God's honour in all things, or to bestow themselves any other way than for God. 2. Men are reckoned by God so to deal with Christ and his blood, and covenant, and Spirit, as they make account thereof, as they have estimation of Christ, and his blood and Spirit. 3. And their estimation is not reckoned by their words, or pretences, but by their deeds, as these do import, so are they judged to esteem. 4. Because apostasy from Christ importeth as much as he and his doctrine are unworthy to be avowed or maintained, by consequence it importeth also, that Christ was not the man he called himself, and that all his Spirit had taught them was untruth; and therefore justly here doth the Scripture challenge the apostate of counting Christ's blood no better than the blood of a common malefactor, and of giving the lie to the Holy Spirit. So fearful a thing is it to make defection from any known part of true religion.

VER. 30. For we know him that hath said, Vengeance belongeth unto me, I will recompense, saith the Lord. And again, The Lord shall judge his people.

In that he proveth the certainty of their punishment out of Deut. xxxii. 35, 36. Learn, 1. That the justice and constancy of God's truth in general threatenings, is sufficient to prove the certain punishment of particular sins. 2. The punishment of apostates of one kind, may evidence the punishment of apostates of another kind; for it is the Jews' apostasy to idolatry and worshipping of images, which in that place the Lord doth threaten. 2. He maketh the knowing of God who speaketh, a proof sufficient for the certain performance of his word.

Then, as men understand God's nature, so will his word weigh with them; and such as know him best will stand most in awe of him, believe his word most.

VER. 31. It is a fearful thing to fall into the hands of the living God.

From this knowledge of God's nature, he pronounceth how fearful a thing it is to fall into the hands of an adversary to be punished. Then, 1. It is presupposed that such as reject the mercy of Christ shall not be able to reject justice, but must fall into his hand. 2. The eternity of God maketh his wrath terrible; for he liveth for ever to avenge himself on his foes. 3. The terror of the Lord, what torment he is able to inflict, and that for ever, is a fit mean to make men beware to make apostasy from Christ.

VER. 32. But call to remembrance the former days, in which, after ye were illuminated, ye endured a great fight of afflictions;

For a mean to help them constantly to go on, he directeth them to make use of their former patience, and experience of troubles for the gospel. Then, 1. Even they who have suffered for Christ have need to be stirred up to constancy, and to be terrified from apostasy. 2. The more men have suffered for Christ, they ought to be the bolder in the profession of his truth, and the more ready for new sufferings. 2. He maketh the time of their first troubles to be after illumination.

Then, some do enter into troubles for religion at their very first conversion, and are yoked in battle against persecutors, besides other onsets of Satan, and their own nature.

VER. 33. Partly, whilst ye were made a gazing-stock, both by reproaches and afflictions; and partly, whilst ye became companions of them that were so used.

He maketh their troubles in their own persons, by reproaches and afflictions, the first part of their fight, wherein they were a gazing-stock to the world.

Then, 1. Such as are called to suffer for Christ are set upon a theatre, to give proof of their faith and love to Christ, before the world. 2. The blind world wondereth at such as adventure to suffer any thing for the truth of Christ, and think but ignominiously of Christ and his cause, and of those that maintain the same. 3. Reproaches and taunts of the godly by the world, are reckoned up to them for parts of their Christian cross, and of their glory before God.

2. The next part of their fight was their partaking with such as did suffer the like.

Then, 1. It is the part of true Christians to countenance them that confess Christ, yea, and to join with them that suffer for him. 2. Communion with the sufferings of others is reckoned up for a part of our sufferings. 3. To suffer patiently ourselves, or take a part with others in their sufferings, will cost us a battle.

VER. 34. For ye had compassion of me in my bonds, and took joyfully the spoiling of your goods, knowing in yourselves that ye have in heaven a better and an enduring substance.

He cometh to particulars; and first, their compassion towards himself in his bonds, is remembered by him.

Then, 1. Compassion with sufferers, especially when it is manifested to the afflicted party for his comfort, maketh the compassionate person a partaker with the sufferer. 2. Such compassion should be remembered by the sufferer thankfully, and recompensed by seeking their eternal welfare who have showed them such great kindness.

2. Another particular is, their joyful enduring the spoliation of their goods.

Then, 1. When trial cometh of men's faith in Christ, such as mind to be constant must prepare themselves to quit their goods if God please so to honour them with employment. 2. When we see we must lose our goods for Christ's sake, or suffer any other inconvenience, we ought to do it cheerfully, and count our gain in Christ more than our loss in the world; and if we find trouble, to let our adversaries know as little of it as we can; namely, seeing there is no cause of grief, if our eyes were opened, and our earthly affections mortified. 3. Their encouragement and cause of joy was the sensible feeling within themselves of the comfort of eternal riches in heaven keeping for them.

Then, 1. It is the assurance of our heavenly inheritance which must make us ready to quit our earthly movables. 2. Whoso getteth a heart to quit any thing on earth for Christ, shall have better in heaven than he can lose here. 3. God useth to give earnest of what he is to give, in sensible feeling of spiritual riches to such as believe in him. 4. When men can esteem of things heavenly, as they are; that is, enduring goods; and of things earthly as they are; that is, perishing movables; then shall they readily quit the earthly in hope of the heavenly.

VER. 35. Cast not away therefore your confidence, which hath great recompense of reward.

Now he exhorteth them to go on in this bold avowing of Christ; for this confidence in the original is such as hath with it a full and free profession of all their faith.

Then, confidence and bold avowing of the truth is required; a plain and full testimony must we give to Christ's truth; our confidence in profession is in part casten [lost] when our testimony is sparing.

2. The encouragement he giveth is the hope of a reward.

Then, 1. Constancy in avowing of Christ shall be well rewarded, although not of deserving, yet of God's grace. 2. He that quitteth his profession, renounceth the reward promised to the constant.

Question. But doth not this exhortation import the elect's unsettledness and uncertainty of perseverance?

I answer, Not; but only his weakness of himself, and need of such exhortations to further his constancy. 2. The danger of dishonouring God in some particular slip or fall is ground sufficient for this exhortation, and this is the most of necessity it can import. 3. Exhortation being given to the common body of the visible professors teacheth them properly, and not the elect formally.

VER. 36. For ye have need of patience, that, after ye have done the will of God, ye might receive the promise.

He giveth a reason, because they have need of patience, therefore they must not cast away their confidence.

Then, 1. The reward will not be given till a time intervene. 2. And troubles will lie on in the mean while to make the time seem the longer. 3. Patience is needful, as a mean, to fit us to attend. 4. Confidence of the truth must support our patience.

2. The time of their patience he setteth as long as God thinketh good to employ them, and after that the reward cometh.

Then, 1. The time of patience is as long as God hath any thing to do with us in this world. 2. Patience must not be joined with idleness, but with active obedience of God's will, as he requireth it. 3. After that employment is ended, the promised reward is given.

VER. 37. For yet a little while, and he that shall come will come, and will not tarry.

He encourageth them to patience by promise of the Lord's coming to relieve them shortly.

Then, 1. The term of patience is until the Lord come to deliver. 2. The patient attender on his coming shall not be disappointed; for he will come, and will not tarry beyond the due time of our necessity. 3. It should strengthen us unto patience that the time is short and the delivery certain.

VER. 38. Now the just shall live by faith: but if

any man draw back, my soul shall have no pleasure in him.

How shall they fend in the mean time? He answereth from Hab. ii. 4, The just shall live by faith; that is, the man who will be found righteous, must not look to present sense, but sustain his soul with the word of promise.

Then, 1. In the midst of troubles, and God's felt absence, faith will content itself with the only promises of God. 2. Looking to God's word by faith is able to keep a soul in life and patience.

2. He threateneth the misbelieving apostate that chooseth to draw back and not to live by faith. The words of the prophet are, "He whose soul is lifted up in him is not upright." The apostle betaketh him to the meaning, which being compared with the prophet's words, doth teach us,

1. That he who refuseth to live by faith is lifted up with the false confidence of some other thing than God; he hath some strong hold within himself wherein he doth trust. 2. He that lifteth up himself in his vain confidence will draw back from believing in God's word in the time of trial. 3. He that draweth back in the time of trial bewrayeth the want of this sincerity. 4. A backslider from the profession of the truth is loathsome both to God and to his saints.

VER. 39. But we are not of them who draw back unto perdition; but of them that believe to the saving of the soul.

He mitigateth the threatening lest he should seem to suspect them of inconstancy.

Then, 1. Such threatenings and exhortations as have been given here, do not import the uncertainty of their perseverance who are threatened, but standeth with the assurance of the contrary. 2. He who threateneth should be as wary to weaken his hearers' faith as his own. 3. Hearers must understand that the right use of threatening is to rouse men out of security, and not to discourage them.

2. We are not of them, saith he, who draw back unto perdition.

Then, 1. They who draw back from constant avowing of the faith draw near unto perdition. He that forsaketh the cross runneth himself on the rock of his own destruction, which is worse. 2. The elect are not of that kind or sort of men who fall into apostasy unto perdition. They may fall for a time, but are not of them that draw back unto perdition.

3. We are of them, saith he, who believe to the salvation of the soul.

Then, 1. True believers are of that kind of whom all do persevere. 2. Persevering in the faith is a going on to salvation.

THE SUM OF CHAP. XI.

Now that you may know the better how to live by faith, consider that faith apprehendeth things to come as present and subsisting, by holding them in their original fountain, which is the word of promise, and beholding in the mirror of the word the clear certainty of things as yet not seen to sense, ver. 1. For so were the elect be-

holders and partakers of Christ before he came, and were justified, ver. 2. And so have we certainty of the creation of the world of nothing, ver. 3. By it was Abel's person and sacrifice accepted and preferred before his elder brother, ver. 4. By it was Enoch made ready for heaven, ver. 5, 6. And Noah, by it, saved both in body and soul, ver. 7. Faith made Abraham leave his country in hope of heaven, ver. 8—10. By it Sarah, being old, got strength above the course of nature to become a fruitful mother, ver. 11, 12. All these, unto their dying day, were contented with the foresight of the performance of God's promises, and in hope thereof renounced the world; therefore God honoureth them as his confederates, ver. 13—16. Faith made Abraham to offer his only son, ver. 17—19. Isaac and Jacob and Joseph by faith, at their death, comforted themselves and others also, in hope of the performance of God's truth. ver. 20 —22. The parents of Moses overcame the fear of man by faith, ver. 23. Moses, by faith, got strength to choose the cross of Christ before the riches and honours and pleasures of Egypt, ver. 24—26. Faith made him constant in his choice and patient, ver. 27. By faith he got the people of Israel to be saved when the first-born of Egypt were slain, ver. 28. By faith the deep sea gave open way, ver. 29. High walled towns were thrown down, ver. 30. Rahab was saved when others perished, ver. 31. By faith numbers of God's children did wonderful things, and received wonderful comforts, and overcame all persecutions, ver. 32—38. All these died in the faith of Christ, and were justified, albeit Christ was not yet come, ver. 39. God having reserved the accomplishment of the prophecies and types in the coming of Jesus Christ, until our time, that the fathers might not get salvation, except by looking to our times, and joining with us in the faith of Jesus, in whom they and we also are perfected, ver. 40.

THE DOCTRINE OF CHAP. XI.

VER. 1. Now faith is the substance of things hoped for, the evidence of things not seen.

He pointeth out the nature of faith, to help them to live by it. Then, he that would live by faith had need skilfully to search out the nature thereof.

2. In describing faith, he ascribeth unto it the property of the word which faith layeth hold upon: for, it is the Word properly, which is the substance of things not seen.

Then, there is such a union betwixt faith and the word, that what the word is in force and effect, that faith is said to be in force and effect also. As faith honoureth the word, so God honoureth faith, in giving it the like commendation for force with the word. What is the original of the being and existence of any thing, but this? God willeth it to be, or promiseth that it shall come to pass, or commandeth that it may be. Therefore, let faith get a hold of the promise or word, and it taketh hold of the thing promised by the root thereof. And in the hand of faith doth truth bud out, and flourish unto the ripe fruit of full satisfaction in performance.

3. The word evidence, in the original, is a term of logic, importing that it is the nature of faith, by dispensation, to convince.

Then, it were wisdom, for helping of our weak faith, to make syllogisms from the word, and to reason so convincingly against all opposition of incredulity in us, as there might be a consent and yielding to the truth extorted from us.

As for example : When we cannot take to heart the danger we are into, by entertaining any known sin, from Rom. viii. 13, we may reason thus : The scripture saith, " If ye live after the flesh, ye shall die ;" but if I forsake not and mortify not this known sin in me, I live after the flesh. Therefore if I forsake not and mortify not this known sin, I shall die. Again, the scripture saith, " If ye, through the Spirit, do mortify the deeds of the body, ye shall live." Therefore if I, by the Spirit, mortify such and such lusts, I have God's promise that I shall live. And so in other particulars.

Ver. 2. For by it the elders obtained a good report.

He proveth the nature of faith to be as he hath said, because the elders were approved of God as blessed in their believing, who could not otherwise be partakers of the promised blessing in the Messiah to come, except faith had furnished unto them the substance and evidence of that hoped for blessing.

Then, 1. The fathers under the law were endued with justifying faith, and accepted of God, even as we. 2. Men, how base soever, are brought into credit with God and into good estimation with his church by faith.

Ver. 3. Through faith we understand that the worlds were framed by the word of God, so that things which are seen were not made of things which do appear.

Another proof to show that faith is the evidence of things not seen, because we can have no other evidence of the world's creation but by looking thereupon in the word, as it were in doing before our eyes.

Then, 1. Faith must not stand whether there be appearances or probabilities, or not, of such things as are promised in the word, or else it could not believe the creation, which is the making of all things of nothing. 2. The whole works of creation are pawns and evidences of the possibility, yea, certainty, of every thing promised ; for the works of creation stand upon no better ground than God's word. This sentence, " God shall make our vile bodies like unto the glorious body of Christ Jesus," is as powerful to make us so as this sentence, " Let there be light," was powerful to create light when there was none before.

Ver. 4. By faith Abel offered unto God a more excellent sacrifice than Cain, by which he obtained witness that he was righteous, God testifying of his gifts : and by it he being dead yet speaketh.

In the catalogue of believers he beginneth at Abel, the first persecuted man for righteousness, and that by Cain, professing the same worship with him. Wherein we learn,

1. That the wicked may join in the outward worship and pure forms of religion with the godly, as Cain did with Abel. 2. That faith putteth the difference betwixt their persons and service. 3. That a man's person must first please God, before his actions can please him ; for therefore was Abel's sacrifice accepted, because by faith his person was justified. 4. Faith maketh Abel still a speaking doctor to the church, directing all who love to have such reward, to cleave unto God as he did ; and albeit they should die for it, by the hand of their persecuting and bloody brethren, not to wonder at it.

Ver. 5. By faith Enoch was translated that he should not see death ; and was not found, because God had translated him : for before his translation he had this testimony, that he pleased God.

Enoch's full felicity is expressed by God's translating of him.

Then, if we ask where Enoch went to, we must search for him by scripture warrant, only in the company of God, the translator of him. For before he was translated, he lived a blessed man in fellowship with God ; and it is injurious to God and Enoch both, to put him out of God's fellowship as not blessed, when he is translated.

2. Enoch's translation beareth witness, 1. That the blessedness of everlasting life with God, after death, was known in the Old Testament. 2. That the fathers got possession of it. 3. That this felicity could not be attained unto but by flitting and removing out of this life. 4. That the body is a partner with the soul of life eternal. 5. That howsoever it be appointed for all men once to die, yet God can make, when he pleaseth, translation or a change to stand in room of death.

3. Before Enoch was translated, he had this testimony, that he pleased God. Then, whosoever desireth to be blessed with God, after they are removed from this life, must first learn to please God, before they depart hence.

Ver. 6. But without faith it is impossible to please him : for he that cometh to God must believe that he is, and that he is a rewarder of them that diligently seek him.

He proveth that Enoch's translation and pleasing of God was by faith : because pleasing of God cannot be without faith. He nameth no other of God's graces in him, but faith only ; because it only, of all other graces, strippeth a man naked of the worth of any thing in him, and sendeth him to God's mercy in the Mediator.

Then, 1. Whatsoever glorious virtues be found in God's children, yet it is not by any of these that they are justified or acceptable to God, but only by their faith ; for it is by faith, that it may be by grace ; and if it be by grace, it is not by worthiness of works. 2. In the matter of justification, and acceptation with God, to be justified by faith, or accepted not without faith, is all one to be justified and accepted by virtue of nothing in a man beside faith; else the apostle's reasoning were not strong. 5. Except a man have this commended faith in God's mercy, he cannot please God. Let him do else what you can name, without this faith, it is impossible to please God.

2. He expoundeth what the faith is of which he meaneth: to wit, a coming to God, all-sufficient and merciful.

Then, 1. God is self-sufficient and all-sufficient. 2. God is so gracious, as none can seek unto him by that way which he hath revealed, but he will give them that which they seek. 3. Except a man believe God's all-sufficiency and merciful bountifulness, he cannot come unto him to seek supply of wants, or relief from evil.

3. From these words also we may observe the nature of faith.

1. It maketh a man sensible of his indigence and misery, else it could not send him begging. 2. It maketh him to acknowledge his natural alienation and farness from God; else it could not set him on work to seek God, and to come unto him. 3. It emptieth him of the confidence in his own, and all the creature's help; else it could not send the man away from all these to God. 4. It pointeth out God, both able and willing to help; else it could not encourage to take course for relief in him. 5. It setteth a man on work to use the appointed means to find God. 6. It certifieth a man of God's impartiality towards every one that seeketh to him; and maketh him to hold on the way, seeking diligently, and never to give over. And so it bringeth a man to deny himself, and to have communion with God.

Ver. 7. By faith Noah, being warned of God of things not seen as yet, moved with fear, prepared an ark to the saving of his house; by the which he condemned the world, and became heir of the righteousness which is by faith.

In Noah's example, observe, 1. He believeth the deluge is coming, and feareth, and prepareth the ark. Then,

1. Faith apprehendeth judgments threatened in the word, as well as mercies in the promises. 2. Faith apprehending the threatening, moveth to fear. 3. That is right fear, which setteth a man on work to prevent the danger.

2. By his diligence he condemned the world. Then,

The pains which the godly take to eschew wrath, condemneth careless beholders of their diligence.

3. By this he became heir of the righteousness which is by faith, that is, came evidently to be seen to be such. Then,

1. There is a righteousness which is only by faith. 2. That righteousness is heirship to all true believers. 3. Some special point of faith may bring this heirship unto light, and give evidence of a man's right thereunto.

Ver. 8. By faith Abraham, when he was called to go out into a place which he should after receive for an inheritance, obeyed; and he went out, not knowing whither he went.

Abraham's following of God's calling, and leaving of his country, is counted a work of faith. From Abraham's example, then, let us learn, 1. That faith in God will cause a man to quit his country and parents, and every dearest thing, at God's calling. 2. Faith counteth God's promises better than present possessions, and is content to quit the one for the other. 3. Yea, it is content with a promise of better in general, and for the special manner of performance standeth not to be blind. 4. Faith is willing to obey, as soon as it seeth a warrant.

Ver. 9. By faith he sojourned in the land of promise, as in a strange country, dwelling in tabernacles with Isaac and Jacob, the heirs with him of the same promise:

Abraham's sojourning in Canaan is counted another work of his faith. Wherein we learn, 1. That faith can for a while suffer to be a stranger even from that whereunto it hath best right. 2. When faith hath certainty of a heavenly inheritance, it can be content with a small portion of things earthly. 3. A man who sojourneth amongst idolaters should be sure of a calling thereunto, and being amongst them, ought to behave himself as a stranger and sojourner. 4. Yea, where he hath best right on earth, he ought to have a pilgrim's mind.

Ver. 10. For he looked for a city which hath foundations, whose builder and maker is God.

That which moved Abraham to behave himself as a sojourner on earth, was the hope of a settled during-place with God, in the society of the saints in heaven. Then,

1. Heaven is a settled, commodious, and safe dwelling-place: all places here are but moveable tabernacles. 2. The fathers under the law looked for entry into their eternal rest in the kingdom of heaven, after the ending of their pilgrimage here. 3. The hope of heaven is able to make a man content with pilgrim's fare and lodging here-away.

Ver. 11. Through faith also Sara herself received strength to conceive seed, and was delivered of a child when she was past age, because she judged him faithful who had promised.

Sara is reckoned in the catalogue of believers, and her laughing, through unbelief, is not remembered, but her victory over her misbelief is commended. Then,

1. Even women are made patterns of believing, and wisely walking with God: worthy to be imitated of men. 2. God marketh not the defects of faith, but the soundness thereof, how small soever it be; what good is in his children, and not what sins they are clogged with.

2. When she is past age, by faith she getteth strength to conceive.

Then, 1. Faith resteth on God's promise, albeit carnal reason seem not to second it. 2. Faith maketh us capable of benefits which otherwise we could not receive. 3. The more hinderances that faith hath, it is the more commendable.

3. That which upheld her, was the faithfulness of God. Then,

1. The consideration of the properties of God, who promiseth, is a special help to make us rest on the promise which he maketh. 2. He that giveth unto God the glory of faithfulness, shall receive for a reward the full performance.

VER. 12. Therefore sprang there even of one, and him as good as dead, so many as the stars of the sky in multitude, and as the sand which is by the sea-shore innumerable.

The promise was of innumerable children, as the stars of heaven: and so was the performance. Then,

Justifying faith not only believeth the great promise of redemption, but also other inferior promises which depend thereupon, the believing whereof giveth evidence of believing the main promise of salvation through the Messiah. And therefore it is, that by the faith of such promises the faithful are here declared to be justified.

Question. How can this be, that Abraham's seed should be so many?

I answer, 1. Because the one is as innumerable as the other; for they are compared together in this respect. 2. Superlative speeches are to be expounded according to the scope, and not captiously to be wrested beside the purpose of the speaker, and beyond the common acceptation of the hearer. Now, the scope of the speech is to raise the dulness of the mind, in weighty matters, to the due consideration of a truth, in the due measure, which otherwise should have been undervalued. This is the proper intent of the figure hyperbolic, in the ordinary use of rhetoric.

VER. 13. These all died in faith, not having received the promises, but having seen them afar off, and were persuaded of them, and embraced them, and confessed that they were strangers and pilgrims on the earth.

He commendeth the faith of the patriarchs and Sarah, that they died in the faith, not having obtained the promises. Then,

1. Faith loseth the commendation, except we persevere therein even until death. 2. Where we have a word of promise made to the church, or to ourselves, albeit we see it not performed in our time, we may go to death in assurance that it shall be performed. 3. They who would die in faith, must live in faith.

2. Though they received not the promises, yet they saw them afar off, and were fully persuaded of them, and embraced them. Then,

Albeit faith came not unto a possession, yet it cometh unto a beholding of the possession coming, unto a persuasion of the possession, and a sort of friendly salutation thereof, as the word importeth; such as friends give one to another, whilst they are drawing near to embrace one another after a long separation.

3. They confessed in their lifetime, that they were strangers and pilgrims on the earth. This we read only of Jacob before Pharaoh: but the mind of one of the faithful, in the main matters, maketh evident what is the mind of the rest. Then, 1. It is the part of true believers, to profess their faith before all, even before idolaters, amongst whom they live. 2. They who know heaven to be their own home, do reckon this world a strange country.

VER. 14. For they that say such things declare plainly that they seek a country.

VER. 15. And truly, if they had been mindful of that country from whence they came out, they might have had opportunity to have returned.

VER. 16. But now they desire a better country, that is, a heavenly: wherefore God is not ashamed to be called their God: for he hath prepared for them a city.

From their profession, that they were strangers, he draweth consequences thus; that they desired a homely country; and if a country, then either their own earthly country or a better. Not their own earthly country: for they might have returned when they pleased, therefore they desired a better country; and if a better country, then a heavenly country; that is, they desired even heaven itself for their country.

1. This deducing of consequences, from the profession of the patriarchs, that they were strangers, teacheth us,

1. So to read the Scriptures, as we may mark, not only what is spoken; but also what is thereby imported by consequence. 2. That what is imported by a speech, is a plain declaration of the mind of the speaker; and not an obscure deduction, as mockers call it. They who say they are strangers, declare plainly, that they seek a country, saith the apostle. 3. Yea, that it is lawful to proceed, drawing one consequence after another, till we find out the full mind; providing the collection be evident in the course of sound reason, as here it is.

2. The apostle hath proved here, that the patriarchs sought heaven for their country, because they sought a better than any on earth.

Then, 1, The apostle knew no place for residence of departed souls, better than the earth, except heaven only. If there had been any other place, such as is feigned to be, his reasoning had not been solid. 2. The patriarchs, after the ending of their pilgrimage here on earth, went home to heaven.

3. Because they counted themselves strangers, till they came home to heaven, God is not ashamed to be called their God.

Then, 1. God will honour them that honour him. 2. God will avow himself to be their portion, who for his cause do renounce the world. 3. Yea, that the Lord may honour such as honour him, he will even abase himself to exalt them. 4. When the Lord hath so done, he thinketh it no dishonour to himself to do any thing that may honour his servants.

4. God did prepare them a city, which the apostle before hath called heaven, or the heavenly country.

E

Then heaven was prepared for the patriarchs, and the rest of God's saints, before they had ended their pilgrimage on earth. And to put them into hell, or any other place [than] there, must be a doctrine not from heaven.

Ver. 17. By faith Abraham, when he was tried, offered up Isaac: and he that had received the promises offered up his only begotten son,

Ver. 18. Of whom it was said, That in Isaac shall thy seed be called:

Another commendation of Abraham's faith from the proof given thereof in his trial about Isaac. Whence we learn,

1. That where the Lord giveth faith, there trial must be expected: and the greater faith the greater trial. 2. That faith is most commendable when it standeth long in trial.

2. He is said to have offered up Isaac by faith. Then, 1. There is nothing so dear, but faith in God will make a man quit it at God's command. 2. The Lord counteth that to be done which a man is about to do. Isaac is counted offered, because so was he in Abraham's purpose.

3. His receiving of the promises is here in another sense, than verse 13. For there to receive the promises, is to receive the thing promised, or the promises in performance. But here it is to have the promises first, and immediately made unto him.

Then the meaning of forms of speech in scripture, is to be found by consideration of all circumstances of the place, where they are spoken, and not of some circumstances only.

4. It serveth to the commendation of his faith, that he obeyed God's command, when it seemed to make the promise null. Then, 1. To adhere to the promise, when by appearance of reason it is likely not to be performed, is tried faith indeed. 2. When reason fighteth against faith, it is wisdom to quit that reason which would make us quit the promises. 3. When God's commandments and promises unto us, seem to cross one another, it is wisdom for us to justify them both. All his words are truth.

Ver. 19. Accounting that God was able to raise him up, even from the dead; from whence also he received him in a figure.

Abraham's looking to God's fidelity, and omnipotency, made him victorious over every difficulty, and so to give obedience to this hard commandment.

Then, 1. When we get hard commandments, we must lay our reckoning how we may obey them, and not how we may shift them. 2. Difficulties and impossibilities, as would appear, must be rolled over upon God. 3. God's omnipotency maketh that his promise cannot miss, but take effect.

2. Abraham as he expected, so he found; he expected Isaac's resurrection from the dead; and in a figure, or similitude, he received Isaac back from the dead: that is, from the jaws of death, no less unexpectedly, than from the dead.

Then, 1. The believer shall find as much as he can expect from God's word. 2. If the performance be not as he doth forecast, yet it shall be by a way as comfortable and profitable.

Ver. 20. By faith Isaac blessed Jacob and Esau concerning things to come.

Isaac's blessing of his sons, is said to be by faith.

Then patriarchal benedictions were given by ordinary faith, albeit from the ground of extraordinary revealed truth. For faith ordinary believeth God's truth revealed, howsoever ordinarily or extraordinarily.

2. In that this example is propounded for ordinary imitation, in believing of God's ordinary revealed word, it teacheth us,

That he who hath the ordinary word of God, hath as sure a ground to rest upon, as if he had a particular and extraordinary revelation.

Ver. 21. By faith Jacob, when he was a dying, blessed both the sons of Joseph; and worshipped, leaning upon the top of his staff.

Jacob a dying, blesseth his offspring, and worshippeth God in bodily weakness.

Then, 1. Faith can look through the cloud of death, and behold both its own and other's felicity. 2. In the solid assurance which it hath, it can worship or glorify God for things to come, as if they were already past.

2. It is not said that he worshipped the top of his staff, but upon the top of his staff, leaning, for his weakness' cause, by approaching death: because he would, for this foreseen blessing of God upon his posterity, testify by signs of worship in his weak body, how he esteemed of that favour.

Then, 1. Faith will make the body, albeit it be weak, concur with the spirit in the Lord's worship. 2. When the infirmity of the body maketh it unable to concur with the spirit, it must be helped with a stone, as Moses praying against Amalek; or staff, as Jacob here; or any thing else, which may enable it to perform the worship the better; being put under breast, or arms, or knees. 3. Jacob's bending of his body in so great weakness thereof must bear witness against the profane ease which many men nowa-days take unto themselves, both in private and public worship.

Ver. 22. By faith Joseph when he died made mention of the departing of the children of Israel; and gave commandment concerning his bones.

Joseph also testified his faith in his death, concerning the delivery of Israel out of Egypt, by giving direction for transporting his bones, in sign of his assurance of their going to Canaan; because God had promised so.

Then the Lord's promises are sure comforts in death, whereby faith both sustaineth itself, and is able to encourage and strengthen others: and faith maketh a man to keep them in memory, and to make use of them in due time.

Ver. 23. By faith Moses, when he was born,

was hid three months of his parents, because they saw he was a proper child; and they were not afraid of the king's commandment.

How great weakness Moses's parents did bewray, the history maketh evident: yet is their faith commended as victorious over the fear, wherein their weakness did most appear. Whence we learn, 1. That nothing is commendable, but because done in faith. Their natural love is not mentioned, but their faith. 2. That God so loveth faith in his children, that he commendeth it in the measure it hath, albeit it go not so far as it ought, and marketh what faith hath, and not what it wanteth of the perfection. 2. The evidence of their faith he maketh this; That they were not afraid of the king's commandment.

Then, 1. God alloweth not that kings' commandments should be regarded when they command impiety and wickedness; for then should they be honoured above God, if for their commandment we should do that which he forbiddeth. 2. Nothing but faith in God is able to make a man overcome the fear of that which potentates may do unto him: and it is a commendable work of faith to get this victory. 3. The beauty of the child stirred up his parents to this work of faith, thinking with themselves, that it behoved to be for some special end that God had so fashioned the child.

Then, 1. The Lord hath ways enough to excitate the faith of his own, and bring it forth to act. 2. Where special endowments are given, there is good evidence of special employment to follow.

Ver. 24. By faith Moses, when he was come to years, refused to be called the son of Pharaoh's daughter;

Moses refusing the honour which he might have had in Pharaoh's court, because it might have hindered him from the honour of one of God's people, is commended for a work of faith.

Then it is better to be a member of God's church, amongst God's people, than to be a prince in a great kingdom without the church. 2. Because he would not have chosen to be the son of Pharaoh's daughter, therefore he refused to be called so. Then,

That which a man dare not avow himself to be, or may not lawfully choose to be, he must refuse to be esteemed to be; he must refuse to be called such. 3. His manner of refusing this unhallowed honour, is expounded to be by joining himself with the people of God, and so forsaking of Pharaoh's court.

Then, 1. That is the true way of refusing unlawful honour, to quit the place whereunto the unlawful honour is annexed, and betake themselves to what they may brook with God's approbation, how mean soever it seem before the world. 2. When honour and a good conscience cannot be kept together, let the honour be quitted and the preferment go. 4. When he was come to years he did this.

Then, 1. What one hath done in his non-age,

or ignorance, is not reckoned, when after riper consideration he amendeth it. 2. The more ripely and advisedly a good work be done, it is the more commendable.

Ver. 25. Choosing rather to suffer affliction with the people of God, than to enjoy the pleasures of sin for a season;

The reason of his refusal is, the estimation which he had of the estate of God's people, how afflicted soever, above the pleasures of sin.

Then, 1. He who chooseth the privileges and fellowship of God's people, must choose their affliction also. 2. The riches, honour, and pleasure which a man enjoyeth with the disavowing of true religion, and want of the society of God's people, which he might have, are but the pleasures of sin. What pleasure a man can have by sin is but for a season. 4. It is better to be afflicted for a season with God's people, than to live with the wicked with pleasure for a season; and it is greater misery to be in a sinful state than in an afflicted state.

Ver. 26. Esteeming the reproach of Christ greater riches than the treasures of Egypt: for he had respect unto the recompense of reward.

He commendeth the work of Moses's faith by the motives thereunto; whereof the first was, the high estimation of the reproach of Christ.

Then, 1. Moses, and God's people in his time, did know Christ, else they could not have borne his cross, and suffered for him. 2. Christianity is as old as true religion. 3. The cross, and reproach, hath attended on true religion in all ages. 4. What reproach men suffer for true religion is reckoned to be Christ's reproach, and not theirs. 5. Reproach and shame is the heaviest part of the cross, for under it is all comprised here.

2. The next motive was, his respect unto the recompence of the reward; which also made him to esteem the reproach his riches.

Then, 1. There is a reward for such as suffer reproach for Christ. 2. It is lawful, yea, needful for men to have respect unto this reward, and to draw encouragement from it, even for their own strengthening. 3. Though the cross seem terrible, yet faith can pierce through it, and behold the reward following it. 4. When sufferings for Christ are rightly seen, they are the richest and most glorious passages in all our life.

Ver. 27. By faith he forsook Egypt, not fearing the wrath of the king; for he endured, as seeing him who is invisible.

Another work of faith is, his leading of the people from their dwelling-places in Egypt to the wilderness, with the hazard of the wrath of Pharaoh if he should overtake them.

Then, whatever it seem unto us now, after it is done, it was no small faith at that time, to undertake such a business, to turn his back upon a fertile land, and go with such a company, without provision, to the wilderness. 2. His faith is commended for not fearing the wrath of the king, Exod. ii. 14. Moses feared the wrath of Pharaoh, and fled. After that,

Exod. x. 29, he feared not another Pharaoh, as terrible as the former.

Then, where natural courage would succumb, faith will sustain; yea, and make a man endure, (as it is spoken in the next words) where natural courage, having led him on a little, would forsake him at length.

3. The encouragement unto this work was, he saw him that is invisible; that is, he apprehended by faith God more powerful than Pharaoh, and more terrible.

Then, 1. Faith openeth the eyes to see God in a spiritual manner, who by sense, or imagination carnal, cannot be conceived. 2. The beholding of the invisible God is able to support a man's courage, against the terror of men, and all things visible; and nothing else can do it.

VER. 28. Through faith he kept the passover, and the sprinkling of blood, lest he that destroyed the firstborn should touch them.

Another work of his faith is, his keeping of the passover; that is, the sacrament of the angel's passing over, and not destroying the people.

Then, 1. It is usual for Scripture, speaking of sacraments, to give the name of the thing signified to the sign, because the sign is the memorial of the thing signified. Circumcision is called the covenant, Gen. xvii. 13, because it is the memorial thereof. The paschal supper, for the like cause, is here called the passover, which was the work of the angel, because it was, by appointment, the memorial of it. So the cup in the Lord's supper is called "the new testament in Christ's blood;" and the bread, in the same supper, is called "the broken body of Christ," because it is the memorial thereof. 2. It is the work of faith to celebrate a sacrament rightly. 3. As Moses celebrated the passover in assurance that the destroying angel should not touch the people of Israel, so may every believer be certified, by using the sacrament, that the grace promised and sealed in the sacrament shall be bestowed.

VER. 29. By faith they passed through the Red Sea as by dry land: which the Egyptians essaying to do were drowned.

He joineth the faith of the true Israelites with the faith of Moses, for whose sakes the rest of the incredulous multitude got the benefit of delivery also through the Red Sea, which was the fruit of the believer's faith. Whence we learn,

1. That faith will find unexpected deliveries and outgates, where it might seem altogether impossible. 2. Yea, means of destruction by faith may be turned into means of preservation.

2. The fruit of faith is evidenced by the drowning of the Egyptians, essaying themselves to follow that way which faith had opened to Israel.

Then, 1. Presumption in unbelievers will set them on work to go through the same dangers which believers pass through; but without all success, for believers shall escape where unbelievers shall drown. 3. The benefit of faith is best seen when the evil of unbelief is seen.

VER. 30. By faith the walls of Jericho fell down, after they were compassed about seven days.

He ascribeth the downthrowing of the walls of Jericho to faith, making the believers only to compass them seven days.

Then, 1. What God doth for believers is reckoned the work of faith, because faith setteth God on work so to say, and his power, employed by faith, worketh the work. 2. Faith will throw down strongholds, and overcome seeming impossibilities. 3. Faith must use such means as God appointeth, albeit they seem but weak. 4. It matters not how weak the means be, if faith have a promise to prevail thereby. 5. The means must be constantly used during the time that God appointeth them to be followed.

VER. 31. By faith the harlot Rahab perished not with them that believed not, when she had received the spies with peace.

Rahab the harlot's faith is commended by the fruit of her safety, when misbelievers perished.

Quest. How heard she God's word to beget faith? Or how heard they of Jericho God's word, that they should be called unbelievers?

I answer, the common report of God, and his works, joined with God's blessing, was sufficient to beget faith in her: and the same report, albeit carried, as other news, by common messengers, being despised, and counted unworthy to be further inquired for and sought after, was sufficient to make them guilty of misbelief.

Then, 1. In this example it is evident that faith is as acceptable in a heathen, and a harlot, as in a professor and person of better condition. 2. That faith can change a heathen, or vile person, into a saint. 3. That the faith of women is to be observed and imitated, even as well as men's faith. 4. That the unworthiness of the party believing giveth commendation so much the more unto the excellency of faith.

2. No word here of her lie in receiving the spies, but only of her faith and peaceable behaviour towards them.

Then, 1. Where God seeth faith, he hideth his eye, as it were, from any thing that might deface the glory thereof. 2. He gathereth up the smallest good fruits which faith bringeth forth, and maketh not small reckoning thereof, how small soever they be.

VER. 32. And what shall I more say? for the time would fail me to tell of Gideon, and of Barak, and of Samson, and of Jephtha; of David also, and Samuel, and of the prophets.

Having reckoned a number, and having more to produce, he stayeth his course to teach,

1. That prudency must moderate, and make seasonable use of, the abundance of man's knowledge and memory. 2. That the Scripture giveth us to make use of the faith of all that are recorded therein, albeit they be not in this catalogue.

2. The diversity of those that are here recorded teacheth us, that albeit there be difference of believers, some stronger, as David; some weaker, as the rest; some base bastards, as Jephtha; some of better sort, some of them notable in holiness and conversation, some of them tainted with notorious falls in their lives; yet are they all enrolled by

God, in a catalogue of honour, amongst his saints.

Ver. 33. Who through faith subdued kingdoms, wrought righteousness, obtained promises, stopped the mouths of lions:

Ver. 34. Quenched the violence of fire, escaped the edge of the sword, out of weakness were made strong, waxed valiant in fight, and turned to flight the armies of the aliens.

He reckoneth the works of their faith, whose names he suppresseth, of whom some subdued kingdoms by their faith, as Joshua and the Judges; some wrought righteousness, that is, attained unto a righteous behaviour, in their difficile [difficult] employments, as David and Samuel, in peace and war; some obtained promises, as Gideon, Barak, &c.; some quenched the violence of fire, as the three children; stopped the mouths of lions, as Samson, Daniel; escaped the sword, as David, Elijah; of weak were made strong, as Hezekiah; waxed valiant in fight, as Joshua, Samson, David; put to flight the aliens, as Jonathan, Gideon, Jehoshaphat; women received their dead alive, as the widow of Sarepta, and the Shunammitess, &c.

Whence we learn, that in the old church, under the law, when the grounds of believing were not so clear as now they are, excellent things are recorded to be done by faith, for upstirring such as are under the light of the gospel to make use of faith. 2. That neither fire nor water, nor man nor beast, is so strong but faith may make a weak man victorious over them all. 3. Yea, nothing so terrible, or difficile, [difficult] but a man who hath God's word to be a ground for his faith, may adventure upon it, with assurance of prevailing. If he be called, he may encounter with the hardest party.

Ver. 35. Women received their dead raised to life again: and others were tortured, not accepting deliverance; that they might obtain a better resurrection:

Ver. 36. And others had trial of cruel mockings and scourgings, yea, moreover, of bonds and imprisonment:

Ver. 37. They were stoned, they were sawn asunder, were tempted, were slain with the sword: they wandered about in sheepskins and goatskins, being destitute, afflicted, tormented:

Whether the apostle hath taken these particulars from the records extant in the time, from the books of Maccabees and others, or not, it matters not much, seeing this standeth sure, that the certainty of the truth thereof was from Divine inspiration, the ground of all scriptures' outgiving. And hence we learn, 1. That as faith enableth men to do, so also to suffer. 2. That there is no trouble in the flesh but God's children may fall thereinto; no torment so cruel, no terror nor allurement, but they may be essayed in them by persecutors. 3. That there is no pain, nor grief,

nor loss, so great, but faith knows how to make gain of it, and to despise all in hope of the reward. 4. That the old church believed the resurrection, and comforted themselves in martyrdom by the hope thereof.

Ver. 38. (Of whom the world was not worthy:) they wandered in deserts, and in mountains, and in dens and caves of the earth.

In calling the world unworthy of the company of these children of God, learn, 1. That one believer is more worth in God's estimation than all the world beside. 2. None despise God's children but worthless and despiseable souls. 2. In that he reckoneth the solitary and hermitical life of God's children, and their apparel suitable to their dwelling, amongst their troubles, sufferings, and persecutions, which they did not choose, but were driven unto of necessity, by the cruelty of the time, he teacheth us, 1. That the hermitical and solitary life and separation from amongst the society of men is only then commendable when men being driven thereunto of necessity, do bear it in a Christian manner. Otherwise, to sequestrate ourselves from the fellowship of men, to whom we owe the duties of love, so long as we may do them any good, or so long as they will suffer us to live amongst them, is in short to loose from our necks the yoke of the second table, under pretence to keep the first table the better. 2. The saints shall find peace amongst the wild beasts rather than amongst wicked men.

Ver. 39. And these all, having obtained a good report through faith, received not the promise:

By the promise is meant the main and chief promise of Christ's incarnation, wherein they were inferior unto us, and yet both were contented to rest by faith upon the promise with the light which they had, and obtained a good report thereby; that is, were approved and justified of God.

Then, the faith of those who lived before Christ having less clearness of the ground than we, and yet sufficient to support them in all troubles and to obtain justification before God, is a great encouragement unto us under the gospel to believe, and a great conviction if we believe not.

Ver. 40. God having provided some better thing for us, that they without us should not be made perfect.

He giveth a reason thereof: Because God hath appointed the accomplishment of the promise of sending the Messiah to be in the last times, that they should not be perfected, that is, justified and saved by any thing done in their time, but by looking to our time, and Christ's satisfaction made therein, whereby they and we are perfected together.

Then, 1. Christ's coming in these last times is a better thing than all the glory of the old church and service and prerogatives thereof. 2. All the shadows in their time without Christ, who is the substance of them all, in our time exhibited, was unable to perfect the fathers, that is, to justify and save them. 3. The perfecting of the fathers in the Old Testament, and the perfecting of us in the New Testament, do meet together in that one better thing, Christ Jesus, by whom they and we both are saved; and so they are not perfected without us.

2. In that he leadeth us unto God foreseeing and foreproviding of this, he looseth all curious questions about this course which God hath taken, to make the case of his church better now than of old.

Then, that God hath thought good so to do, is sufficient for stopping our minds from all curious inquiring of the Lord's dispensation.

THE SUM OF CHAP. XII.

The use of all these examples is, that we hold on in the course of Christianity whatsoever trouble may meet us in the way, ver. 1. Looking on Christ for your pattern, ver. 2. And for your encouragement also, lest you faint, ver. 3. For you have not suffered so much as you must be ready to suffer, ver. 4. And you have forgotten that chastisements are tokens of God's favour, ver. 5. For he loveth whom he chasteneth, ver. 6. And your enduring thereof shall prove you sons, ver. 7. But immunity should prove you bastards, ver. 8. We have borne our parents' correction, and why should we not now bear God's? ver. 9. For they chastened us to satisfy their own passions, but God for our profit, ver. 10. And albeit affliction be grievous now, yet the fruits shall be sweet afterwards, ver. 11. Wherefore take you comfort, ver. 12; and courage to go stoutly on, lest by discouragement you fall into apostasy; but rather seek to recover the courage which you have lost, ver. 13. Follow peace with all men; but holiness also, as you would be saved, ver. 14. Beware of the unmortified roots of sin, lest they break out in scandals, ver. 15. Beware lest there be any filthy or profane body suffered among you, as Esau was, ver. 16, who sold the blessing for a short pleasure, and could never recover it again, ver. 17. And to this you are obliged, because the old church was not so privileged as you are; but for their external estate and manner of religion in a great deal of more bondage, ver. 18—21. But you, by the light of the gospel, are brought into the highway to have society with heaven and angels, and the catholic church of elect souls, and God the Judge, and Christ the Mediator, and his benefits. So clear now is the doctrine, ver. 22—24. Therefore beware, lest by your apostasy you reject Christ's offer, and be destroyed more fearfully than the despisers of the law, ver. 25. For Christ is a terrible Lord to his foes, his voice shook the earth in giving of the law; but he hath promised to shake heaven and earth once more, ver. 26. And once more importeth the removing of these and making of a new heaven and a new earth, wherein dwelleth righteousness, for the settled and perpetual remaining of his kingdom, ver. 27. Therefore, let us keep a fast hold of his grace, that we worship him with fear, ver. 28. For if we do not so, even our God is a consuming fire, ver. 29.

THE DOCTRINE OF CHAP. XII.

VER. 1. Wherefore seeing we also are compassed about with so great a cloud of witnesses, let us lay aside every weight, and the sin which doth so easily beset us, and let us run with patience the race which is set before us,

That right use may be made of all the former examples, he exhorteth to a constant and patient persevering in the course of Christianity.

1. The similitude is borrowed from a race. To teach us to endeavour for overtaking all the duties of the Christian man with all the skill and strength and speed we can.

2. The original importeth a strife or race. To advertise us both of our spiritual adversaries against whom we must fight still as we go on, and of our compartners who run in the race with us, with whom we may strive in holy emulation who shall go foremost in the course of pleasing God.

3. It is a race limited, the race set before us. To teach us what way we should hold on our course, not doing that which pleaseth us, every man running his own way of religion, but all running the beaten way, the royal way of God's commandments.

4. For the motives unto this race, he useth the examples rehearsed in the former chapter, who compass us about as a cloud of witnesses, to teach us,

1. To hearken to the deposition of these worthy witnesses who are recorded in Scripture, who can best show what is the best Christian way which we must hold in our course towards happiness. 2. Then all our behaviour is marked by spectators, God, angels, and men. 3. That albeit there were none to see us, except our conscience, the examples of God's saints in Scripture should stand as witnesses against us if we run not as becometh.

For direction how to run, he teacheth, 1. To lay aside all weights which do press our minds downwards, such as is the setting of our affection upon things which are on earth, either wittingly upon unlawful objects, or inconsiderately exceeding the bounds of Christian moderation upon things lawful. 2. To lay aside the sin which so easily doth beset us; that is, by studying to mortify the body of our corrupt inclination, to cut off the wood-bind growth of violent predominant and wily sins which most frequently get advantage of us. 3. Because we cannot end our race but after some progress of time, and must meet with many impediments in the way, and troubles and temptations to arm ourselves with patience.

VER. 2. Looking unto Jesus the author and finisher of our faith; who, for the joy that was set before him endured the cross, despising the shame, and is set down at the right hand of the throne of God.

With direction he joineth encouragement, by setting our eye on Jesus, who shall both guide us in the way, and carry us on when our strength faileth.

Then, 1. The Christian race-runner hath Jesus before him in the way to help him in every thing that may befall him in his course. 2. Christ must be looked upon by him who would be helped in the race ; the eye of the soul being drawn off of every thing which might divert the man or discourage him, (such as are the multitude of backsliders, the multitude of mockers, the multitude of by-ways and runners therein, the multitude of fears from our own unworthiness and sinfulness, and temptations on all sides,) and our minds fixed on Christ with loving and longing looks, which may draw life and strength from him. 3. We must look on him as Jesus, the deliverer from sins and giver of salvation, even him who saveth his people from their sins. 4. We must look upon him as the author and finisher of our faith; that is, as our God, who hath begun his good work in us and will also perfect it, who hath given us grace to believe, and will surely continue this grace with us, even to the end, lest the fears of our faith failing make us to faint. 5. We must look upon him as our pattern and example, who having run the race before us, hath set forth himself for our imitation, that in him we might find all whereof we stand in need.

2. How Jesus ran this race he showeth for our example. 1. He had joy set before him, which he was to receive by our salvation wrought. So have we joy set before us also. 2. For the hope of that joy he ran with courage. So must we. 3. He ran with the cross upon his back all the way, being a man acquainted with sorrows. So must we resolve also. 4. In his griefs and sorrows, shame set upon him from the world and poured out contempt upon him. So must we resolve to find it. 5. For the hope of the joy he endured patiently, and went on under the cross and wearied not. So must we. 6. Albeit shame was the sharpest of his griefs from the world, yet he regarded it not, but despised all despising, and shamed shame, as unworthy to be taken notice of in comparison with his design. So must we. 7. He overcame all at length. So shall we through him also. 8. He hath gotten the joy and the glory for which he ran. So shall we with him. If we suffer with him we shall also reign with him. 9. He is set down on the right hand of the throne of God ; that is, is joined with the Father in the glorious government of heaven and earth and all things therein, for the good of all his followers. So that we need to fear nothing in our way, seeing he hath the government of all.

VER. 3. For consider him that endured such contradiction of sinners against himself, lest ye be wearied and faint in your minds.

He pointeth forth a special part of his suffering, namely, the contradiction of sinners, willing them to ponder this well for their uphold [support].

Then, 1. Nothing more forcible to discourage a persecuted Christian than contradiction. A man will suffer much if he know it be for truth ; but if the truth for which he suffereth be called in question, and scribes and Pharisees and chief churchmen shall contradict him and brangle [lessen] his faith in the truth, it is more pitiful than a rack-stock unto him. 2. The considera-

tion of our Lord Jesus, his being exercised this way, is a special mean to guard us in such a temptation. 3. If we be not armed against contradiction by certain knowledge of the truth and faith in Jesus, we cannot hold out, but upon force weary under the cross, and be lost or dissolved like water, and fall by, as the word importeth.

VER. 4. Ye have not yet resisted unto blood, striving against sin.

These Hebrews were somewhat dashed and discouraged by the persecution which they had already borne, and were like to faint. Therefore he setteth them on to prepare for suffering to the blood, that every suffering less nor [than] that might be the more tolerable in their eyes.

1. He maketh their party, sin. Then, 1. Christians must remember, in their troubles, that they are tried, whether they will choose to sin or to suffer. 2. When they disobey their persecutors, they must not be interpreted to be strivers against them, so much as against sin. 3. With what colour or pretence soever sin be urged upon Christians, they must not yield, but resist in a Christian manner, and fight Christianly against that sin whereunto they are tempted. The more stedfastly they resist, they must prepare themselves for the more suffering, and resolve at length to lay down their blood in suffering. No yielding to sin must be, while life is in us.

2. He maketh the greater sufferings which remain, a reason to make them bear the present the better.

Then, 1. Suffering in a man's person is the highest degree of suffering. 2. Resolution for the worst that can come, maketh lesser troubles more comportable. 3. Except a man prepare himself for the worst that can be done unto him by man, for the truth, he will faint in lesser sufferings.

VER. 5. And ye have forgotten the exhortation which speaketh unto you as unto children, My son, despise not thou the chastening of the Lord, nor faint when thou art rebuked of him.

From the general doctrine of bearing afflictions, Prov. iii. 11, 12, he stirreth them up to Christian patience in persecution and every other trouble.

Then, persecution for righteousness cometh in the account of chastisement, and is appointed, among other ends, to amend our faults.

1. He maketh these Hebrews the party to whom the Proverbs were directed, and God the speaker thereof.

Then, 1. Whosoever be the penmen of the Scripture, it is God who speaketh in it. 2. The Scriptures do direct their speech to every age, and church, and person, no less than to those who lived in the church of old, when it was first written.

2. He chargeth them for their forgetting of such a kindly speech, as is the styling of the afflicted by the names of sons.

Then, 1. The special point of faith, which the Lord will have fostered under the cross, is the faith of our adoption, that we never mistake our Father's affection, nor our gracious state by calling, for any hard dealing wherewith possibly we may be exercised. 2. He will have us assured of our adoption by God's manner of speaking unto us, as a father to his children. 3. He showeth us, that the not remembering of the word of God speaking unto us according to our estate, is the cause of fainting and of mistaking.

3. The exhortation dischargeth despising of the rod, and fainting under the rod.

Then, 1. These are the two evils which we are inclined unto, either to harden ourselves against corrections, and count light of them, or else to be discouraged and cast down by them; both of which we must eschew. 2. Though the Lord both strike and rebuke for sin, yet esteemeth he us to be sons not the less.

VER. 6. For whom the Lord loveth he chasteneth, and scourgeth every son whom he receiveth.

He giveth a reason to confirm the afflicted, in the certainty of their sonship; teaching us,
1. That neither chastisement, yea, nor scourging, which is the sharpest measure of correction, is a sign of God's hatred, but of his love rather. 2. That God's dealing with all his children in general, being considered, may mitigate the case of any of them in particular.

VER. 7. If ye endure chastening, God dealeth with you as with sons; for what son is he whom the father chasteneth not?

From this he urgeth the patient bearing of God's chastisements, that they may know adoption the better.

Then, though God be the afflicted person's Father, yet is he not perceived to deal as a father, but when the affliction is patiently borne and endured.

VER. 8. But if ye be without chastisement, whereof all are partakers, then are ye bastards, and not sons.

Albeit men desire naturally to go free from trouble, yet he showeth that this is not to be chosen; and to this end teacheth,
1. That it is the common lot of all God's children, without exception, to be acquainted with some cross, and exercised with some correction, of one kind or other. 2. That to be exempted from the cross, and common handling of God's children, is to be put out of the roll of children. 3. That in the visible church all are not freeborn children, but some are bastards, which the church holdeth possibly for children, but God reckoneth to be none. 4. That among other marks, this is one of a bastard: If God let him alone, and suffer him, without discipline, to follow his own ways.

VER. 9. Furthermore we have had fathers of our flesh which corrected us, and we gave them reverence: shall we not much rather be in subjection unto the Father of spirits, and live?

From submitting to our parent's correction, he urgeth to bear the Lord's correction. Whence we learn,
1. That as it is a part of the parents' duty to correct their children, so it is a part of that reverence due to parents, that children receive their correction without change of affection towards their parents. 2. That God is the Father of spirits in a special manner, because they are immediately created by him, and do not run in the material channel of fleshly descent, and because they have a more near resemblance unto his divine nature. 3. That receiving correction is counted subjection to God, and refusing correction is refusing of subjection. 4. That submission to chastisement is the way to life.

VER. 10. For they verily for a few days chastened us after their own pleasure; but he for our profit, that we might be partakers of his holiness.

He compareth the chastisement of our earthly parents with God's chastisement. Whence we learn,
1. That parents sometimes chastise their children out of mere passion, and at the best have some mixture of their own humours in chastising; but God never mixeth passion with his rod, but intendeth our profit therein only. 2. The special profit intended by God in our correction, is the making of us partakers of his holiness; partly while he driveth us thereby to seek our righteousness in himself, and partly while he mortifieth our nature, and reneweth our affections, and sanctifieth us for himself.

VER. 11. Now no chastening for the present seemeth to be joyous, but grievous: nevertheless afterwards it yieldeth the peaceable fruit of righteousness, unto them which are exercised thereby.

He meeteth the doubt of the felt grief of present affliction, by showing the fruit which followeth thereupon at after [afterwards], and teacheth us,
1. That it is the pain of present affliction which maketh us unwilling to endure. 2. That we must not, like children, judge of affliction by our present sense, but by looking to the fruit which doth follow, must season to ourselves the felt bitterness. 3. That the fruit of affliction is righteousness, or sanctification, which bringeth peace with it. 4. That this fruit possibly will not be found incontinent after one affliction or two, but after we be exercised, acquainted, and made patient in bearing the yoke.

VER. 12. Wherefore lift up the hands which hang down, and the feeble knees;

From these considerations he will have them to draw comfort and courage, and to recover themselves from their dejection of mind. Teaching us,
1. That afflictions bring discouragements with

them, whereby hand and heart fail in God's service. 2. That discouragements must be resisted by consideration of God the author, and his wise ends of afflicting of us.

VER. 13. And make straight paths for your feet, lest that which is lame be turned out of the way ; but let it rather be healed.

Under a similitude borrowed from walking in a narrow and dangerous path, he exhorteth them boldly to avow the truth, lest their fearfulness and apparent doubtfulness should tend at length to defection. Then,

1. No trouble must so dash us, as to make us seek by-paths, for eschewing thereof. 2. In a good course we must not halt, nor walk feebly, nor fearfully, but stoutly and straight up, avowing what is right. 3. As a man in a dangerous path, by halting, may be swayed to the one side, and thrown over the bray [brae, the side of a hill] ; so a man that fairly maintaineth a good cause may be overcome at length, and driven from it.

The apostle's diligence and prudence to recover these fainting Hebrews, teacheth,

1. That we must not cast down our countenance on weak brethren, who do not so boldly avow the truth as they should do, but rather ought to strengthen and heal them, and hold their staggering faith on foot. 2. That such feeble souls must be timeously dealt with, that they may be healed, as long as they are yet in the way, and have not shaken hands with an evil course.

VER. 14. Follow peace with all men, and holiness, without which no man shall see the Lord.

Having thus dealt with them, for strengthening them in the faith, and bold profession thereof, he giveth them a number of wholesome precepts for ordering of their life and conversation.

From the precept for following of peace and holiness, learn,

1. That we must beware of all provocation of any amongst whom we live ; for we have troubles enough, albeit we make none to ourselves. 2. That how wicked soever the world be, we may follow a course of living in peace with them, and if peace flee from us, we may and should pursue after it, as far as is lawful. 3. The farthest we may follow peace with men, is as it may stand with holiness and duty towards God. 4. It is more dangerous to quit holiness than to quit peace ; for he that followeth holiness shall see God, albeit he find not peace amongst men. But if any man prefer men's peace before holiness, while he gaineth men, he loseth God. 5. To see God, that is, to enjoy God's fellowship, is the sum of our blessedness.

VER. 15. Looking diligently lest any man fail of the grace of God ; lest any root of bitterness springing up trouble you, and thereby many be defiled.

He giveth direction here for eschewing a fall from grace ; that is, from the doctrine of grace in begun knowledge, faith, love, renovation, or any measure thereof.

Then, 1. Albeit the elect cannot fall away fully and finally, yet some professors in the visible church may fall away from their profession, and what degrees of grace they had attained unto ; for whose cause warning must be given to all, as a mean to keep the elect from a fall. 2. Albeit the elect cannot fall away finally from grace, yet may they fall, for a time, from the purity of the doctrine of grace, and from some degrees of the work of grace ; from the measure of their first love and zeal, and at length fall into scandalous sins.

He joineth another point of advertisement with the former : that they beware lest any bitter root break forth, whereby many be defiled : that is, lest any scandalous sin break forth amongst them.

Then, 1. As men do fall from any measure of the work of grace, so doth the bitter root of unmortified sin spring out and grow. The one's decreasing is the other's increasing. 2. When any scandal breaketh forth in the church, it troubleth the whole body, and polluteth them, by the contagion thereof, till it be removed. 3. Watch must be kept diligently, by every man, to curb this bitter root, preventing the outshooting thereof.

VER. 16. Lest there be any fornicator, or profane person, as Esau, who for one morsel of meat sold his birthright.

He expoundeth this "bitter root," in the example of fornication and profanity, like Esau's.

Then, 1. Fornication and profanity are the bitter roots of other evils, and able to defile a congregation. 2. Such as count more of the satisfaction of their sensual lusts than of their spiritual prerogatives, do prove themselves profane persons, and are justly ranked in with Esau.

VER. 17. For ye know how that afterward, when he would have inherited the blessing, he was rejected : for he found no place of repentance, though he sought it carefully with tears.

He showeth God's judgment on Esau, to terrify all men, to hazard upon the sinful satisfaction of their own lusts, at any time.

Then, 1. Esau's judgment should be a terror to all men, to keep them from presuming deliberately to commit that sin, which they know may cut them off from the blessing ; because sundry times (albeit not always) God doth punish presumptuous sinners with giving over the man to his own ways, and final impenitency. 2. Esau's example showeth how justly they may be deprived of the blessing annexed to any sacred symbol or gracious mean, who do despise the mean whereby the blessing is conveyed. For the birthright amongst the patriarchs was a pawn of the blessing of being an heir of promise, and therefore was Esau counted to reject the blessing when he counted light of the birthright. 3. His example showeth how little sinners consider for the present what merchandise they are making with Satan when they meddle with known sins, and how they will be made to know it afterwards.

2. He saith that afterwards he would have inherited the blessing, but was rejected.

Then, it agreeth with the profane man's disposition to desire the blessing, and yet despise the means whereby the blessing is gotten; to satisfy his fleshly lusts for the present, and to desire the blessing withal afterwards. But God will neither sever the means from the blessing, nor join the blessing with the satisfaction of men's lusts. Therefore, he who will have the blessing must use the means to obtain the same, and renounce the satisfaction of his sinful lusts, or else be rejected when he thinketh to get the blessing.

3. He saith, he found no place of repentance, albeit he sought the blessing with tears; that is, he could not obtain that his father should repent the bestowing of the blessing beside him; nor that God should repent his righteous judgment on him. For repentance, here, is recalling the sentence given out. And why? Because he, for all his tears, and untimous seeking of his sold blessing, repented not himself of his sin; for he continued as profane as before, and resolved to murder his brother as soon as he found opportunity.

Then, 1. Esau did rue his deed, but repented not his sin. It is one thing to rue a deed done, and another thing to repent the sin in doing of the deed, and every known sin for that sin's cause. 2. Tears may follow upon ruing, as well as on repenting; and it is possible that the loss or harm procured by sin may draw forth the tear, and not the sorrow for the offending of God by the sin. 3. Esau here is not brought in dealing with God for pardon of sin, and the heavenly inheritance, but with the man who had the ministry of dispensing the earthly blessing only.

We read, then, that a blessing was sought carefully from a man, with tears, and not obtained; but we read not that God's mercy and blessing was ever sought from himself, carefully, and not obtained.

VER. 18. For ye are not come unto the mount that might be touched, and that burned with fire nor unto blackness, and darkness, and tempest,

Beside the example of Esau's judgment, here is another reason to move us who are under the gospel, to beware of licentiousness and profanity, because we are delivered from the terror of the law, ver. 18—21, and brought by the gospel to the society of so holy a company as beseemeth no profane man to enjoy, ver. 22—24. The sum tendeth unto this, You are not under the law, but under grace. Instead of saying whereof, he sayeth, "You are not come unto Mount Sinai, but unto Mount Sion." For the Lord's manner of dealing with the people at Mount Sinai represented the state of men in nature, under the law, liable to the curse. His manner of dealing with them at Mount Sion represented the state of men reconciled through Christ, and under grace. Let us take a view of both, as the apostle setteth them before our eyes; and first, how the state of man unreconciled, in nature, and under the law, and curse thereof, was represented.

1. Before we come to Christ, we have to do with God, as a terrible judge, sitting on the throne of his justice, shadowed forth by Mount Sinai. 2. Our Judge is offended with us, his wrath is kindled, ready to consume us, as his adversaries, in our transgressions, represented by the burning of the Mount. 3. When God beginneth to show himself as our Judge, offended with us, we are filled with confusion, and perplexity, and fire; represented by blackness, and darkness, and tempest.

VER. 19. And the sound of a trumpet, and the voice of words; which voice they that heard intreated that the word should not be spoken to them any more:

VER. 20. (For they could not endure that which was commanded, And if so much as a beast touch the mountain, it shall be stoned, or thrust through with a dart:

What further? 4. There is no flying from compearance [appearance] before our Judge: summons and citation go forth from him, and powerfully seize upon the conscience, to cause it acknowledge the Judge; represented by the sound of the trumpet. 5. The killing letter of the law read out unto us, showing us our dittie [doom], what we should have done, and what omitted, and what we should not have done, and have committed; without giving any strength to obey for time to come; represented by the sound of words. 6. By this charge, and new exaction of the law, an unsupportable weight lieth upon the conscience, pressing it down to desperation and death; that we would give all the world, if we had it, to be free of the terror of the Lord, and challenge of the conscience upon so fearful a dittie [doom]; represented by the people's entreating that the word should not be spoken to them any more. 7. There is an impossibility to help ourselves by any thing we can do, or to do any better than we have done; and the seen impotency of our cursed nature maketh the commandment, for time to come, a matter of desperation, as well as the challenge for breaking the law in time bygone; represented by their inability to endure the thing which was commanded. 8. No drawing near to God here, such terror in his majesty; justice being only seen, and no mercy; represented by their debarring from touching the mountain. 9. Such uncleanness, and vileness, as not only ourselves but our beasts and cattle, and all that we have, is counted unclean for our cause, and liable to the curse with us; represented by the debarring of the beasts from the mount. 10. Such a loathsome abomination in the guilty, as the Judge will not put hand on the malefactor himself, nor employ any of his clean angels, but give them over to death, if they remain in that state, to be destroyed ignominiously; represented by stoning or darting, where the stone or dart lighteth upon the malefactor, but not the hand which threw it.

VER. 21. And so terrible was the sight, that Moses said, I exceedingly fear and quake:)

Yet further. 11. If God deal with us as Judge, and by the rule of the law examine our works, were we, like Moses, the meekest men under heaven, the least harmful and innocent in the world, richest in good works, for service done to God and to his church, yet could we not stand before this tribunal; all that ever we had done, all our works, were not able to free us from the curse of the law, and God's fearful wrath for our sinfulness mixed amongst our works; represented by Moses' professed fear and quaking. 12. And, with all this, no place to flee unto, no place to remain in; no company but an evil conscience within, and matter of terror without; represented by the wilderness, wherein this throne of justice was set up. And this is the estate wherein we are by nature, according to the law; from which we are delivered by Christ, according to the gospel, as followeth.

VER. 22. But ye are come unto Mount Sion, and unto the city of the living God, the heavenly Jerusalem, and to an innumerable company of angels,

This is the estate whereunto we are advanced under the gospel, by Christ; which by comparison with the former shall be more clear, thus: 1. Before we come to Christ we have to do with God, as Judge, sitting upon his throne, terrible. After we come to Christ we find God upon a throne of grace, reconciled unto us; resembled by Mount Sion. 2. Without Christ we are kept under, upon the earth, depressed in the valley, and may not touch the Mount, to ascend; but through Christ we get access to climb up towards God, and to advance, piece by piece, above the world, and sin, and misery, towards heaven; resembled by going up Mount Sion. 3. Without Christ, vagabonds, wandering abroad in a waste wilderness; but through Christ collected together under a head, and brought to a place of refuge and rest, and commodious dwelling, to the kingdom of heaven; resembled by the city where Mount Sion stood. 4. Without Christ, exposed to the wrath of the living God; through Christ, admitted to remain, as reconciled, in the city of the living God. 5. Without Christ, afraid, by the terrible sight of wrath and judgment; through Christ, brought into Jerusalem, the vision of peace, not only in this world by faith, but in heaven by fruition; resembled by Jerusalem. 6. Without Christ, heirs of hell; through Christ, citizens of heaven. 7. Without Christ, exposed to the fellowship of devils, in sin and torments: through Christ, admitted to the society of innumerable angels; resembled by the inhabitants of Jerusalem on earth. 8. Without Christ, angels our foes; through Christ, our fellow-citizens.

VER. 23. To the general assembly and church of the firstborn, which are written in heaven, and to God the Judge of all, and to the spirits of just men made perfect,

9. Without Christ, we are as scattered sheep in the wilderness, a prey to all the ravenous beasts: but through Christ, gathered together in one, to the society of the true catholic church of the elect, under the government of one head, even Christ. 10. Without Christ, living with the world, in the suburbs of hell: through Christ, made members of the true church, and company, which is called out of the world, by the effectual calling of his word and Spirit. 11. Without Christ, forlorn children, who have deprived ourselves of our inheritance, and wasted all our father's benefits on vanities: through Christ our fore-faulting [misery] is reduced, our inheritance redeemed, we brought back to the family, restored to the inheritance, dignified with the first born, and made priests to our God, as his portion from amongst men. 12. Without Christ, living amongst them whose names are written in the earth, and whose portion is beneath: through Christ, our names are enrolled in heaven amongst those who are written in the book of life, elected and predestinated unto grace and glory. 13. Without Christ, without God in the world, having God our judge against us: through Christ, we are reconciled to God, get access unto him, and have our God, judge of all, upon our side, to absolve us, and to plead for us against all our foes. 14. Without Christ, we are for guiltiness, in the rank of those who are already damned, and brethren to those whose spirits are in prison: but through Christ we are brethren to those who are already saved, whose souls and spirits are freed from sin and misery, and made perfect in holiness and glory; having the same grounds of right to heaven, through Christ, which they have who are entered already into possession.

VER. 24. And to Jesus, the Mediator of the new covenant, and to the blood of sprinkling, which speaketh better things than that of Abel.

He goeth on. 15. In our natural estate we are under the law, and the covenant of works, which bindeth us to perfect obedience, or to the curse. When we come to Christ, we are under the covenant of grace, which proclaimeth remission of sins unto all who are in him. 16. Yea, now under the gospel, coming unto Christ, we are in better case than they who lived before Christ, because they were bound to all the ceremonial and typical ordinances of the law under the old covenant, but we are exempted from that old covenant, and are entered into the new, which freeth us from that yoke which the Israelites could never bear. 17. Without Christ, we stand alone, and none to plead for us before our Judge: but when we come to Christ, we find him a Mediator both to deliver us from the old covenant, and to take burden for us for keeping of the new covenant. 18. Without Christ, unrighteous and unholy: when we come to Christ, we come to be sprinkled with his blood, for justification and sanctification also, and for receiving of all other benefits bought by that blood.

He compareth this blood with Abel's, as speaking better things. For albeit we by our sins have made our Lord to serve, yea, and to die also, yet doth his blood not speak against us, as Abel's did speak against Cain and the earth, for drawing down of a curse on both, but speaketh to God still to pacify his wrath, and to pardon us, and to our conscience to cleanse it, and make it quiet within us.

From this comparison of men under the law and under grace, we learn,

1. That the impenitent and unrenewed man, how secure soever he sit, yet he is in a fearful estate, the wrath of the Judge, from his justice seat, being ready to break out upon him. 2. That the awakened conscience, lying in the sense of its own sins, and fear of the offended Judge, is much to be pitied. 3. That the holiest man on earth, if God reveal unto him the terror of his justice, he will be shaken with fear. 4. That the only remedy against the challenge of the conscience, and fear of the law and wrath, is to have recourse to Jesus Christ. 5. That he who is fled, as a true penitent, to Jesus Christ for refuge, to be saved, and directed and ruled by him, is a true member of the true catholic church of the elect, whatsoever be men's estimation of him. 6. That the more graciously we be dealt with under the gospel, the more must we beware of fleshliness and profanity. For to this end all his speech doth tend.

VER. 25. See that ye refuse not him that speaketh. For if they escaped not who refused him that spake on earth ; much more shall not we escape, if we turn away from him that speaketh from heaven :

From these considerations he chargeth them to beware lest they make light account of Christ's doctrine. The word importeth a shifting of Christ, speaking by some excuse or pretence.

Then, 1. The way to eschew profaneness and apostasy, is to embrace and make much of Christ's speaking unto us in his word. 2. Whatsoever pretences and excuses a man use to cloak his not giving hearty obedience to the doctrine of Christ, it is but a refusing of him, and a turning away from him, make of it what he will.

2. He urgeth this by threatening more certain and heavy judgments than upon the despisers of Moses, who is said to speak on earth, because he was but the earthen vessel which carried God's will to his people, and by earthly types and figures made offer of grace unto them. But Christ, as God, by his own authority casting heaven open, in the plainness and spirituality of the doctrine, is said to speak from heaven.

Then, as much as Christ's person is more excellent than Moses, and his authority above his, and the heavenly clearness of Christ's gracious offer above his dark types ; as much more heavy and certain wrath shall overtake the despisers of his doctrine, than the despisers of Moses' law.

3. He joineth himself in the same danger with the people, if he should turn away or refuse.

Then, preachers shall do well to lay the edge of their threatenings to their own hearts, and to enroll themselves amongst the threatened, that bitterness towards the people may be seen to be removed, and their own sluggishness may be roused up, seeing they have none to preach unto them but themselves.

VER. 26. Whose voice then shook the earth : but now he hath promised, saying, Yet once

more I shake not the earth only, but also heaven.

To put an edge upon the threatening, he showeth how terrible Christ is in shaking of the earth by his voice at Mount Sinai, and by the shaking of heaven and earth at the day of judgment.

Then, 1. The terrible quaking of the earth, and burning of Mount Sinai, was pronounced by the voice of Christ, who therefore is declared to be the Lord God ; for so, Exod. xix., is he called. 2. His terror at the day of judgment may be seen in that little resemblance of Mount Sinai. 3. The terribleness of Christ should make us stand in awe of his word.

VER. 27. And this word, Yet once more, signifieth the removing of those things that are shaken, as of things that are made, that those things which cannot be shaken may remain.

He commenteth upon the testimony of Haggai, chap. i. 6, and from this word " once," concludeth that heaven and earth shall pass away, and be changed at the power of Christ's uttering of his voice ; that these changeable heavens and earth being removed, he may make a new heaven and a new earth, wherein his subjects, and his kingdom over them, may remain for ever settled.

Then, 1. It is a good mean to get the understanding of God's mind in Scripture, to consider and weigh the force of the words thereof, and what they do import by due consequence. 2. No more change shall be of any thing after the day of judgment, because " once more," and no oftener, is Christ to shake the same. 3. It is for the standing of Christ's kingdom that the creature is moved, shaken, and changed. All things made shall be shaken ; but Christ's kingdom, and the salvation of his subjects, shall never be shaken.

VER. 28. Wherefore we receiving a kingdom which cannot be moved, let us have grace, whereby we may serve God acceptably with reverence and godly fear ;

From the nature of this kingdom, granted unto us in Christ, and from his terribleness, he exhorteth us to stedfastness of faith and humble obedience. He saith, We have received it, because we have received the right and title by the gospel, and some beginning of it.

Then, as we receive Christ in the gospel, we receive the kingdom of heaven with him in right and title ; yea in begun possession, which groweth by degrees. 2. He requireth of a receiver of this kingdom a reverent serving of God.

Then, right is given to this kingdom before our service be done ; not because we have served heretofore, but to oblige us to serve God hereafter.

3. He will have us to serve God acceptably, that is, pleasantly and cheerfully. Next with reverence, or shamefacedness, and godly fear.

Then, 1. It is not enough that we do such works which belong to God's service, but we must take heed to the manner of doing of them, that they may be done with a ready affection and good will. 2. Next, that they be done in the sense of our own weakness, vileness, and unworthiness. 3. And thirdly, that they be done with reverend regard to God, in such a godly fear as may make us circumspectly handle and meddle with his service, as the word importeth. 4. That this may be the better done, " let us have grace," or hold fast the grip of " grace, whereby we may serve God," saith he.

Then, he that would have strength to serve God, must study by faith to lay hold on God's grace in the gospel, and having laid hold thereon, to hold it fast, for otherwise we can neither have heart nor hand to serve God. But he that is fastened on the grace and good will of God towards him, will draw courage and strength from this believed grace, to serve God cheerfully and reverently.

VER. 29. For our God is a consuming fire.

Because the holiest men have need of the spurs of God's terror to stir up their lazy flesh, he closeth with a watchword of Moses, Deut. iv. 24, terrifying the people from idolatry, or imagery, which he applieth for making men circumspect in their manner of worship.

Teaching us thereby, 1. That to serve idols, and follow a false religion, and not to serve God in reverence and godly fear, in the true religion, will be both alike plagued. 2. The words do teach us, that God's entering into covenant, and laying down of the feud and enmity against us, maketh him not to lay down his awful majesty over us. 3. And therefore we must be so confident of his love towards us, as we remember in the mean time that he is a consuming fire to the ungodly and profane professors of his name.

THE SUM OF CHAP. XIII.

Now, that you may be fruitful in the faith, I recommend to you, in short, brotherly love, ver. 1. Hospitality, ver. 2. Compassion, with sufferers for the truth, ver. 3. Chastity, ver. 4. Contentation, ver. 5, 6. Stedfastness in the truth, which God's messengers have taught you, ver. 7. For change who will, Christ, in himself, and in his doctrine, changeth not, ver. 8. Beware of the leaven of Jewish doctrine, such as is distinction of meats, and others like, ver. 9 ; for they who maintain the Levitical service cannot be partakers of Christ with us, ver. 10. This was prefigured in the law, ver. 11. So was Christ's contemptible usage, ver. 12. And we must follow him, and be contented of reproach for him, ver. 13 ; for we have no place of rest here, but look for it hereafter, ver. 14. Therefore let us follow the spiritual signification of those ceremonies, and sacrifice unto him our prayers, and praise, and good works, ver. 15, 16. Obey your ecclesiastical governors in their office, for their charge is great, and you have need not to grieve them, ver. 17. Pray for me, for I shall be found an honest man, whatever be men's speeches of me, ver. 18. But pray you for me, for your own good, ver. 19. And I pray God to finish his begun work in you graciously, ver. 20, 21 ; and because I have but touched things

briefly in this short epistle, take exhortation in good season, when your teachers do press such doctrine upon you more at length, ver. 22. It may be, that Timothy and I see you shortly, ver. 23. Deliver our commendations, ver. 24. And grace be with you all, Amen, ver. 25.

THE DOCTRINE OF CHAP. XIII.

VER. 1. Let brotherly love continue.

From this first precept, learn, 1. That the first fruit of faith which God requireth, is love, and constant love, amongst his children. 2. That our mutual love must be sincere and kindly ; as if it were grounded on bands of nature.

VER. 2. Be not forgetful to entertain strangers; for thereby some have entertained angels unawares.

From this precept, learn, 1. That we are ready to forget charity to strangers, especially to be hospitable unto them. 2. That the possibility of finding strangers better men than we take them to be, should overbalance the suspicion of their sleightness [artifice], and should set us on to do the duty. 3. That if a man intending to do good, do more than he intended to do, it shall be imputed unto him no less, than if he had intended the same.

VER. 3. Remember them that are in bonds, as bound with them ; and them which suffer adversity, as being yourselves also in the body.

From this learn, 1. That it is no new thing for the world, to put bonds on them who seek to bring them out of bondage. 2. That prisoners for Christ, are readily forgotten of such as are at freedom. 3. Such men's bondage should be esteemed, as our own, even until God set them free. 4. That other distressed people also shall be helped by us, if we consider what may befall ourselves, before we die.

VER. 4. Marriage is honourable in all, and the bed undefiled; but whoremongers and adulterers God will judge.

From this we learn, 1. That breakers of wedlock, and unclean persons in a single life, are both reserved unto God's judgment, how lightly soever men let them pass. 2. That marriage being provided of God, for a remedy of incontinency, maketh uncleanness the heavier sin. 3. That seeing it is God's doctrine to commend marriage for honourable, and hath pronounced it not only lawful, but commendable in all persons of whatsoever place or calling, and hath justified it for undefiled; to traduce this estate of life as not holy or not beseeming a holy man, or a holy calling, and to forbid marriage to persons of any calling, must be, as it is called, 1 Tim. iv. 1, 2, the doctrine of the devil.

VER. 5. Let your conversation be without covetousness ; and be content with such things as ye have : for he hath said, I will never leave thee, nor forsake thee.

Here we are taught, 1. That the enlargement of our desires, to have more and more worldly goods, whether we be rich, or poor, is disallowed of God. 2. That God requireth contentation with our present estate, how mean soever it be; and counteth it covetousness, not to be contented.

2. To make us contented, he giveth us God's promise made to Joshua, chap. i. 5, for our provision in necessaries. Then,

1. The promises made to Joshua, or any other holy man, in Scripture, for furniture in his calling, may be very well applied unto us, for help and furniture in our calling. 2. Faith in God's promise, for our maintenance, must both stay our fear of want in time to come, and give us contentment with that which we have for the present. 3. A general promise of God's being with us, and assisting of us, is as sufficient for all particulars whereof we stand in need, as if they were expressed.

VER. 6. So that we may boldly say, The Lord is my helper; and I will not fear what man can do unto me.

By applying of the promise made to Joshua, he concludeth, warrant to apply David's gloriation, against all perils, Psal. cviii. 6.

Then, 1. He that can apply one promise to himself, may confidently apply another also. 2. The weakest true believer, hath as good ground of confidence in God, for every good, needful for soul or body, as the Lord's chief prophets, and as good warrant to apply the Scriptures to their own use which speak of them. 3. He who believeth in God, needeth not to fear what flesh can do unto him. 4. Faith then doth its part duly, when it glorieth in the Lord, against all opposition.

VER. 7. Remember them which have the rule over you, who have spoken unto you the word of God: whose faith follow, considering the end of their conversation:

That they may be stedfast in the faith, he setteth before them the example of God's messengers, who had instructed them in the truth, and led a life conformable thereunto.

Wherein he teacheth us, 1. Who is worthy to be a guide to a people; to wit, the man who speaketh the word of God, and not his own dreams; believeth the truth which he teacheth, and hath his conversation answerable. 2. The best respect that a preacher can crave, or that a people can give to a preacher, either in his lifetime or after, is to remember the truth of God taught by him, and to make use thereof. 3. In as far as preachers have spoken the word of God, and made it the end of their conversation, people are commanded here to remember them, and imitate their faith, but no farther.

VER. 8. Jesus Christ the same yesterday, and to-day, and for ever.

This sentence serveth, first, To show the eternity and immutability of Jesus Christ, in himself, and all his properties, of truth, and love, and pity, &c. Again, it serveth for a reason of keeping fast the doctrine taught from him, by our faithful leaders; because Jesus Christ will still

allow and maintain that truth once given out by himself, and cannot choose to change his truth, being first and last, like himself. And thirdly, It serveth to encourage us to be constant in the faith, because Jesus Christ is unchangeably the same, in love and care towards those who believe in him, in all ages, for their preservation and deliverance; in all cases wherein they can fall, for his truth; as he hath given proof in former times towards others.

VER. 9. Be not carried about with divers and strange doctrines; for it is a good thing that the heart be established with grace, not with meats, which have not profited them that have been occupied therein.

That they may be stedfast in the faith, he warneth them to beware, that they be not carried about with divers and strange doctrines.

Then, 1. Doctrine which agreeth not with the word of God, uncouth and strange doctrine, which the apostles did not acknowledge and recommend unto us, must be rejected. 2. There was such uncouth doctrine beginning to creep into the church, even in the apostle's time. 3. Apostolic doctrine, such as they acquainted the church with, must be stedfastly believed, and stood unto; and not loosely laid hold upon, lest we lie upon the wind of false doctrine.

2. He bringeth in, for example, the doctrine of distinction of meats, wherein the Jewishly affected did place some holiness, and help to salvation: and yet they who most leaned to the same were least profited thereby.

Then, 1. To place some holiness in distinction of meats, and to count the observation thereof helpful to salvation, is an old error, which even in the beginning did trouble the church. 2. Never man got profit by leaning any thing to [relying upon] the observation of distinction of meats. For under the law, distinction was commanded, for the leading of men to some duties, signified thereby; but never did God give way, that men should esteem of this observation as a thing conferring any whit to the purchase of salvation.

3. To keep out this error of leaning to ceremonial observations, he opposeth the doctrine of grace; wherewith he will have the heart established, and not with meats.

Then, 1. The ground of devising and urging of superstitious ceremonies, is the unquietness and unstableness of men's hearts wanting satisfaction in God and his ordinances; and therefore seeking to support themselves by means of their own devising. 2. It is the doctrine of justification by grace only, and nothing of our doings, which getteth true rest to our hearts, and quiet settling to the consciences.

VER. 10. We have an altar, whereof they have no right to eat which serve the tabernacle.

Such as pertinaciously did plead for the standing of the Levitical service, and ceremonies thereof, he secludeth from the enjoying of Jesus Christ, who is our altar.

Then such as maintain the Levitical ceremonies, and do urge them on the Christian church, do cut themselves from right to Christ. 1. Because they deny, in effect, that he is come, seeing they will have those figures to remain, which did serve to prefigure his coming; and will have his church still under ceremonial pedagogy, as it was under the law. 2. Because they join unto Christ their own devices; as if either Jesus were not sufficient for salvation, or his ordinances were not sufficient for means to attain thereunto. 2. The observation of the distinction of meats, is a point of serving the tabernacle; for so doth the apostle reckon. 4. Such as will eat of Jesus, and be partakers of him, must beware to serve the Jewish tabernacle, by keeping on foot, and continuing the ceremonies, and appurtenances annexed thereunto: such feasts, such jubilees, such altars, such sprinklings, and holy water, such priests and vestments, &c. as Levi had.

2. He calleth Christ by the name of the altar; because he is the thing signified by the altar, and by the sacrifice, and by the rest of the Levitical ceremonies.

Then, 1. Those ordinances of Levitical service were figures of Christ, some in one part and some in another; and he is that accomplishment of them, even the truth of them all: the true tabernacle, the true priest, the true sacrifice, the true altar, &c. 2. Christ's self is all the altar that the Christian church hath. Our altar is he only, and nothing but he. The apostle knoweth no other.

3. In that he saith, They have no right to eat, learn, 1. That Jesus is our food who believe in him, by whom our souls are kept alive, and maintained every day spiritually, as the priests were maintained by the old altar bodily. 2. That before a man attain to eat, or draw benefit from Christ, he must have a right unto him. There is a possession following the right, and the right tendeth to the possession. 3. He who loveth to have the right, must take the course which Christ prescribeth, without mixing any thing therewith.

VER. 11. For the bodies of those beasts, whose blood is brought into the sanctuary by the high priest for sin, are burnt without the camp.

He showeth, that this was prefigured in the law; for Levit. xvi. 27, the sin-offering was burnt, and none of the priests, the servants of the tabernacle, did eat thereof. To show,

1. That such as adhered to the tabernacle and Levitical service, as needful to their salvation, (especially after Christ, the sin-offering that was offered) should not be partakers of him. Again sin-offering was offered without the camp; to show that such as would be partakers thereof, must forsake the Jewish synagogue, and come out of it towards Christ, who will not have his church mixed with the forms of the Jewish church. Thirdly, the bodies of the sacrifices of sin were then taken from the use of the priests of the tabernacle, when the blood was now brought into the sanctuary: to show that Christ should be taken from them, who, after his blood was shed, and had made atonement within the sanctuary of heaven, should not relinquish the Jewish tabernacle, and the shadowing figures thereof.

VER. 12. Wherefore Jesus also, that he might sanctify the people with his own blood, suffered without the gate.

Another end of the burning of the sin-offering without the camp, he showeth, first, to be, the prefiguration of the ignominious usage of Christ's body, cast out of the city of Jerusalem. 2. Again, like as the sin-offering, howbeit the body thereof was burnt without the camp, yet the blood of it was brought within the sanctuary, to make a figurative atonement. Even so, how basely soever men did use Christ's body in casting of it without the city, yet was his blood in high estimation with God, made atonement for the people, and sanctified them.

VER. 13. Let us go forth therefore unto him without the camp, bearing his reproach.

Hence he draweth an exhortation to be ready to renounce the world, and to take up our cross and follow Christ.

Wherein he teacheth us, 1. That Christ's sufferings without the city represented the state of his mystical body and kingdom, thrust forth and contemptibly rejected of the world. 2. That such as will be partakers of Christ must resolve to be so handled also, and must sequestrate their affections from the world, and must be contented to be crucified unto the world, with our Lord and Master Christ Jesus. 3. That what reproach is suffered for Christ's sake is not the man's, but Christ's reproach, for whom it is suffered. And so the reproach is as honourable before God as it is ignominious before the world.

VER. 14. For here we have no continuing city, but we seek one to come.

He giveth a reason of this exhortation, teaching,

1. That the instability of this present world, and our short and uncertain time of pilgrimage therein, should be a motive to make us loose our affections off it in time. 2. That the hope of a quiet and sure and blessed place of rest hereafter should be another motive to make us renounce this world with a better will. 3. That the true pilgrim's employment in this world is to be seeking how to come home to his country and city prepared for him.

VER. 15. By him therefore let us offer the sacrifice of praise to God continually, that is, the fruit of our lips, giving thanks to his name.

Another exhortation to offer spiritual sacrifices, wherein we learn,

1. That as Christ hath abolished all properly called priests by office, so hath he made all Christians spiritual priests by common duty. 2. As Christ hath offered the propitiatory sacrifice of his own body once for all that are to be saved, and hath left no properly called sacrifice, no offering for sin, no propitiatory offering, now to offer, so hath he appointed the spiritual sacrifice of thanks to be offered by every faithful man and woman, such as is prayer, praises, and thanksgiving to God. 3. That these our sacrifices of prayer and praise, is the spiritual service of saints,

answerable to the thank-offering of the first fruits, and calves and bullocks, which was the external sacrifice of the old church. 4. That the offering of these spiritual sacrifices is not tied unto set hours, as the legal, but to be done continually. 5. That these our sacrifices of prayer and praises are not to be offered by the mediation of saint or angel, but by Jesus Christ only. 6. That albeit they be unworthy as from us, yet being offered by Christ's mediation, they will be accepted for service at our hands.

VER. 16. But to do good and to communicate forget not, for with such sacrifices God is well pleased.

Another exhortation to good works and alms deeds, teaching us,

1. That good works and alms deeds are appointed to be of the number of spiritual sacrifices, and a part of the thank-offerings of the saints.

2. That because they are sacrifices, they must not be offered to the idol of our own credit and estimation, or our own private ends, but unto God, even in obedience unto him and for the glory of him. And because they are a part of the thank-offerings of the saints, they must not encroach upon the sin-offering of the Saviour, the only expiatory, the only propitiatory, and the only meritorious sacrifice.

3. That being so offered, they are well pleasing unto God; the smell of Christ's sin-offering once offered making our thank-offering to be sweet smelling unto God.

VER. 17. Obey them that have the rule over you, and submit yourselves; for they watch for your souls, as they that must give account, that they may do it with joy and not with grief, for that is unprofitable for you.

Another exhortation, to obey such as had the rule over them, their guides and leaders, as the word importeth. That is, public office-bearers in the church, appointed of God, to teach and govern them by the word and ecclesiastical censures.

Then, 1. The churches of Christ are not dens of confusion, but houses of order having some to be guides and rulers, and some to be instructed and guided by the direction of God's word and ordinances.

2. Even the meanest and poorest churches, albeit no more powerful than were the churches of these scattered Hebrews, must be so provided.

3. The right duty of the office-bearers in the church is, first, to be guides, pointing out the way in God's word, which the people should keep towards heaven. Next, to be leaders going before them in the example of faith and the fruits thereof, in their conversation. And thirdly, rulers by the rod of discipline, to take order with the scandalous, and to recall wanderers, to encourage the obedient, for thus much doth the word import.

4. The duty of the people is to obey the direction of such guides and rulers, and to submit themselves unto their censures, and to maintain them in their office every way, that this order may be continued, and not fall by any want which the people may supply.

2. The reason which he useth to induce them is, they watch for your souls, as they who must give account.

Then, 1. The charge of church rulers is the heaviest of all charges, because of souls.

2. The most assiduous and painful, setting not the body only, but the spirit on work, because it is a charge of watching.

3. The most dangerous of all charges, because the account of lost souls within the church shall be craved at their hands, whether they have done all that which became them to do to save them or not.

4. The weightiness of their charge should affect their people, and move them to concur for their parts, as they are able, for their encouragement.

3. Another motive is, that they may do their work with joy, and not with grief, for that is unprofitable unto you, saith he.

Then, 1. Churchmen's chief joy should be their people's obedience unto God's directions in their mouth, and their chief grief if it be otherwise.

2. Whether they will get joy or grief from their people, they must do their work, and follow their charge.

3. The less comfortable people be unto their leaders, their teachers, and rulers, the less profit shall they have by their ministry.

VER. 18. Pray for us: for we trust we have a good conscience, in all things willing to live honestly.

His craving the benefit of their prayers for him, teacheth us,

1. That albeit the Scripture giveth no warrant to seek the benefit of the prayer of saints departed, or of angels; yet it giveth warrant for seeking of the mutual concurrence in prayer, of these that are living together, and militant here on earth together. 2. That the greatest apostle hath need of the prayers of the meanest Christian, and may be helped thereby.

2. He giveth a reason, answering all the calumnies which were spread of him by his adversaries; that they might, with greater freedom, pray for him as for an honest man.

Then, 1. They who are unjustly reported of, must comfort themselves in the testimony of a good conscience. 2. An honest heart may expect the better fruit of their own prayers and others. 3. And such as we know are sincerely set to serve God, we may, with the better courage, pray for them.

3. He expoundeth what he calleth a good conscience, by saying that he was willing to live honestly.

Then, the purpose, desire, and endeavour to live honestly, is the evidence of a good conscience, and the ground also of the good testimony; because such a disposition escheweth to do evil, and is careful to do good.

VER. 19. But I beseech you the rather to do this, that I may be restored to you the sooner.

He joineth a reason, for their own good, to pray for him, that the impediments of his coming unto them being removed by their prayers, he might come the sooner.

Then, 1. When our own good is joined with the good of such as call for our prayers, we have the more inducements to set us on work. Many hinderances of our good and comfort do stand in the way, which by prayer might be removed.

Ver. 20. Now the God of peace, that brought again from the dead our Lord Jesus, that great Shepherd of the sheep, through the blood of the everlasting covenant,

Now he prayeth for them whom he hath in the former words requested to pray for him.

Then, 1. Prayer is a mutual duty, and ought to be made by us for such as we desire to pray for us.

2. He styleth God, to whom he prayeth, first, the God of peace ; to teach us,

That peace proceedeth from God, and is preserved by him in his church, and that it doth please him well that his children should be in peace, and should study thereunto.

3. Again, he describeth God by the great work of Christ's resurrection wrought by him.

Then, 1. As Christ's resurrection is the work of his own power, John x. 18, so also is it the work of God the Father, in this place ; for, John x. 30, the Father and Christ in power are one.

4. The props of his faith in prayer are, first, the office of Jesus, who is the great Shepherd of the sheep.

Then, 1. Those who come under the reckoning of Christ's sheep are the only people of whom he, by special office, professeth to take charge. 2. Howsoever he employ the ministry of men, to feed his flock under him ; yet doth he keep the place and style of Arch Pastor, or Great Shepherd, to himself. 3. People, howsoever they be furnished by ministers, yet they have the Great Shepherd to acknowledge and rely upon; of whose care and fidelity for their feeding, and preservation, they may be confident.

5. The next prop of this prayer is, the power of God, who brought again from the dead the great Shepherd.

Then, 1. The sheep must not think to be above the Shepherd, but must resolve for bearing witness to the truth, and to be put to death, as he was, if God please. Nor need they fear to be used so, seeing he is risen again ; because, he that raised the Shepherd, for the sheep's cause, can raise the sheep from death also for the Shepherd's cause.

6. The third prop of confidence, for obtaining this prayer, is, the blood of the everlasting covenant, through which he seeketh his petition to be granted.

Then, 1. It is Christ's blood which hath ratified the covenant, and established our reconciliation, to endure for ever, because the virtue of that blood is perpetual. 2. It is through that blood that every thing is purchased for which we can pray. It is the price of the purchase of sanctification unto us, as well as salvation.

Ver. 21. Make you perfect in every good work to do his will, working in you that which

is well pleasing in his sight, through Jesus Christ : to whom be glory for ever and ever. Amen.

That which he prayeth for here is, that they may be made perfect in every good work to do the will of God.

Then, 1. Only the doing of God's will, and what he hath commanded is to be reckoned for a good work. 2. It is not enough to be given to some sort of good work, but we must endeavour ourselves to work every sort of good work, having a due respect unto all God's commandments. 3. Whatsoever measure we have attained unto, we must not stand there, but perfection must be aimed at, which is still before us, until we come to heaven.

2. The way how this may be done he showeth to be, by God's working in us that which is well-pleasing in his sight, even through Jesus Christ.

Then, 1. It is not by any strength of our own whereby good works are wrought, but even by the power of God working in us graciously. 2. It is through Jesus Christ that this working is procured, conveyed unto us, and made acceptable unto God.

3. He closeth his prayer with ascribing of glory unto Jesus, " for ever." Amen.

Then, 1. Christ Jesus is true God, worthy of divine glory, for ever. 2. The prayer and praises which we offer unto God must come from so advised a mind as we may seal the same with faith, and hearty affection, imported in " Amen."

Ver. 22. And I beseech you, brethren, suffer the word of exhortation, for I have written a letter unto you in few words.

Last of all, he exhorteth them to take in good part the word of exhortation from their ordinary teachers, who behoved to dilate, and urge, and inculcate these things, even at length, unto them. The reason whereof he giveth ; because he had written this letter but in few words unto them, and might not insist on those points at large, as they had need of, but behoved to leave this unto their teachers.

Then, 1. There is need of preachers, by the word of exhortation, to dilate and inculcate that which the Scripture hath in short. 2. It is very irksome for men to have their sluggishness stirred up by exhortation, and the same things inculcated again and again ; but their own profit should make them to suffer it patiently. 3. The writing of Scripture prejudiceth not the use of preaching, but both keep their own room; the Scripture serving for a short laying down of the grounds to be taught, and exhortation serving to dilate and urge the truth delivered in Scripture, as their case requireth.

Ver. 23. Know ye that our brother Timothy is set at liberty, with whom, if he come shortly, I will see you.

From this learn, first, That the delivery of one Timothy, out of the hands of his persecutors, should be a matter of comfort and joy unto as many churches as do hear of it. Secondly, Good

F

news should be spread abroad, and are a fit matter for Christian epistles.

VER. 24. Salute all them that have the rule over you, and all the saints. They of Italy salute you.

From this learn, first, That as it is the mutual duty of Christians to send forth commendations one to another, so is it a Christian duty to carry them, not unbeseeming even an apostle.

2. His directing of the people for to carry his commendations to their rulers, maketh it evident that the apostle ordained this epistle to be first read unto the people. And so was far from their minds who will not suffer the Scripture to come into the people's hands.

VER. 25. Grace be with you all. Amen.

This closing of the epistle, usual to the apostle, teacheth, 1. That grace is the common good of the church, whereunto every saint hath interest.

2. That grace is all that can be desired; for if the fountains of God's grace or favour run towards a man, what can the man stand in need of which the overrunning stream of God's good-will shall not carry unto him?

THE POSTSCRIPT.

Written to the Hebrews, from Italy, by Timothy.

Some inconsiderate hand hath put to this postscript, appearingly; for this epistle was ordained by the apostle to carry the news of Timothy's liberation, and a promise of his coming to them afterwards, possibly, as the 23rd verse of this chapter showeth, and not to be carried by Timothy.

And again, the apostle was bound by this letter to come with Timothy, if he had been to come shortly after the writing of this epistle.

And thirdly, Timothy was not yet come to that place where the apostle Paul was, when this epistle was directed; for, then, had he been certain of Timothy's purpose, and behoved, if not to go with Timothy, yet to have written the reason of so sudden a change of his purpose and written promise; or else to have deleted the promise of his coming out of the epistle, by writing it over again, or some way else.

Whence we collect, that postscripts are not a part of the text, nor of the apostle's own writing; neither ought they to have such authority or credit as the text hath, which always agreeth with itself, as proceeding from the inspiration of the Holy Spirit: to whom, with the Father, and his Son Jesus Christ, our Lord, be glory for ever. Amen.

THE END.

John Eadie Titles

Solid Ground Christian Books is delighted to announce that we have been privileged to republish several volumes by John Eadie, the great Scottish minister of the nineteenth century. We have brought the following back into print:

Commentary on the Greek Text of Paul's Letter to the Galatians
Part of the classic five-volume set that brought world-wide renown to this humble man, Eadie expounds this letter with passion and precision. In the words of Spurgeon, "This is a most careful attempt to ascertain the meaning of the Apostle by painstaking analysis of his words."

Commentary on the Greek Text of Paul's Letter to the Ephesians
Spurgeon said, "This book is one of prodigious learning and research. The author seems to have read all, in every language, that has been written on the Epistle. It is also a work of independent criticism, and casts much new light upon many passages."

Commentary on the Greek Text of Paul's Letter to the Philippians
Robert Paul Martin wrote, "Everything that John Eadie wrote is pure gold. He was simply the best exegete of his generation. His commentaries on Paul's epistles are valued highly by careful expositors. Solid Ground Christian Books has done a great service by bringing Eadie's works back into print."

Commentary on the Greek Text of Paul's Letter to the Colossians
According to the New Schaff-Herzog Encyclopedia of Religious Knowledge, "These commentaries of John Eadie are marked by candor and clearness as well as by an evangelical unction not common in works of the kind." Spurgeon said, "Very full and reliable. A work of utmost value."

Commentary on the Greek Text of Paul's Letters to the Thessalonians
Published posthumously, this volume completes the series that has been highly acclaimed for more than a century. Invaluable.

Paul the Preacher: A Popular and Practical Exposition of His Discourses and Speeches as Recorded in the Acts of the Apostles
Very rare volume intended for a more popular audience, this volume begins with Saul's conversion and ends with Paul preaching the Gospel of the Kingdom in Rome. It perfectly fills in the gaps in the commentaries. Outstanding work!

DIVINE LOVE: A Series of Doctrinal, Practical and Experimental Discourses
Buried over a hundred years, this volume consists of a dozen complete sermons from Eadie's the pastoral ministry. "John Eadie, the respected nineteenth-century Scottish Secession minister-theologian, takes the reader on an edifying journey through this vital biblical theme." - Ligon Duncan

Other Solid Ground Titles

In addition to the book in your hand, Solid Ground is honored to offer other uncovered treasure, many for the first time in more than a century:

THE SECRET OF COMMUNION WITH GOD by Matthew Henry
THE COMMUNICANT'S COMPANION by Matthew Henry
THE CHILD AT HOME by John S.C. Abbott
THE LIFE OF JESUS CHRIST FOR THE YOUNG by Richard Newton
THE KING'S HIGHWAY: *10 Commandments for the Young* by Richard Newton
HEROES OF THE REFORMATION by Richard Newton
FEED MY LAMBS: *Lectures to Children on Vital Subjects* by John Todd
LET THE CANNON BLAZE AWAY by Joseph P. Thompson
THE STILL HOUR: *Communion with God in Prayer* by Austin Phelps
COLLECTED WORKS of James Henley Thornwell (4 vols.)
CALVINISM IN HISTORY *by Nathaniel S. McFetridge*
OPENING SCRIPTURE: *Hermeneutical Manual by Patrick Fairbairn*
THE ASSURANCE OF FAITH *by Louis Berkhof*
THE PASTOR IN THE SICK ROOM *by John D. Wells*
THE BUNYAN OF BROOKLYN: *Life & Sermons of I.S. Spencer*
THE NATIONAL PREACHER: *Sermons from 2nd Great Awakening*
FIRST THINGS: *First Lessons God Taught Mankind* Gardiner Spring
BIBLICAL & THEOLOGICAL STUDIES *by 1912 Faculty of Princeton*
THE POWER OF GOD UNTO SALVATION *by B.B. Warfield*
THE LORD OF GLORY *by B.B. Warfield*
A GENTLEMAN & A SCHOLAR: *Memoir of J.P. Boyce by J. Broadus*
SERMONS TO THE NATURAL MAN *by W.G.T. Shedd*
SERMONS TO THE SPIRITUAL MAN *by W.G.T. Shedd*
HOMILETICS AND PASTORAL THEOLOGY *by W.G.T. Shedd*
A PASTOR'S SKETCHES 1 & 2 *by Ichabod S. Spencer*
THE PREACHER AND HIS MODELS *by James Stalker*
IMAGO CHRISTI: *The Example of Jesus Christ by James Stalker*
LECTURES ON THE HISTORY OF PREACHING *by J. A. Broadus*
THE SHORTER CATECHISM ILLUSTRATED *by John Whitecross*
THE CHURCH MEMBER'S GUIDE *by John Angell James*
THE SUNDAY SCHOOL TEACHER'S GUIDE *by John A. James*
CHRIST IN SONG: *Hymns of Immanuel from All Ages by Philip Schaff*
DEVOTIONAL LIFE OF THE S.S. TEACHER *by J.R. Miller*

Call us Toll Free at 1-877-666-9469
Send us an e-mail at sgcb@charter.net
Visit us on line at solid-ground-books.com
Uncovering Buried Treasure to the Glory of God

Printed in the United States
94761LV00002B/1-4/A

9 781599 250199